Home Extensions

THE COMPLETE HANDBOOK

PAUL HYMERS

NEW HOLLAND

For Melanie, Karina and Rochelle for their endless support, patience and tea-making skills, and in memory of my Dad and best friend, Doug Hymers. Back in the 1950s, the Building Inspector visiting our home advised my Dad that his newly built asbestos-panel garage was too close to the house. With the help of his brothers, he picked the garage up and carried it down the garden until it wasn't.
I live in hope that life will one day again be that simple.

Reprinted in 2007
First published in 1999 by
New Holland Publishers (UK) Ltd
Garfield House, 86–88 Edgware Road
London W2 2EA
United Kingdom
London • Cape Town • Sydney • Auckland
www.newhollandpublishers.com

13 15 17 19 20 18 16 14 12

ISBN 978 1 84330 373 2

Editor: Ian Kearey
Editorial Assistant: Kate Latham
Designer: Casebourne Rose Design Associates
Illustrator: Sue Rose
Cover photography: Mark Asher
Managing Editor: Coral Walker

Reproduction by R&B Creative Services
Printed and bound by Kyodo Printing Co (Singapore) Pte Ltd

ACKNOWLEDGEMENTS

With thanks to my colleagues, past and present, in Building Control, Structural Engineering, Planning and Environmental Health, who have been more than willing to share with me their knowledge and experience.
Thanks to Mr D W Hosegood for allowing us to photograph his home extension for the cover of this book and to Connections of Grahams for the kitchen illustration on page 150. To my sister Anne and her family for the use of their superior computer equipment, and last but not least to my Mum for sanctuary, coffee and homemade cake — how can anyone write a book without these ingredients?

The views expressed in this book are those of the author and do not necessarily reflect those of his employers.

Contents

4 **Introduction**

SECTION 1 **Planning**

6 *Chapter 1* Preliminaries

14 *Chapter 2* Plans

42 *Chapter 3* Builders

SECTION 2 **Building**

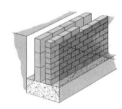

56 *Chapter 4* Substructure

76 *Chapter 5* Superstructure

120 *Chapter 6* Internal work

152 *Chapter 7* External work

168 Glossary

172 Useful contacts

174 Index

Introduction

If you found this book in the 'DIY' section of your local bookshop, let me begin by offering you an apology, because this isn't a DIY book – it is just that the bookshop didn't know where else to put it. It is a guidebook for people who are having an extension built onto their home, whether they are employing a general builder to carry out the whole thing or employing individual tradespeople for the various stages. They may even be working on parts of it themselves – even in DIY-crazy Britain, few people are reckless enough to attempt to build an entire extension themselves without the benefit of some experience in the building industry.

This is a guide that will take you from the conception right through to the decorating. (In Building Control, we have this theory that, for many people, the home extension is conceived over the kitchen sink just after Christmas. From this spot, the lady of the house orates on just how difficult it has been to prepare the festive fare in a kitchen so hopelessly small and ill-equipped, or how wonderful it would be if next year they could eat in a separate dining area or entertain the relations in a family room. As if by design, nature conspires to reinforce the idea with the January garden, seen from the kitchen window as a dead and lifeless space, just waiting to be built on.)

Along the way, this book will alert you to the hazards and pitfalls of which so many fall foul. Not every danger is listed, but as a local authority Building Control Officer since 1984, I have inspected over a thousand home extensions and have noted the most common problems and mistakes made, many occurring time and time again. The book is not intended to put you off the idea of extending, but to guide you safely towards a valuable addition to your home.

Even if you aren't planning to get your hands on the work, there is one particular tool that will be an asset – a 1.2 m-long spirit level, preferably of sturdy construction, with a durable coating and shockproof glass tubes that won't be offended when you swear at them.

Happy building!

CHAPTER 1

Preliminaries

Site investigation and preparation

The fundamental reason for carrying out a site investigation survey is to discover the nature of the land you are to build on, and in particular what possible problems it may hold. With property development this is an essential process before buying a site, but in the building of an extension you inherit whatever ground conditions exist. Even so, this should not deter you from carrying out a proper site investigation. You may think you know your own backyard, but are you sure that you know exactly where the water main runs, or if there are any drainage pipes or soakaways where you intend to build? These things need not come as a surprise when the foundation trenches are dug, and indeed, if you have more than one possible location for your extension, it may help you to decide exactly where you are going to position it.

10 Expert Points

WORTH CONSIDERING BEFORE YOUR PLANS ARE DRAWN UP:

1 TREES
Are there any trees or large woody shrubs nearby? If so, note their position, size and species. In some situations, trees up to 30 m away from the building can have an effect on the design of the foundations.

2 VEGETATION
Note the vegetation on the site and be aware of any sudden changes in its appearance which may give a clue towards ground conditions. For instance, in summer a strip of dead grass across a lawn will show where a shallow drain, usually bedded and covered with pea-shingle, runs below ground.

3 FLOOD
If you are new to the property, are there any signs of past flooding or a high-water table in evidence? Are you near to a river or on the coast? Consult with neighbours to find out the history of the area. Is the water table high? Flood damage has to be one of the most destructive and disheartening things that can happen to your home, and if all you need to do is raise your floor level a few extra courses to be on the safe side, it must be well worth the work.

Maps or advice from the Environment Agency are of some help when it comes to established flood plains, but every year global warming seems to bring record flood levels to parts of the UK that were never previously considered at risk.

If your existing home has a low ground-floor level, do not be inflexible about continuing it into the extension. Building the new ground-floor level higher may mean you are also building a refuge.

4 SERVICES
Will your extension cover the outside wall of the kitchen? The majority of water mains enter the building below the kitchen sink. Will it cover electricity or gas meter boxes, and telephone entry points? The relevant service companies will be able to give you the location of their pipes and ducts by an on-site survey or plan. Drainage should also be investigated. Local authorities hold records of public sewers, but not private drains, unfortunately. Only site surveys can trace them accurately, and the technique of using coloured vegetable dyes mixed with water is useful in finding out what goes where.

5 SLOPES

Will your extension be constructed on or close to a steep slope? If the answer is yes, you should employ a competent engineer to ensure that the slope will not become unstable when the extension adds weight to the top of it; if it's at the bottom, the engineer should check that the excavations will not cause the ground to become unstable by removing the slope's support. The nature of the subsoil will make a good deal of difference.

6 SUBSOIL

To help you investigate the subsoil, a trial hole between 1 and 4 m deep can be dug. If this is positioned 5 m away from any building, including the new extension, it could later be used as a soakaway for the rainwater disposal. Even if the hole reveals nothing else, it will tell you what the subsoil conditions are, whether they are clay or chalk, etc.

7 NEIGHBOURS

If you are new to the property, ask the neighbours what experiences they have had with the ground conditions; for example, does the soil dry out quickly in summer, shrinking and cracking? If they have lived in their property for some time, their knowledge will be invaluable.

8 ORDNANCE SURVEY MAPS

Consulting large-scale Ordnance Survey maps of the area may reveal previous buildings on the site, the foundations of which could still exist underground, or an old pond or pit that may since have been backfilled.

Copies of 1:2500- or 1:1250-scale OS maps are only obtainable from retail outlets licensed by Ordnance Survey, but they can also be viewed in most public libraries. If

there is any doubt as to exactly where the boundary of your property lies, the Land Registry will provide a marked-up map on application with a fee.

9 EXISTING HOUSE FOUNDATIONS

Most importantly – and even if you do none of the above – dig a small hole down alongside your outside wall, sufficiently deep to reveal the type and depth of your existing house foundations. This is ideally done where your extension will abut the existing house, so that the hole may be subsequently incorporated into the new foundation excavations.

10 RIGHTS OF WAY

If you have recently purchased or remortgaged the property, a Local Land Search will have been carried out by your conveyancer; this should tell you whether or not there are any public footpaths or private rights of way across your land. They need not be obvious on site.

Your extension should not obstruct a public right of way. If it does, quite apart from rendering your property unmortgageable or unsaleable, you may be fined and required to pull it down. The fact that you may have obtained Planning Consent to build the extension would be no defence.

As a separate matter, you should have obtained an order to do away with or divert the path (on receiving an application for such an order, the planning authority is required to advertise the fact for 28 days, to allow any objections to be made).

All public footpaths are recorded on Statutory Conclusive record maps that are maintained at council offices and may be viewed by the public – if you are in any doubt, it is an easy matter to go and check. Private rights of way, if obstructed for whatever reason, are enforceable through civil law.

Restrictive covenants

These covenants are clauses in a contract which was drawn up for the sale of the land previously and are binding on all future purchasers. They may require, for example, home-owners to seek consent from the original developer for any extension or alteration they wish to make to the property; in so doing, they aim to control the character of the estate as a whole. They may prevent any building at all, so it is important to check the deeds of your property to see whether any exist. It is possible for covenants to be removed by application to the Lands Tribunal under Section 84 of the Property Act 1925.

Drainage

If your new extension includes a bathroom, WC or kitchen, you will need access to your drainage system for the new appliances. Before you start is the time to investigate where your drains are and where they run to. Although previous plans can be of some help, the only sure way to find out is to lift manhole covers and measure depths from the bottom of the channel to the cover. Needless to say, it is absolutely necessary to ensure that your existing drains are deep enough to allow any new pipes to be connected at a reasonable fall, and that the connection can be made in the general direction of the flow or at no less than 90° to it.

For 'emergency' situations where it is not possible to supply conventional drains, mini-pumped systems will allow extra toilets and other appliances to be installed. Because the pumps run on electricity, these systems should only be used where you have other conventional WCs and facilities that dispose of foul water by gravity.

Trees

If you wish to fell a tree that is in the way of your development, you must first check to ensure that it does not have a **Preservation Order** placed upon it. Most local authority Planning Departments have a tree or landscape officer who can advise you.

In **Conservation Areas** it is an offence even to lop or top trees without obtaining the consent of the council and giving them **six weeks' notice**. The same also applies to **uprooting or felling**. It is not a sufficient defence to claim that your extension would be affected by the tree if it was retained. Advice on building near trees can be found in Chapter 4.

Mines

In some parts of the UK mine workings are prolific, and although the collieries may be long closed the shafts and tunnels are still there underground, albeit capped off at the surface. If you live in such an area, it should be possible to obtain the exact position and depth of these workings from British Coal (or the current site owners).

It is surprising just how close properties can be. A few years ago much media attention was given to the fact that some properties had been blighted as a result of shafts not being declared on land searches when the houses were bought – only when the owners tried to sell them did the search reveal the proximity and thus ruined the sale.

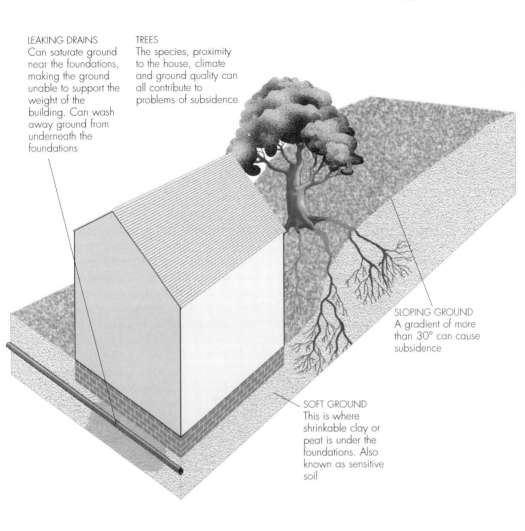

LEAKING DRAINS
Can saturate ground near the foundations, making the ground unable to support the weight of the building. Can wash away ground from underneath the foundations

TREES
The species, proximity to the house, climate and ground quality can all contribute to problems of subsidence

SLOPING GROUND
A gradient of more than 30° can cause subsidence

SOFT GROUND
This is where shrinkable clay or peat is under the foundations. Also known as sensitive soil

Trees account for between 50-60% of subsidence claims each year. However, they are not the only cause.
This diagram shows some other common causes of subsidence.

Services

Many service companies – gas, electricity, water and telephone – now offer a free site survey to determine the exact position of their service pipes before you start digging. They are able to do this by using sensitive detection equipment. In the past, they were only able to issue marked-up location plans, which were often inaccurate. If you can't

9

get a site survey done and have to settle for a plan or nothing at all, then be prepared to dig carefully!

Dig and see

The United Kingdom has a good deal of geological diversity. The highly shrinkable clays that cause so much trouble in the south-east of England are unheard of in Scotland, where metamorphic rocks prevail. In some counties, such as Kent, the diversity in ground conditions exists from one town to another: rock chalk, found nowhere else in the world, sits alongside Wealden clay, clay alongside green sand, or gravel beds or sand.

Large-scale geological-survey maps, produced for regions throughout the country, can provide a useful guide. However, they only provide a generalised assessment of the situation. To discover the secrets of the ground beneath your garden, you must dig, as only by excavating can you become sure of what you will find.

Among some of the most common findings are wells, old soakaways, backfilled ground, redundant water tanks and foundations of long-demolished buildings. Those of the hole-in-the-ground nature, such as wells and soakaways, are best filled up and 'bridged over'. If they lie within the footprint of the extension, this can invoke some structural design work. If they are shallow and dry, it may be best to fill them with concrete and reinforce the foundation that passes over them with steel bars. As you have created a 'hard spot' by providing a lump of concrete under one part of the foundation, the reinforcement would go near the top of the foundation concrete to act against the compressive stress.

If, on the other hand, the hole is of indeterminate depth, it may be wiser to fill it with hardcore, topping it off with some suitably level material to form a soft spot (that may well settle), and then reinforce the foundation concrete with steel bars near the bottom to act against tensile stress. If you intend to bridge over such a hole in this way, you will need to find some good load-bearing ground on either side, and you should bear in mind that a brick-built well is likely to have had some excavated ground around the outside, for working space during its construction, and the ground must be assumed to be backfill. A more generous bearing is thus required to overcome it.

The soil around wells or soakaways may be softer, due to water seeping out over a long period of time. Any drainage should always be diverted well away from the house and extension before work proceeds further.

Old tanks may represent a bigger problem – while they may have been backfilled, they may not have been properly treated or capped off. It is advisable to have any newly redundant septic tank or cesspool thoroughly emptied, doused with lime to settle the gases, and filled with hardcore before capping it off with reinforced concrete. The actual foundation or ground floor above such an old tank will need an engineer's structural design to bridge over it.

In addition to these man-made obstacles, nature can also throw up its own natural ones: you may, for example, be unfortunate enough to have a fissure in the ground. This is basically a crack found in sedimentary rock that has opened up, perhaps due to mine workings or natural forces like underground streams. Alternatively, there may be a geological slip-plane below the site, where one subsoil condition collides with another.

Perhaps the worst situation is to find backfilled ground, partly because it may not be all that obvious. Apart from being a little softer and perhaps variable in colour, backfilled ground is sometimes only recognised by finding tiny fragments of unnatural material in the sides and bottom of the trench. Look for pieces of house brick or china – these do not occur anywhere naturally, and are conclusive proof that the ground is backfill, consolidated backfill maybe, but nonetheless backfill.

The dilemma is made worse by the uncertainty of how deep the backfill is. It could be extremely deep, making excavation impossible or uneconomical, but on the other hand it may be that virgin ground is just beneath it, waiting to be discovered. A cautious trial hole in one corner of the foundation will prove to be a way forward.

Building near basements

Excavating foundations alongside basements can be problematic, largely because you might not know they are there – and it isn't just basements to your own house that are concerned, it is any house close enough to make a difference. The load spread from your new foundations runs down and out

into the soil below at a 45° angle. If a basement wall occurs within this spread, it will not only rob your extension of the support it needs, but it will also place loads onto the basement walls which they were never designed to have. If you live in a terrace or in close proximity to older properties, check with the neighbours if they have any basements, whether used or not, beneath the house. Excavating your foundations to a depth where this does not occur is the usual remedy. It means taking some on-site measurements and combining them with some basic mathematics or a simple section drawn to scale. This way you can see just how deep your footings will have to be dug in advance.

Refer to Chapter 2 for advice on building near boundaries, even where there are no basements.

Percolation testing

Subsoil varies in porosity to a tremendous degree: chalk and gravel beds are usually free-draining, and are excellent for soakaways from either rainwater drainage or septic tank run-off. Clays, on the other hand, can be very sticky, holding water like a sponge and thus making it necessary to spread soakaway drains over a much wider area.

A percolation test on the subsoil will enable you (or your septic tank manufacturer) to design your soakaway drainage so that it works effectively. The standard test is to make three trial holes with 100 x 100 mm sump holes dug in the bottom and filled with water; the time taken for the water to drain completely away is measured. You can then calculate from this time how much storage (i.e. how big in volume) your soakaways will need to be to effectively drain your extension's roof of rain arriving at the rate of 75 mm in an hour.

If you're very lucky, your local Building Control Officer will be able to give you a Percolation Test form to complete and will help you fill it in.

Hedgerows

Over the latter half of the twentieth century we have managed to lose over 150,000 miles of England's indigenous hedgerows, a great many miles of which were ancient and dating back to Anglo-Saxon times, and every mile of which was a rich haven of wildlife. Staggeringly, a third of them went in the six years between 1984 and 1990, and in the true government style of bolting the stable door after the horse has gone, the Hedgerows Regulations were introduced in 1997 to help protect what is left.

If you intend to remove even part of a hedgerow to accommodate your extension, you may well need to apply to your local authority for permission. I say may, because the criteria for whether regulations apply is complex, to say the least. They involve not only the position of the hedgerow, but also what number and type of woody species it consists of (in any 30-metre length), whether it is home to certain species of birds or animals, and whether it associates with certain other features in the landscape.

Because of these individualised conditions, I suggest that you write to your local planning authority seeking their consent well in advance of commencing work —under the regulations, they have six weeks to

respond. The penalties for removing or destroying a hedgerow or even part of one without consent are severe.

Before concluding this section, mention must be made of two other site problems which, although relatively uncommon, are extremely important.

Radon gas

This is a natural radioactive gas which is produced in the breakdown of components present in a site's geology. It is therefore only prolific in specific parts of the country where the geology is conducive, the main areas being Devon and Cornwall, where granite is present, although it is not wholly restricted to these two counties. At the time of writing, nobody seems to know just how widespread radon pollution is, but in some areas of Britain it should be included within site surveys.

Radon can not be smelt, seen, heard or felt, but it has nevertheless been recognised as harmful, and it is listed as the second biggest cause of lung cancer in this country. Government has now addressed the fact that it is harmful, and has established an 'action level' at which radon-proofing works become necessary to seal the building and protect the occupants against exposure. There is, of course, little benefit in sealing an extension to a building if the existing building is not likewise sealed.

Radon-proofing basically involves sealing floors at ground level, if timber-constructed, with polythene, and making airtight seals around any service openings. Rooms within the house should be kept well ventilated to prevent the build-up of radon gas, and any basements may need to be mechanically ventilated. Positioning a fan at ceiling level has been claimed to reduce the build-up of gas by pressurising the atmosphere.

No requirements currently exist for the enforcement of radon-proofing in existing dwellings, but your Building Control Authority may require precautions to be taken in the building of an extension where a problem is known to exist. Largely speaking, the responsibility lies with the home-owner. Further advice can be obtained from the National Radiological Protection Board. Grant aid may be available from your local council's Environmental Health Department if you have discovered that your home is exposed to radon beyond the action level stipulated. The council may be able to carry out a survey of your property for you and advise on what precautions, if any, you need to take.

A leaflet entitled 'Radon and Buildings 3: Protecting New Extensions and Conservatories' has been published by the Building Research Establishment; this covers principal routes of radon entry and gives guidance on prevention and measuring radon levels before starting work. It is available from the BRE's bookshop (see page 172).

Methane (marsh gas)

This is another invisible threat, which has largely come about by a cruel twist of environmental fate. Years ago, the introduction of the Clean Air Act stopped us burning our domestic waste, and so available holes, pits and hollows were filled with refuse and termed landfill sites. The trouble is that much of our waste is organic; being organic, it decomposes, and in doing so it produces a cocktail of gases, one of which is methane. In a 5–15% mixture with air, methane can be highly explosive. In lower percentages it can cause headaches and even asphyxia. To date, it should be noted that only one death has been attributed to a build-up of methane gas, but this was enough to generate positive action on the subject.

The sites at risk are those where landfilling has taken place or where natural (marsh) gas occurs. It is not enough to only take precautions when building directly on landfill sites, as methane gas has been known to migrate through the ground for up to 500 m from the actual site. The precautions to be taken are similar to radon-proofing. Foundations should, if possible, avoid puncturing layers or pockets of gas laying dormant in the ground.

Controlled venting away from homes is usually required, and may be achieved by open (French) drain runs. Ground floors should be sealed with gas-resistant membranes, and any sub-floor space should be kept well ventilated. Guidance on this subject is available from local authorities and from the waste-disposal section of some county councils.

The next step is to find somebody to prepare the plans after they have visited your home for a feasibility study. Some surveyors and architects offer a brief appraisal free of charge, during which the findings from your site investigation can be discussed, along with your design ideas and queries.

CHAPTER 2

Plans

Finding a Designer

Choosing the right person to draw your plans is just as important as choosing the right builder, and the prospect can be just as daunting. A badly drawn plan can be confusing and misleading, if not impossible to read. As with builders, the best method of selecting your designer is by personal recommendation, but you may not be fortunate enough to have a host of friends who have all benefited from the professional design services of one local person.

As is the case with builders, designers do not have to be registered or licensed.

They may voluntarily belong to a professional institution, but there are a whole host of different ones to choose from. Most of them require full members to have relevant academic and technical qualifications, but you should be aware that they all have varying levels of membership. For example, a student membership may be obtained with a school-leaving qualification, an associate membership with half-completed technical studies, while a corporate or full membership may only be attained after completing the full qualifications and after so many years of experience. As if this isn't enough, some of these bodies represent a broad range of

HERE ARE A FEW EXAMPLES OF THE INSTITUTES TO WHICH DESIGNERS MAY BELONG:

ROYAL INSTITUTE OF BRITISH ARCHITECTS (RIBA)
Only those registered with the Architects Registration Board, principally RIBA members, are entitled to use the declaration 'Architect'. Otherwise 'architectural technician' is frequently used.

ROYAL INSTITUTION OF CHARTERED SURVEYORS (RICS)
This has a wide membership, with categories ranging from building surveyors to quantity surveyors, arbitrators and even auctioneers. The only relevant discipline for designers may be building surveyors, although these can often be more specialised in the inspection of existing properties and advising on repairs and maintenance, rather than the design of new extensions.

ASSOCIATION OF BUILDING ENGINEERS (ABE)
Formerly the Incorporated Association of

Architects and Surveyors (IAAS), this is again a wide-ranging association that incorporates different disciplines, including planning and surveying, but is largely made up of Building Control Surveyors.

INSTITUTE OF BUILDING (IOB)
This is a general base institute for members of the building industry, which is often patronised by non-trade employees of building contractors, such as site agents, contracts managers, etc.

INSTITUTION OF STRUCTURAL ENGINEERS (ISE)
Some structural engineers may also prepare structural design plans as well as making calculations, but ifor the most part they have no expertise outside of structures and would usually restrict their professional services to these elements.

There is also an Institution of Civil Engineers (ICE), but their field of structural design is often confined to roads, bridges, tunnels, etc., and is removed from the design of small buildings.

professions, so it is not only important to know which 'club' the designer belongs to, but to which discipline within it and the level of his or her membership. Of course, membership of any group is not essential – after all, it may only rely upon an annual subscription being paid to maintain it and little else.

Some bodies may encourage continuing professional development, but not many insist upon it. They are therefore, in effect, trade organisations for white-collar professionals, and should not be used as a measuring stick to judge the quality or otherwise of a designer. Having said that, most encourage their full members to at least follow a basic code of conduct in their professional activities.

Those employed in the field of building design may have a variety of titles: surveyor, engineer, architectural surveyor, building consultant, and so on. It matters not what they call themselves if the quality of their work is good. When it comes to building design, a good designer (for the purposes of this book, I shall call them all 'designers') is one who possesses the necessary skills of draughtsmanship and is familiar not only with the details of construction, but also with the problems and regulations relating to the work. It is possible to make the mistake that somebody who designs hydroelectric dams in Zimbabwe for a living is going to be more than qualified to draw up a small extension to your house. However, it is more likely to be the case that a local 'plan draughtsman', who has done hundreds of other kitchen extensions in your area

and is conversant with local planning policies, is more qualified for the job at hand. Domestic building work is a field all of its own, so find somebody who works in it.

Most designers offer a free consultation period, when they will visit your house to discuss with you the feasibility of extending it. When making this appointment, ask them to bring along to the meeting some examples of extension plans drawn for their previous clients. You should always view the standard of their work before agreeing the terms of their engagement.

If you are happy that the plans satisfy all of the criteria on the following page, then you may well be in the hands of a professional. Even so, it is still worth comparing the drawings of several designers before appointing one. You may be astonished to see just how different the quality of plans can be, and it will give you a good idea of the wide variety of drawing standards around.

Agreeing the terms of engagement

Ask your prospective designer if their price includes all structural calculations or details that may be required by Building Control. They may reply that calculations would not be needed, but if your scheme involves the forming or widening of a structural opening through to the extension, it is likely that a beam will be needed over the opening and calculations will be required to prove its adequacy. This would apply whether it was a timber or steel beam, and even perhaps if it was an existing lintel retained, but subjected to increased loads.

10 Expert Points

LOOK FOR THE FOLLOWING TEN EXPERT POINTS IN FINISHED PLANS:

1 CLARITY
How clear and easy to read are the plans? Is the specification writing legible? You may not understand what is written, but if it isn't printed clearly, neither will anyone else.

2 TRUE ELEVATIONS
Are there elevations of all aspects, showing the extended property as a whole, in addition to floor plans? Elevations are the one aspect where the designer can display artistic flair alongside his or her technical draughting abilities. Often well-drawn elevations can help to 'sell' the design.

3 SCALE
Are the plans drawn to an appropriate scale – proposed plan layouts/elevations 1:50; sections 1:25; block plan 1:500; location plan 1:1250?

4 PLAN COPY SIZE
Are the plans reproduced on A1 or AO paper? Having to refer to several different sheets of A3 or A4 paper during the work is not going to be helpful.

5 MEASUREMENTS
Are the plans annotated clearly, with plenty of measurements in the same units? The external dimensions for all outside walls, positions of windows and doors are most important.

6 SPECIFICATIONS
Are the Building Regulations plans comprehensive and detailed? Are they annotated with a detailed and bespoke specification? In other words, do they look busy and worth the money being paid for them?

7 LEVELS
Do the plans show a representation of the outside ground levels, either as existing or as proposed? Those that always show a perfect level site, even when in reality it is sloping, can cause problems. Are invert levels for proposed drainage shown?

8 DETAILS
Are there separate large-scale details of connections or critical areas of construction (e.g. abutments between the new extension and the existing building)?

9 RED HERRINGS
Are the plans free from statements like '... work to comply with Building Regulations – Approved Document...'? This is generally an indication that the designer is trying to palm off his or her responsibilities to somebody else and avoid having to detail some elements. You, the client, do not need to know what the references of the Building Regulations are, only that your scheme complies with them. Most Building Control Officers will not accept such bland statements, and will request that the details of the project are shown in the specification or on the drawings. Pre-printed standard specifications are also to be avoided. Some designers use these as a labour-saving tool, but this procedure is far from helpful to their clients or the builders, since it usually contains some notes that will not apply to your project. All extensions are unique in some way and deserve a bespoke specification.

10 PRESENTATION
Do the plans look as though they have been drawn with care and pride? In other words, are they clear – have they been drawn with black drawing ink and in a variety of pen nib thicknesses? Do they show plenty of detail? Are they presentable?

Calculations may be an expensive 'extra' in the design process, since the designer may have to engage the services of a structural engineer on your behalf, and you need to know this in advance. Extensions which involve rooms in the roof similar to loft conversions (although this book doesn't cover loft conversions in detail) require a fair amount of structural design. Indeed, it may represent as much as half the designer's work, so knowing how much of the job is included in the cost is critical. The same could be true if 'special foundations' are required due to site conditions (see Chapter 4).

Agree a fixed fee with your designer before they commit drawing pen to paper, and establish whether this includes plans for Planning Permission and Building Regulations or just one or the other. Will the fee also include Planning and Building Regulations fees, which are not insignificant (currently they total around £500 for an average-size extension), or will you be paying these separately? Many disputes have arisen between clients and their agents over who was due to pay council fees. It is worth remembering that in the eyes of the local authority the responsibility lies with the home-owner, and it would be there that they would look in the event of a bad debt. If you do agree for your designer to pay the fees on your behalf, make it a written contract between the two of you – a statement jointly signed and copied would suffice, and may save many arguments later. Your best option may be to write out personal cheques to the council for the exact amounts required by them, and hand them to

your agent for inclusion with his submission. I say cheques: Planning and Building Regulation applications are entirely separate, and lumping their fees together on one cheque may give rise to confusion.

The second problem is more often to be encountered with less honourable agents – those who regard minor amendments to the plans, required by the council, as 'extras', even though the amendments are needed as a result of their lack of knowledge or absence of information on the original drawings.

Do not be fooled into believing that the 'council' is insisting upon an extraordinary amount of detail for your scheme. Although this can be a grey area, which clients do not often go into beforehand, it should always be possible for designers to include in their price any minor alterations or revisions to the plans without charging extra. The professional designer will have drawn up the plans on a negative which can easily be amended by scratching out and reworking. Some councils only require a written note for a specification change, while others may insist upon amended plans. Check which yours prefers.

Should any changes take place, request an amended plan. A letter detailing the changes to the project may become separated from the project details once the builders start work, resulting in the amendments being overlooked. If they have been requested, then they are important: have them put on the plans, and label the old plans 'Superseded' to avoid confusion. An alphabetical suffix to the plan number identifies the latest revision. This same

10 Expert Points

TEN EXPERT POINTS TO DRAWING IT YOURSELF ARE:

1 MATERIALS

Use tracing paper of at least 90 gsm weight and a drawing pen containing indelible black ink. Thinner tracing paper will not tolerate much 'scratching out' if changes are to be made. Use A1 paper. Dyeline prints can be made from the negative at a relatively low cost.

2 PENCIL LINING

Mark out as much as you can in 2H pencil before inking in.

3 LOCATION PLAN

You must include a location plan to a scale of not less than 1:1250, showing your site outlined in red. Note that Ordnance Survey maps can only be copied by an OS-authorised supplier – the penalties for breach of OS copyright are expensive! Some satellite-produced maps are becoming available from other sources, such as redundant Soviet spy satellites; come to that, your own hand-drawn rendition of your location could be used.

4 BLOCK PLAN

You should include a block plan to a scale of 1:200 or 1:500, showing the position of the extension on the existing house and the position of any other nearby buildings or roads. It may be sufficient to combine this with the location plan in one, depending on the locality.

5 FLOORS AND ELEVATIONS

Include 1:50- or 1:100-scale elevations from all aspects, showing the proposed extension and the existing house. The floor layout of plans of each level should be included again, both of the existing house and as extended. The reason for this is that it may be the case that the extension will have some effect on the ventilation or fire escape route from the existing rooms, for example.

6 USE OF ROOMS

Mark on all floor plans the use of each room – this has an effect on what requirements will be imposed on the extension and how it will be judged.

7 CROSS SECTIONS

Include at least one cross section through the proposed extension, drawn at a scale of 1:20 if possible, but no greater than 1:50. Cross sections are the most valuable of building plans, since they expose the details of the construction, indicating the materials and their thicknesses, as well as heights and dimensions within the property. It is a good idea to include much of the specification alongside the cross sections.

8 LEVELS

Indicate the outside ground levels and the invert levels of the drains, where new drainage is to be connected, on the section and the elevations. This is normally done at manholes or inspection chambers. Even if you don't have the national datum level measured from a local bench mark (datum levels are measured from Newlyn, Cornwall), you can still take your own levels from the existing drains by measuring the depth between the manhole cover and the bottom of the channel (invert level). If you intend to keep your ground-floor level the same throughout the extended house, you can reference these levels from the floor level measured from the existing house. Be aware of the ground level when drawing up plans.

9 SPECIFICATIONS

These should include the position,

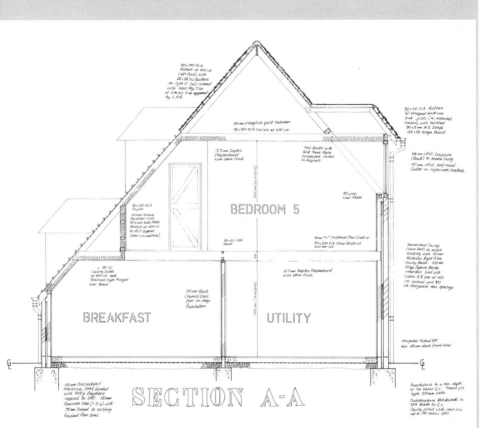

When drawing up a plan, make sure that you label everything clearly and with no room for confusion.

form and dimensions of the foundations, walls, windows, floors, roofs, chimneys, etc.; the provision made in the structure for insulation to the floor, walls, and roof; the position of drains, their fall, access points for rodding, and manholes; and the protection of any drains passing under the structure. In all cases the specificationsshould describe the materials to be used and, where appropriate, their thickness.

10 COPIES

Be prepared to have many copies printed up. Councils will require at least six sets for Planning Permission, and up to four (usually two) for Building Regulations. Leave at least two in a safe place for yourself, and prepare several for builders to quote with. Once the work starts on-site, it is often worth laminating the approved plan in weather-resistant plastic to make sure that it sees the whole job through.

process should be applied to Conditional Approvals issued for the Building Regulations. Make sure that your designer resolves these conditions (which are usually listed on an attached schedule with the plans approval notice) as soon as possible. Leaving them unaddressed until the work starts is likely to lead to subsequent problems for the builder.

However, it may be the case that the plans are required to be completely redrawn, for example if the scheme is fundamentally unacceptable for planning consent, and in such cases the designer may be justified to charge extra for the total redraw. Again, agree the principles beforehand!

An experienced and knowledgeable designer should be able to give you some warning of any possible problems with your requirements before he or she draws up the scheme, based on his or her knowledge and experience.

DIY (draw it yourself)

If you intend to draw the plans yourself – and there is no reason why you shouldn't – bear in mind that the Building Regulations plans are fairly onerous in respect of the detail that must be shown.

Submitting your applications

There is one very important point to get across here, a point which is the cause of much angst and confusion amongst the public. This isn't surprising, as there is a wealth of misinformation available to the public. Every book printed that mentions either Planning or Building Regulations seems to mix the two

together or suggest that they are one and the same thing.

They are not.

The most they have in common is that their officers work in the same building. Planning has a public image, with its officers sometimes being portrayed (with stunning mimicry) on TV soaps and sitcoms. Building Control, on the other hand, hardly ever gets a mention, and when it does a lot of people wrongly assume it is another name for Planning. The two disciplines are entirely separate, so try to disassociate the two of them in your mind, and forget about anything you may have read in other books that touch upon the subject.

If you are in any doubt over the questions contained on the application forms for Planning and Building Regulations – and some of them do look pretty odd, it must be said – it is wise to ask for assistance at the council offices rather than to guess. Incomplete or incorrect submissions will only delay your approval.

On receipt of the application for Planning Permission, you will be given a date eight weeks ahead, which is the statutory date by when the application is due a decision, but be warned, they may need to extend it with your consent. Building Regulations work to a statutory five-week date (which again may be extended, with your consent, to two months) and may write to you, setting out a list of defects or amendments to the plans required before approval. Alternatively, they may simply make these points the subject of a Conditional Approval. Either way, they should be addressed before work starts, to avoid problems on-site. In Scotland, you must have a Building Warrant before starting on any work.

If you do intend to submit your own plans, it is quite likely that unless you are familiar with current Building Regulations and construction, they will need amending. If you have some faith in your builder's knowledge and abilities, you may wish to avoid a **Full Plans Application** under the Building Regulations and submit a **Building Notice** (not available in Scotland).

Building Notice

This is a statement form which basically says that you will be complying with the Regulations in building your extension, and gives the Building Control Surveyor 48 hours notice of your intention to start the work. Surveyors will inspect the work at various stages on notification by you or your builder, and will advise you on any problems. There is a certain element of risk with the Building Notice method, because you do not have the benefit of an approved plan to work to, and the Building Control Surveyor may only know if you have contravened a regulation requirement after you've done it, so it could be an expensive way to build. Consequently, it is only advisable to adopt this procedure after discussing with your builder and Building Control Surveyor the scheme in detail, and only then if you are satisfied that they can agree on the details before each stage of the work. If you are proposing to build your extension yourself, it would be advisable to have an approved set of plans to work to.

Structural Design Certificates

Only available in Scotland, these certificates can be submitted by either a full or corporate member of the Institute of Civil Engineers (ICE) or the Institute of Structural Engineers (IStructE) as a statement of compliance. They are, in effect, self-certifying the structural design of the scheme. A 'supporting statement' must be submitted with them regarding the stability of the property, and a new design certificate must be submitted for any amendments affecting the structure that are made later. Plans showing the structural design are still required to be submitted for reference, showing the conditions that the design is based on, e.g. wind load assumed, bearing capacity of subsoil assumed, etc. These conditions will then be verified on-site by inspection once the work has got under way.

Local authority approvals and exemptions

The following gives an indication of some exemption categories. It should be considered only as a guide, because the law in this respect is prone to change. For a full and definitive statement of the law, consultation should be made to the relevant current statutory instrument.

Planning Permission may or may not be required for your proposed extension. A house which has not been extended before might still have permitted **development rights** which would allow you to extend without needing Planning Permission. The law as to what constitutes permitted development changes regularly, and you should **always check with your local**

planning authority and apply for a **Lawful Development Certificate** for your particular project. Needless to say, they will only do this on receipt of detailed plans as mentioned above, and in some cases a fee.

Under the Town and Country Planning Act 1990 (General Development Order), current guidelines for Permitted Development of domestic extensions in England and Wales are as follows; variations in Scotland under the Town and Country Planning (General Permitted Development) (Scotland) Order 1992 are shown in brackets:

Porches:
No more than **3 sq m** ground area (measured externally), and no more than 3 m height above ground; and at least **2 m from a public highway** (which means a public road, public footpath, public bridleway or byway).
Small extensions which are:
1) No higher than the highest part of the existing house. When within 2 m of your property boundary, in no part higher than 4 m.
General cases:
2a) No bigger than 15% of the existing house in volume or 70 cu m (Scotland –

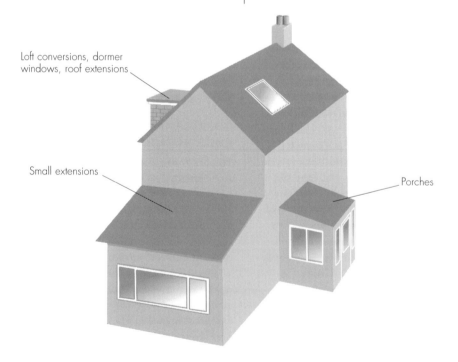

Loft conversions, dormer windows, roof extensions

Small extensions

Porches

Permitted development – small extensions may include loft conversions, dormer windows, roof extensions, conservatories, porches and bay windows.

20% or 24 sq m floor area) (whichever is the greater), and definitely no bigger than 115 cu m in volume (Scotland – 30 sq m floor area).

2b) **Extensions to the roof**, such as dormer windows – the roof extension will add less than 50 cu m to the volume of the house; the roof extension is to a roof slope which does not face the highway; the roof extension does not increase the height of the roof.

Special cases: terraced houses and also properties in the following designated areas: **Area of Outstanding Natural Beauty, National Park, Conservation Area, Norfolk and Suffolk Broads.**

3a) The extension is no bigger than 10% of the existing house in volume (Scotland – in floor area) or 50 cu m (Scotland –16 sq m floor area) (whichever is the greater), and definitely no bigger than 115 cu m in volume (Scotland – 30 sq m floor area).

3b) An extension to the roof, such as a dormer window, is only exempt in the case of terraced houses, providing it is no bigger than 40 cu m in volume. (Note: **in the other special areas listed above, Planning Permission will be required.** In all cases volume is measured externally and includes roof space.)

4) That no part of your extension is nearer to a public highway than any part of the existing house, unless it is at least 20 m away from your finished house (as extended). Public highway definitions are as given under porches. Watch out for public footpaths within 20 m.

5) No more than 50% of the total area of land around your original house has been built on by additions or other buildings (Scotland – a maximum of 30% is permitted).

6) There are **no** permitted Development Rights for extensions to listed buildings.

7) No Article 4 directive is in force on your property, removing Permitted Development rights (these are sometimes used in Conservation Areas or ground-polluted sites where greater control is needed).

Conservation Areas are defined as 'areas of special architectural or historic interest, the character or appearance of which it is desirable to preserve or enhance'. They are designated by the controlling local authority in consultation with parish councils, local amenity societies and the general public.

Areas of Special Control, although too small to be considered as Conservation Areas, have been so designated to protect their architectural or historical value. Permitted Development will be affected.

Farmhouses are not usually considered as domestic dwellings for planning purposes.

Extensions to council houses will also require the consent of the local authority Housing Department. Even recently sold council houses may carry restrictive covenants to this effect.

Because the first Town and Country Planning Act came into force on 1 July 1948, anything built on or after that date in the way of extensions, porches, garages, etc. counts towards your permitted development quota, and if your property has had any add-ons since then, you might not have any rights left at all. If this is the case, you may only recover Permitted Development rights by demolishing some or all of the old buildings. It is not unheard of for someone to knock down an old garage so that they can build a house extension without needing planning permission!

In England and Wales, the local Planning Authority will notify your neighbours of your proposals, either by letter, advertisement in the local press or by a notice displayed nearby. In Scotland, it is the responsibility of the applicant to consult his or her neighbours and submit their signed comments. Forms for this purpose are usually acquired with the planning application forms and should be returned completed when the application is made. In the former, interested parties have a couple of weeks to lodge any objections. It is, therefore, sometimes beneficial to show the Planning Authority your plans and consult with them beforehand.

Many people and organisations are consulted in the planning process – parish councils, environmental groups, etc. – and it takes some time for all comments to be collected. If there are any objections, it does not necessarily mean that your scheme will be refused. It does mean that it will be presented at a planning committee or sub-committee meeting, and will thus be decided by councillors rather than by delegated powers (i.e. planning officers). In reality, the case officer will prepare a short report and make a recommendation which, more often than not, will be adopted. You should be entitled to see any such report together with any

consultees' comments, but you will not be sent them automatically, so make enquiries and ask.

In most local authorities applications can be made and tracked electronically via the internet. Many architects can submit your plans as 'computer-aided designs' through this service which is accessible via the government's 'planning portal' site. The full address is given on page 173.

Planning approval is likely to be given with conditions. One condition is probably to be that work must start within 5 years otherwise the approval becomes invalid. Another may be that samples of materials (a brick and a roof tile) must be submitted for approval before work starts.

Planning authorities must have a good reason for refusing consent. The assumption is always one in favour of an application and not against it.

Refusal of Planning Permission

In the unfortunate event of your application being refused Planning Permission, find out what the exact nature of the objection was from your Planning Officer. The reasons will be printed on the refusal notice, but they are likely to be in planning jargon with policy references, so try to discuss ways with the Planning Officer as to how they could be overcome by revising the scheme. If this isn't possible, your only other recourse is to submit a **Planning Appeal** to the Planning Inspectorate (or the Welsh or Scottish Office or DOE for Northern Ireland as appropriate).

Appeals are currently a lengthy and time-consuming process. After the appeal is submitted, it can take four to five months before the Inspector visits the site, and then another two to three months after the visit before a decision is issued. The Planning Inspectorate does not currently charge for appeals, and so an appeal can be entirely free if you do it yourself. Many people engage their solicitor in this process, but if the solicitor is not fully conversant with local planning policies and DCLG advice circulars (and most won't be), he or she is likely to be only of administrative help. Planning consultants who specialise in planning applications and appeals are the best choice, but their fees may not be proportional to the benefits, so have a long, careful think before engaging one. Appeals may also be made against conditions of approval, if you consider them to be unacceptable.

The appeal is normally dealt with on the basis of a written statement in which you may quote the case for your application to be approved, and request that the council's decision is overturned.

In making your case, it is helpful to draw attention to relevant policies and DCLG circular advice, as well as to other approved schemes in your area which are similar, if not identical. Obviously, it is of advantage to have an expert on your side. Many home-made appeals lack substance and consequently fail. Once you have submitted your appeal, the local council's Planning Officer can respond with a counter-statement explaining why they think their decision should be upheld.

If this raises new issues, you may respond again, but otherwise it is best to leave it at that – exacerbating the

situation with a rhetorical argument will not help. A date will be established for the Inspector to visit the site, and the council's Planning Officer may attend as well. The Inspector will largely conduct his inspection without discussion, and will not entertain a verbal argument between parties. His decision will be notified to both parties at some point in the future by a concluding statement. The decision is final and challengeable only in the High Court.

Bear in mind that Planning Inspectors have complete freedom of judgement in considering your appeal and can, in deciding, make matters worse for you. For example, your application was refused because of a proposed overlooking window which you could have repositioned to gain approval. Instead, you lodge an appeal and the Inspector finds not just against the window but now states that the whole extension is unacceptable. What was a minor, redressable situation is now a major lost one.

Complaints can be made to the Local Authority Ombudsman if you consider that the local Planning Authority has been guilty of maladministration regarding your application. This means that you believe they have mishandled the planning process and, in doing so, jeopardised your application's chances of success. In other words, it is not the decision that is important in these cases but the way in which it was reached.

Obviously, local authorities have a duty to follow legislative procedures in processing planning applications, and such a complaint can only be successful if it can be proved that the Planning

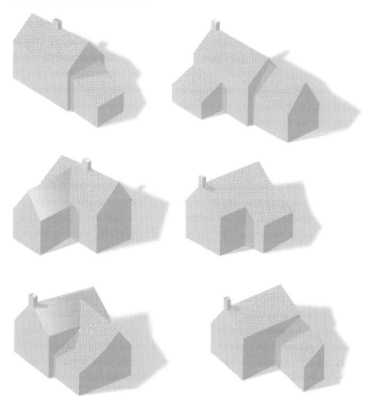

Examples of how a simple house form could
be extended to either the rear or side, and
showing the resultant shadowing.

Authority has neglected those
procedures to your detriment.

A lot of complaints addressed to the
Ombudsman each year are thrown out
as having 'no case to answer' simply
because the appellant has either not
understood this fact and is simply
objecting to the council's decision, i.e.
the initial refusal to grant planning
consent , or has chosen to ignore this
and continue with the objection.

Planning considerations include:

Overshading

If your proposed extension is on the
south side of a neighbouring building,
then the Planning Officer may judge
your proposal to be unsatisfactory
because of excessive overshading caused
by it. Obviously, this is more likely to be
a problem with two-storey extensions
than with single-storey ones.

Overlooking

If your proposal includes windows which overlook a neighbouring property, the Planning Officer may consider that in doing so, they encroach upon the privacy of the people living there.

It is usually not sufficient to suggest glazing the offending window with obscure-glass, unless it is a bathroom and would normally be so glazed. It is relatively simple for future owners to replace the glass with a clear pane. Apart from removing the window and repositioning it on another elevation which doesn't overlook, the only acceptable solution is to design it as a high-level window, with the bottom cill height at least 1.78 m above the finished floor level. This is above an average person's eye level, and therefore is often an acceptable solution. Most window manufacturers produce long, narrow windows for this purpose.

Design

The visual appearance of the extension is a prime consideration and is often the cause of much disagreement. Clearly, 'good design' is a matter of opinion and – believe it or not – some Planning Officers have been known to disagree with home-owners as to what is a good, or appropriate, design.

The only advice I can give you at this stage of the proceedings is that if an extension blends in with the original house, with materials that match and a design that is considerate, if not similar – the same style of windows, roof shape, etc. – then you have a sound basis for claiming that it is a good design, regardless of personal tastes.

Off-street car parking

You may be wondering how your extension – perhaps sited in the back garden – can affect your car-parking space. If the extension contains extra bedrooms, it can. This is because some planning guidelines cross-reference the number of off-street parking spaces required for a house with the number of bedrooms in the house. For example, a two-bedroom house may have needed two car spaces (one on the drive and one in the garage) when built, but a two-storey extension on the back of it proposes two extra bedrooms, making the total four. Your local planning guidelines may require a four-bedroom property to have at least three car spaces. These spaces have to be a given size and agreed with the Highways Officer, who will be consulted on your planning application.

If you intend to build over your driveway, you may have to provide alternative car-parking space on your site. All in all, you may have to find space in your garden for more than just the extension!

Highway visibility

If it is near to the road, your extension must not interfere with the existing 'line of sight' for motorists using the road, or indeed for yourself as you emerge from your driveway onto the road. The details of this line depend on the classification of the road.

Size

The size of your proposed extension is also important, and may relate as much to the amount of available room on your site and how much garden will be left, as to the impact on the neighbourhood. Too big, and the Planning Officer may consider your proposal to come under the heading of overdevelopment.

By now, you might be thinking that you stand a better chance of winning the National Lottery than getting planning consent, but in fact the odds are stacked in your favour – the percentage of all submitted applications approved each year runs around the 80% mark. On the debit side, in recent years only around two-thirds of these were actually approved within the statutory eight-week period.

Listed Building Consent

If you are fortunate enough to live in a listed building, you will need to apply separately for Listed Building Consent as well as Planning Permission. You will also have to apply for it even if your extension does not require an ordinary planning application.

The good news is that at the time of writing, no fee is paid for Listed Building Consent applications, as opposed to ordinary ones, which are at 2002 prices around £100 and going up frequently. The work is zero-rated for VAT purposes, and you should be able to recover the VAT paid on all materials. Labour should not be charged with VAT in the first place if you've advised your builders that it is a listed building.

Like conservation areas, listed buildings can be found throughout the United Kingdom. Your local planning authority will have a copy of the list for their area.

Building Regulations

In constructing your extension you are required to comply with the requirements of the Building Regulations. These regulations impose health and safety, energy conservation and accessibility requirements onto the built environment, and provided that you meet these minimum standards in the design and construction of your extension, you will receive Building Regulation Approval (in Scotland this is referred to as a Building Warrant).

Building Control Surveyors do not often receive plans that are 100% approvable in the first submission, and it is quite normal to receive an amendments letter or conditional approval from them, requiring some additional information or changes. This process may seem like a game of 20 Questions, but it is far better to discuss possible contraventions at this stage, rather than after they have been built in. Some of the points raised may seem insignificant, but remember that the plan checker doesn't know you or the person who will be building it, and is simply trying to iron out potential problems before the work starts. A note added to a plan or a change made at the stroke of a pen is usually less painful than having to knock a wall down!

If you have any doubts or don't understand the reasoning behind the points raised, pick up the phone or go and visit your Building Control Officer, who will be only too pleased to discuss matters with you. In Building Regulation terms, very little is considered impossible – it may be impractical or economically unviable but not impossible, and for every problem there usually exists more than one solution.

In some respects, receiving a conditional plans approval with comprehensive or onerous conditions for Building Regulations is no different to receiving a rejection notice. Some authorities may choose the former method to be more customer-friendly, but at the end of the day, it means the same – the design or specification requires some amendment before it is regarded as being 100% OK.

Incidentally, a rejection notice for Building Regulations may be overcome by re-presenting the plans suitably amended and re-completing the application forms; no extra fee is required for a straight resubmission. If the scheme is drastically altered, even if these alterations were imposed by the Planning Office, another separate fee and application may be required.

Advice on Building Regulations

If you need any advice on particular requirements of the Building Regulations, the Building Control Section of your local authority will be pleased to help. In England and Wales the requirements are contained in 14 Approved Documents, lettered A to P and issued by the DCLG as guides. The Scottish Building Standards have been arranged into a handbook of six parts. (Parts I and O don't exist.) Each one deals with separate issues. e.g. Part A – Structure, Part B – Fire Spread, Part C – Resistance to Weather and Ground Moisture, etc. The Approved Documents can be purchased from the HMSO or any good

bookshop, and have recently been published on CD-ROM. You don't need to buy them for one extension, but if you do need to refer to them, they are usually found in the reference section of public libraries, and at your local authority Building Control Office.

When it comes to building construction, an experienced Building Inspector is a fountain of knowledge, so do not be afraid to tap into it.

Most people will have some idea of what they want their extension to provide, and will instruct their designer accordingly. Often plan-drawers will simply draw up what the customer requires, without offering any advice. **Home extensions need Building Regulations approval, regardless of whether they need planning consent – Building Regulations approval is a separate matter, and is in no way connected to Planning Permission.** Categories for exemption are much fewer, and are simpler to understand. Currently under the Building Regulations 2000, Schedule 2 exemptions for extensions are as follows – in Scotland, variations under the Scottish Building Standards 2005 are shown in brackets:

1 **Porches** under 30 sq m floor area, built at ground level only (Scotland – under 8 sq m and more than 1 m from the boundary).
2 **Conservatories** under 30 sq m floor area, built at ground level only (Scotland – under 8 sq m and more than 1 m from the boundary).
3 And that in both cases the glazing which you may come into accidental contact with (such as in windows less

than 800 mm above floor level and doors and sidelights up to 1500 mm above floor level) is safety glass (toughened or laminated) or protected by guarding.

This in itself should not be a problem, because the glazing industry is self-regulating with its own standards, and suppliers of glass should enquire as to its location to ensure that the correct material is provided.

4 **A covered way or car port** that is less than 30 sq m and is open on at least two sides.

The definitions are usually taken as follows:

Porch – a non-habitable space that covers an entrance to the house but remains as an entrance, i.e. separated from the house by a door. Thus there is no scope for opening your 'porch' up into the lounge.

Conservatory – an extension which is not for year-round habitable use but seasonal, does not have any fixed heating, is used in some part for the propagation of plants, and again is separated from the main house by a door and not opened up to a heated room.

To qualify for these exemptions you must adhere to a set of strict guidelines. These are: Porches or Consevatories can not contain WC's, or flued appliances like fires or boilers which are controlled services. Neither can they adversely affect the property and compliance with other regulations, such as 'access for people with disabilities' by building over an accessible entrance to the house.

See Chapter 5 for more advice on building conservatories.

Building control on-site

It is a requirement of the Building Regulations that the builder notifies the Building Control Officer at various stages of the work, and leaves the work at these stages exposed for inspection before covering it up and continuing. Failure to give such notice may mean that you are required to break open and expose the work for inspection later.

The stages for notification usually include:
1 **Commencement** – 2 days' notice.
2 **Foundation excavation** – 1 day's notice
3 **Foundation concrete** – 1 day's notice
4 **Oversite preparation** – 1 day's notice
5 **Damp-proof course** – 1 day's notice
6 **Drains before covering** – 1 day's notice
7 **Drains testing** – 1 day's notice
8 **Occupation** – 1 day's notice
9 **Completion** – 2 days' notice

Additional inspection notices may be required by some authorities, so check with them before starting.

Notice should be in writing, and most authorities provide cards which can be used for this purpose. A fax machine is an excellent way of giving notice, since it endorses the request with the time and date it is transmitted. Some authorities may operate a telephoned notice system. If you don't receive an inspection within the time limit, it is extremely unwise to carry on without first contacting the Building Control Office, to check why they haven't come out and to give them an eleventh-hour opportunity to do so.

Building Control Officers do not supervise the work on your behalf. They carry out spot checks to ensure that the minimum standards of the Building Regulations have been met. If you are in any doubt as to the quality of workmanship your builder will apply, you should appoint your own surveyor to oversee the project. A private surveyor can ensure quality control of the work, authorising stage payments as the job proceeds.

Completion Certificates

Once the work is finished, a Completion Certificate should be sought from the Building Control Office. This is a valuable piece of paper which will be required should you sell or remortgage the property. It is a statement that the work complies with the Building Regulations. Until this point, you may only have a Plans Approval Notice that says that your plans comply. In Scotland, you may have to submit a certificate of safety for the electrical installation from a competent person before you can receive a Completion Certificate.

Use of materials

Your home extension must be built with approved materials that are fit to do the task required of them. Your designer and builder should be familiar with the products available and their limitations, but you need not rely solely on their knowledge. Their are several ways in which materials and products can be checked for fitness in building:

1 A product that is British Standard-approved is one that has been tested and accepted as being in accordance with the relevant British Standard.

2 British Board of Agreement (BBA) approval is given in the form of a certificate which sets out the performance of a material and the criteria in which it should be used.

3 In respect of both the BSI and BBA approvals above, it should be noted that because we are part of the EC (European Community), similar national and equivalent standards from EC member-state countries may be equally valid, but the onus is on you to establish that they are.

4 EC marks on products that are in compliance with the European Construction Products Directive are considered satisfactory.

The EC mark.

5 The kite mark scheme, operated by the British Standards Institute (BSI) and other independent schemes which exist in the UK for testing and certifying, is regarded as satisfactory, provided that the scheme has been accredited by NACCB (National Accreditation Council for Certification Bodies).

6 Laboratory test results are a way in which a material or product can be

Cottage Dormer Window

Plain Tile Hanging to Cheeks to match Dormer window with 25x38 mm SW Battens on untearable felt to plywood face nailed to studwork frame

Raised Patio Level at Rear

Rear End Elevation

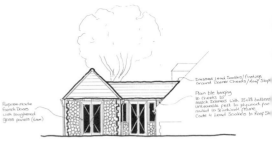

Dressed Lead Soakers/ Flashings around Dormer Cheeks/ Roof Slope

Plain tile hanging to Cheeks to match Dormer with 25x28 battens untearable felt to plywood face nailed to studwork frame. Code 4 Lead Soakers to Roof Slope

Purpose-made French Doors with toughened Glass panels (6mm)

Garden End Elevation

Line Position of new Lobby Link

Purpose-made Window Frames with 4mm Glass panes

Raised Patio Level at Rear

Stone Wall

Cottage Elevation

Scale 1:5

Plan

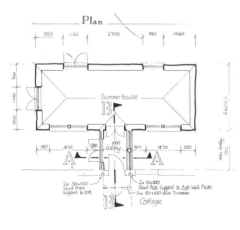

| 1350 | 1150 | 2700 | 990 | 1460 |

Summerhouse

580 | 1870 | 880 | 1000 Lobby | 900 | 1870 | 550

2/50x100 Stud Post Support to Oak

2/50x100 Stud Post Support to Oak Wall Plate

2/50x100 SC4 Trimmer

Cottage

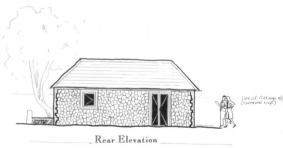

Line of Cottage (Catslide Roof)

Rear Elevation

The illustrations on these pages are taken from actual working plans drawn up professionally. On your plans, make sure that everything has been covered.

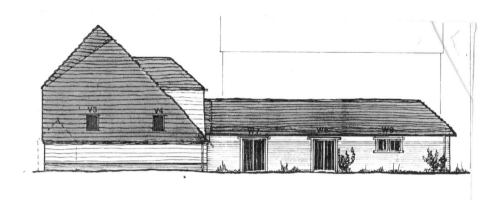

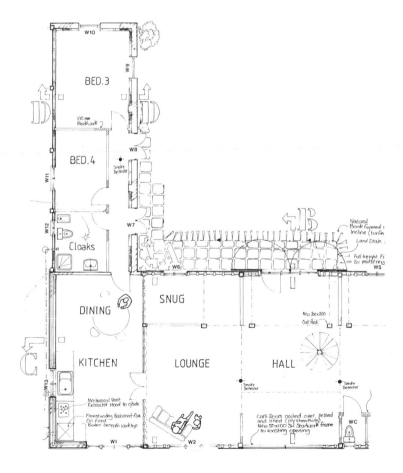

10 Expert Points

HERE ARE TEN EXPERT POINTS OF
GENERAL DESIGN ADVICE:

1 LIGHT

Most extensions are built onto outside
walls which already have a window or
glazed door, and that window or door
opening is often used or enlarged to make
the internal opening to the extension.
Consider how much light you will lose from
that existing room, and try to avoid making
it into a black hole. The Building Regulations
are only concerned with the ventilation to it,
not how dark it is, and you can borrow
ventilation from the extension windows a lot
more easily than you can borrow light. If
possible, design in a new window or
rooflight to the old room, to replace the
daylight. Consider the orientation of the
windows on your extension – south, north,
etc.; south-facing patio doors can heat up a
room quickly with solar energy, and small
windows on a north face can leave it dark
and cold.

2 CORRIDORS AND PASSAGES

Try to avoid overlong corridors or
passages which are windowless. This is
easily done with large extensions comprising
several rooms (particularly in bungalows),
and can look fine on a drawing but end up
like a rabbit warren when built.

3 SECURITY

Security is an important consideration,
but make sure that it doesn't trap you in
your own home. In a fire you will need to
be able to escape quickly. PVC-U double-
glazed and lockable windows can be as
impenetrable from the inside as they are
from the outside. If they have the glazing
beads on the inside and you keep them shut
and locked, there is no reason why you
shouldn't leave the key in the lock so that
you can get out in an emergency, so long as
you don't include fanlights alongside them –

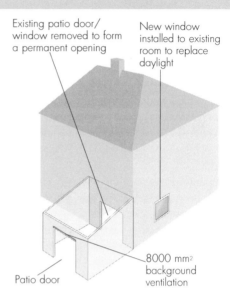

Existing patio door/
window removed to form
a permanent opening

New window
installed to existing
room to replace
daylight

8000 mm²
background
ventilation

Patio door

fanlights have a habit of being left open.
Avoid flat roofs that will provide a
platform for burglars to upstairs windows. Fit
extra locks to patio doors, and make sure
that they can't be lifted off the runners.
Choose laminated, double-glazed units for
added security. (See Chapter 5.) Consider
using garden plants as a line of defence
against intruders – for example, pyracantha
is an attractive and natural form of
protection when trained along a vulnerable
fence or wall (see Chapter 7).

4 ROOM FOR EVERYTHING

Although the Planning and Building
Control Officers do not need to see the
internal furnishings drawn on your plans, it
is a good idea to overmark one set for
yourself with scaled-down outlines. If you're
not sure how you will arrange things, cut out
some cardboard shapes to the scale of
furniture and overlay them on a plan to see
how they fit. This way you can juggle
everything around easily without wrecking

the plan, and you may be surprised to discover that a wall could do with being a bit longer! In the same way, be aware of windows and their cill heights – they may not be obvious on a floor plan and can easily be 'covered' by wardrobes.

Watch out for long, featureless walls. You may want to build in a feature, such as a chimney breast or fireplace, in which case now is the time to plan it before the foundations are dug.

5 POWER POINTS

Consider how many socket outlets you will need and where they should be placed. Apparently, one of the Consumer Council's biggest complaints received from new house-buyers was that there weren't enough power points in new homes (see Chapter 6).

6 HEATING

Give some early consideration to plumbing and heating. Will your existing boiler be powerful enough to supply the extension as well, or will it need to be replaced? Where will you run the pipework to radiators – ducted within the floor structure or out on the surface of walls?

7 FINISHINGS AND CRACKS

Will you be wanting to occupy the extension the minute it is finished? If so, it may be worth considering dry-lining the walls inside with plasterboard instead of wet-plastering them. When dried out quickly with central heating, wet plaster can crack terribly; dry-lining won't. Unless they are structural, cracks are not covered by most warranties, unsightly though they may be.

8 MATCHING MATERIALS

Check with builders' merchants to see if they can match your house bricks. Some specialist brick suppliers offer a 'matching' service. An extension can look awful if the bricks clash with the original house bricks.

The same goes for roof tiles and slates – and be aware that they have minimum pitch requirements. Try to ensure a suitable pitch for your extension roof – one that is too shallow may prevent you from matching the tiles to the house.

9 FENESTRATION

Consider the elevations carefully, and pay particular attention to the position and size of windows. Align the heads of windows to each storey, not the cills. If possible, consider using low-maintenance paint systems, such as stains and microporous paints, unless you are one of the few people who enjoy biannual exterior decorating.

10 SPACE

Consider the amount of free space you are going to create. For most people the reason for extending the house is to create extra space, so make it as spacious and freely accessible as possible. For example, there is no requirement that says you have to have 762 mm wide internal doors. It may be the industry standard, but if you want 838 mm wide doors, design them in and make it easier to get the shopping into the kitchen or invite elderly or disabled friends round. In addition, an overhanging roof can offer shade from the sun and shelter from rain to the wall below.

Remember than the design standard required will be much higher for a Listed Building or in a Conservation Area. Local Planning Authorities may have specific policies aimed at protecting the character of the building or area.

You may be encouraged to re-use existing roof materials and supplement them with natural matching ones; PVC-U windows may not be acceptable. You may be encouraged to replicate the design and material of the original timber windows.

verified fit for a particularly use, but care needs to be taken in reading them. They may actually demonstrate the complete opposite. The fact that a product has a test certificate does not necessarily mean that it is OK – the test criteria may have been determined with the manufacturer to demonstrate what it can do, but that may not reflect the situation that it will be in when installed in your extension. Be sure to have any test certificates checked over by your local Building Control Officer. Ideally, the laboratory should be independent and NAMAS (National Materials Accreditation Service) approved.

From time to time unscrupulous manufacturers make bogus claims about their products' performance; if discovered, these matters should be referred to Trading Standards.

All but a very small minority of the building materials available today are suitable and fit for use. The biggest problem comes from them being installed in the wrong position, fixed or built-in in the wrong way. There is one simple way in which you can insure that any material is properly used, and that is to contact the manufacturers and request their advice. Most manufacturers of building products have technical advisors whose sole aim in life is to try and ensure that their company's products are used correctly. To this aim they produce leaflets, booklets and sometimes manuals along with test evidence, certificates and CDs, all illustrating and describing in clear simple language (their customers are builders) what must be done.

Other matters of law
Covenants

If you are unfortunate enough to have Restrictive Covenants (see Chapter 1) on your property which require you to obtain the consent of other parties, make sure that you do this with enough time to spare before starting.

Who else could possibly be involved? If you live on a fairly new housing estate, the original developers could be. The majority of house-builders employ their own in-house architects to design their homes, and they frequently impose Restrictive Covenants on the deeds to regulate any extensions or alterations. I suppose they feel that the character of the houses shouldn't be adversely affected by poorly designed extensions while their name is still associated with the development. You may have to submit the plans for their approval before you start. Given that they may take a more onerous view than anybody else, you would be wise to obtain their consent first before moving on to submit the planning application.

Party Wall, Etc. Act 1996 (Building near Boundaries)

If your extension is proposed within 6 m of your neighbour's foundations, it may be likely that you have a duty under the Party Wall Act 1996 to notify the owner of that property of your intentions. I say likely, because it does ultimately depend upon the depth of their foundations in relation to yours.

The Party Wall Act was introduced to England and Wales in general in July 1997, but has existed in London under the London Building (Amendment) Act since 1939. It endeavours to prevent neighbour disputes over party walls ending up in the courts by setting down a procedure for consultation. If London is anything to go by, it seems to work, because only 20 cases out of roughly 2000 end up in court each year.

The Act can be divided into two parts, of which only one is covered by this book, that relating to extensions. The other part relates to work carried on existing party walls, such as repairs. Party walls (or separating walls) are those which divide one property from another in the case of semi-detached or terraced properties.

Although the boundary line may run though the middle of such a wall, legally both property owners have rights to the whole wall. This is because they both rely upon the whole wall for protecting their property from fire and sound transference, so both need to know if the other is doing anything to the wall.

Because it is also possible to undermine the stability of nearby foundations by excavating the ground alongside them, the Act also covers excavation of foundations for extensions, or indeed, anything else.

If your extension proposals fall within the Act (as illustrated), you are required to do the following:

One month before you start work, you have a statutory duty to notify the owner of the neighbouring building of your proposals.

What happens if I have agreed with my neighbour already?
The agreement must be in writing. If this is the case, the one month is not an issue and you can execute the works. In the event that, having served notice on your neighbour to do the work and given him a copy of plans detailing your proposals, 14 days have passed without reply, he is deemed to have dissented and you have to appoint surveyors. The neighbouring owner can require you to underpin their foundations, if necessary at your own expense, should they prove to be within the affected zone caused by your excavated trenches.

What happens if my neighbour and I can't agree?
You may jointly in agreement appoint one surveyor to act for both of you, or appoint two surveyors, one to act on each behalf. The surveyor/s draw up an agreement which covers the right to do the work, describes it and the time and manner in which it is to be done, and the costs which you may pay to the neighbour in compensation. If they cannot come to an agreement, a third surveyor can be jointly appointed to act as a final arbitrator. This adjudication by surveyors is intended to relieve the courts of disputes.

If your proposed extension is to be built on the boundary itself, you can only allow your foundations to cross the boundary by virtue of their design spread after giving one month's notice to the neighbouring owner and compensating them for any consequential damage.

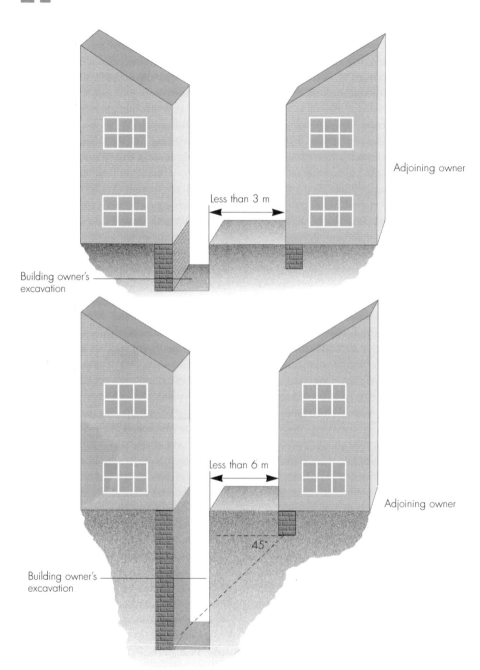

Adjoining owner

Less than 3 m

Building owner's excavation

Less than 6 m

Adjoining owner

45°

Building owner's excavation

Excavations controlled under the Party Wall Act 1996.

If your extension involves the construction of a new party wall on the boundary (perhaps your neighbour has an extension to the boundary already, which you intend to abut), you must give them one month's notice of your intention. If they consent to the wall's construction you can go ahead, the cost being met by both parties proportional to the benefit for each. If they object, you cannot proceed and have no rights to build the new party wall. You do still have rights to set the wall back onto your land and let only the foundations spread across the boundary, as described in the procedure above.

In the case of new extensions, the Party Wall Act 1996 can apply simply to building near (within 6 m) to the boundary. Neighbours with affected foundations up to 6 m away can require them to be underpinned. Generally, all costs would have to be met by you, unless it can be agreed that your neighbour has benefited from the work as a result and should therefore contribute to the costs.

Where is the boundary?

The Party Wall Act has one fundamental drawback: it assumes that both neighbours agree on where the boundary between them is. In a party wall this is not a problem – the wall itself is jointly owned by both of them – but in the garden?

In a cabinet in the British Museum, sitting alongside one of the earliest maps of the world (c. 600BC), is another carved stone from ancient Babylonia. This one sets out the principles for establishing the boundary between you and your neighbour and resolving disputes. You see, this isn't a new problem. Indeed, Babylon's ruler, King Hammurabi – firmly lodged in the annals of history for his harsh but fair law codes – might have been forgiven for thinking that in over 2000 years we might have had this one cracked.

The Land Registry can send you a map extract with a red line drawn around the boundary of your land. The map is reproduced to an impossibly small scale and the line is drawn so thick that it will serve to be of little value if you are fighting for inches. In these situations, the surveyor can be introduced to measure and make a considered opinion. If you still can't agree and consider that your neighbour is in some way trespassing, then you may wish to take the matter to court. I know that every man's home is his castle and all that, but it might be a sobering exercise to work out how much value these few inches of land have on the current market, and compare this to the money that you anticipate spending on claiming it.

I am hopeful that in the next millennium we will be able to sort this one out; the technology for plotting boundaries more accurately already exists with laser (EDM) theodolites that can plot lines straighter than you can care to imagine, and then measure them to a hair's thickness. Satellites that can photograph the earth's surface to 1-m resolution can define hedges and the lines on a tennis court from space. All this information can be digitally stored and reproduced by computers. Who knows, perhaps even one day the Land

Registry will be able to give you a decent scale map that hasn't been overdrawn with felt pen.

Right to light

A rather older piece of private sector legislation, but one that is still in force and effective, is the 'right to light' principle established in the Prescription Act of 1832.

If your extension will cut out some of the light from your neighbour's window, and that window has been there for at least 20 years, then you may be open to legal action. If your neighbours have not already enjoyed 20 years of light at a particular window and you are concerned that this act may jeopardise your plans to build an extension in the future, you may apply to the local Land Registry for a Light Obstruction Notice which allows you to block the light for a period of 12 months. This would mean that you would have to reapply regularly if you wanted to ensure that their right could not become established by the 20-year period.

However, if you live on a relatively modern housing estate, it may well be the case that the deeds of the properties contain a clause removing the 'right to light' of any owner, regardless of how long they have enjoyed it.

Building over drains

If your extension is proposed to be built over the top of drainage pipes, you will need to establish what category these drains fall into: public or private. Public sewers are those which have been adopted by the water authority dealing with the sewerage disposal in your area.

Mostly they are found under the highway, but not always; some public sewers run along under the back gardens of older properties, particularly terraced ones, and are therefore prone to being built over by rear extensions. Your local council holds records of where the public sewers in its area are, and these maps are available for public inspection, so if in doubt – check. Before building over a public sewer, you may be required to enter into a legal agreement with the water authority before work starts. In fact, there is a requirement under the Building Act 1984 to do this before plans can be approved under the Building Regulations. An added complication is that some authorities treat 'building over' as being within a 'certain distance of' and not necessarily on top of.

The agreement you enter into will undoubtedly detail what protection you will need to give the sewer from damage by the building, and what rights of access the authority will have to it after it is built. It may also require that the drain is first inspected by remote camera to determine its condition, so that any repairs are carried out beforehand, and likewise any repairs needed afterwards can be attributed to your building work and appropriately charged.

A 'building-over sewer' agreement can be a costly and most onerous contract for the home-owner to enter into, and you should have your solicitor read it over before you sign. It may well prove to be a disadvantage in any future sale of the property.

Private drainage is less of a problem, particularly if it only serves your house and nobody else's. If it does serve other properties along the run, it is known as 'shared drainage' and means exactly that. You don't own it, you share ownership of it with the other home-owners on the system before it connects to the public sewer. Consequently, you should obtain their consent for building over it, so that they may be satisfied that you are correctly protecting it.

Remember that in the case of shared systems, all the owners have to share maintenance and repair costs between them, regardless of which part of the drain blocks and whose land it was crossing at the time. If it can be established without doubt which owner caused the blockage, they would be legally obliged to pay in whole the costs of unblocking it, even if the blockage has occurred further down the run, on somebody else's property.

Wildlife

You may like to incorporate some wildlife-friendly features in your design to attract certain species. Overhanging eaves for house martins and swifts would be much appreciated – by conservationists as well as the birds – as recent design trends have followed boxed-in eaves details, leaving them homeless. If you do so, a tray fixed to the wall just below the eaves to catch the droppings is advisable.

Owls, particularly barn owls, can be encouraged if you have a high gable end where a built-in cavity can be formed within the loft space. This takes some careful design work, but with a projecting brick detail around a small arched opening it can be made into an attractive architectural feature, as well as a much-needed home. A sheltered gable end is best, with perhaps the benefit of an overhanging verge.

Bat boxes can be secured to a high gable wall too, if the idea of building in a home within your roof space gives you the creeps. Bats don't actually nest, they hang themselves up at night, and pipistrelles, being the smallest species, will do that quite happily in the cavities of old buildings anyway. They don't chew cables or timber, and their droppings consist only of insect remains, so they aren't a health hazard.

Advice on building in these wildlife homes can be obtained from The Hawk and Owl Trust and the Bat Conservation Trust respectively.

Health and safety

Designers have a responsibility under the Construction (Design and Management) Regulations 1994 to minimise the risks associated with building work. They can do this by specifying safe working-practice procedures when risks are involved, such as when forming an opening in a load-bearing wall, by detailing the sequence of work and provision of temporary support.

The house-owner who is having domestic building work carried out on his or her house is exempt from the provisions for 'clients' under these regulations and has no responsibilities. Other parts of the CDM Regulations only apply to domestic building work, where the house is also used as a business premises. If in doubt, contact the Health and Safety Executive.

CHAPTER 3

Builders

Finding a builder

The building industry has unfortunately been the butt of much criticism in this country for a great many years, largely due to the minority of cowboys operating as builders. Regrettably, it has always been the case that anyone who wants to operate as a builder can do so without qualification or, indeed, previous experience. After all, we live in a country where DIY is so popular and materials so easily available that general building is seen by some as requiring no particular skills, apart from the ability to labour hard – in other words, the perfect conditions for cowboys to flourish in. Recently there has been a bit of a media explosion on the theme of 'nightmare builders', as if the situation has suddenly just appeared. It hasn't – it's been here for years, centuries even.

The ancient Babylonians (them again) invented the first building codes, with one simple but effective regulation: your house falls down, we put the builder to death. Sadly, this is no longer considered acceptable, and at least since the Second World War the law for controlling builders has been somewhat ineffectual.

Trading Standards Officers are occasionally featured in these programmes, tracking down cowboys but never being able to stop them. From a Trading Standards point of view, it comes down to a matter of the rogues misrepresenting themselves, like a manufacturer who makes false claims about their product – if they can prove that these cowboys make false claims about themselves or their work to win custom, they can be prosecuted. For the people featured in these horror stories, to have got to the stage where Trading Standards are involved usually means to have got to the stage where they have already become a victim. The wolf is no longer at the door, but is either sitting in their kitchen reading their newspaper or has moved on to a new territory.

Some cowboys have aliases, some of them prey on the elderly, and some of them have advertising campaigns to rival the imagination of the Saatchis, but all of them have a talent for separating people from their money. If they are taken through the courts and prosecuted, it doesn't necessarily mean that the customer will be reimbursed – the cowboy builder may have no definable assets, trusting in the adage that there is little point in suing a man of straw.

In the absence of a licensing system, the only way to find a reputable builder is to find his work and his previous customers. Ideally, it would be helpful to get a recommendation from an independent inspector of his work, such as the local authority Building Control Office, who may have inspected all his work for years and years. However, this is not considered to be acceptable by most local authorities, and consequently their officers are required not to give recommendations or otherwise, which is a shame, because they are almost certainly the only people who know with any certainty. Collectively, local authority Building Inspectors, to use their former name, share the experiences of hundreds of home-owners every year engaged in building work in their districts.

10 Expert Points

HERE ARE TEN EXPERT POINTS TO HELP YOU FIND THE RIGHT BUILDER:

1 SHORTLIST
Draw up a shortlist of four or five builders. Include at least two from your local area, to avoid incurring travelling charges.

2 QUOTES
Invite them to give you a detailed and written quotation for the work (not an estimate) once you have had your plans approved. It will prove difficult, if not impossible, to get anything but a vague estimate without plans.

3 ATTENTION TO DETAIL
Consider how detailed the quotation is. Does it refer to the drawing numbers and details, etc.? Did the builder spend time inspecting the site as well as the plans?

4 TRADE ASSOCIATION
Check to see if they advertise any trade association membership, and check the validity of that membership with the association. Do they offer a warranty?

5 PREVIOUS WORK
Request a list of previous contracts recently completed (within the last 2 years), and once you have received it, select one or two of them and ask if it would be possible to view the work or speak to the owners. Most builders are happy to arrange this if they have satisfied clients. Others may feel unable to make such an arrangement. If so, ask if it would be possible to visit one of their current sites to see the work in progress.

6 SITE VISIT
If you can visit a site in progress, you can gain a valuable insight into the builder's work, even without possessing building knowledge. For example, consider how tidy the site is kept, look to see whether materials are neatly stored and protected or littered around, and check how many workers are on-site – a quiet, undermanned site might indicate slow work lacking continuity, a chaotic, overcrowded site might suggest that work is being rushed and is behind schedule. Is the work protected if the weather is bad?

7 VAT
Check to see if they are VAT-registered. Some builders may offer a cash price by deducting the VAT element, which, after all, is not insubstantial. It should be needless to say that cash deals are best avoided. Quite apart from defrauding the Exchequer, they undermine reputable VAT-paying builders, reducing the industry's standards and affecting your contractual rights in disputes. Try also to imagine that the 'cash-deal' builder has already added in the VAT element without declaring it on paper!

8 INSURANCE
Ask to see evidence of the builder's Public Liability Insurance (which should provide a minimum of £1,000,000 worth of cover), and check that it is valid.

9 BANKER'S REFERENCE
Ask for a banker's reference, and avoid builders who request a deposit for materials or whatever up-front. Those that need it are unlikely to have the financial security necessary to carry out the work, and may already be refused credit at local builders' merchants.

10 LOCAL AUTHORITY
Check with the local authority Environmental Health or Housing Department's Grant Aid Section to see if they have a shortlist of builders who have carried out grant work. This will help you establish the authenticity of the builder. Does the builder carry out work for the local authority themselves?

Contractors' insurance

It is essential that your builder has sufficient Public Liability Insurance, and you should, before appointing him, ask to see his current certificate of insurance. The reason is as follows: should an accident occur which results in your builder injuring a third party whilst he is at work on your property, and he is not adequately insured, you could be jointly liable to pay compensation. For example, your extension is to be built close to the road and a bricklayer accidentally drops a brick from the scaffolding on to the head of a passer-by, injuring or killing that person. Only the builder's Public Liability Insurance may protect you as the owner of the works from action under civil law in a situation like this.

Less dramatic, and perhaps more common, is the case of property damage to a neighbouring building, caused directly or indirectly from the building of your extension. A broken window, damaged roof or knocked-down fence is one thing on your own property, but damage like this can all too often occur to adjoining properties. A builder's third-party insurance cover is intended for instances like this.

Heath and safety

Building sites are dangerous places. Accidents that occur are often serious and all too frequently fatal. Under the Construction (Health, Safety and Welfare) Regulations 1996, the home-owner has no responsibilities for the health and safety of workmen on the home site. Those responsibilities lie with their employer, the builder, or with themselves if they are bona-fide self-employed tradesmen.

Even so, it is essential that you are aware of safety on the site, not only for your own protection around the house, but also for those lawfully visiting your house. If, for example, the postman disappears down an unprotected hole in the ground, action could be taken against you under civil law – over half of all injurious accidents on building sites are caused by falls.

Encourage your builder to keep the site as tidy as possible, and keep an eye open for hazards such as discarded broken bricks, untied ladders and faulty scaffolding. More health and safety advice is given under the relevant chapters in the second section of this book, as well as from the Health and Safety Executive.

Trade federations and guarantee schemes

Builders sometimes belong to trade federations and advertise the fact as a symbol of their professionalism or quality of work. You should be aware that such groups exist to represent the interest of their members, the tradesmen, and not you, the client. They are funded by the annual subscriptions of their members, and there are as many different organisations for tradesmen to join as there are for designers. One report released in 1996 suggested that between 13 and 22% of all building firms made false declarations about membership of trade associations. Even if you check and find a bona-fide member, in practice very little can be interpreted from the fact that a builder carries such a membership.

Having said that, some of these organisations do offer one valuable service: they offer insurance if you employ the services of one of their members. The cost is usually based on a percentage of the contract sum that the builder and you have accepted, and if there are any variations or extras to this sum, the cover and premium can be adjusted as they occur or when the job is finished. The insurance guarantees you – normally for a period of up to ten years from the date of completion – against financial loss as a result of some defects resulting from inferior workmanship or materials, or against the event of the builder becoming insolvent, or dying, before finishing the work.

Three bodies which at time of writing offer an insurance-based guarantee scheme are the Federation of Master Builders, the Building Employers Confederation and the Building Trades Alliance.

Much thought and effort is being put into cleaning up the industry's poor reputation, and more and more schemes are springing up all the time. The government itself has set up a voluntary registration scheme for builders and is still trying to establish this scheme. Developed in partnership with the industry, as well as consumer groups and local authorities, the DTI 'Quality Mark' hopes to provide consumers with a list of professional, reliable firms. The benefits would include an independent complaints procedure, a warranty (available at cost) and the knowledge that the builder has been audited in respect of his financial probity and work. In time the register would develop, the symbol would be nationally recognizable, incompetent builders would be booted off it and cowboys would be out-marketed by the government – at least that's the plan. It has been slow to start because builders could see no benefits in it for them, the registration paperwork was too complex and the joining fee too high. Those issues have now been addressed and, with the help of local councils, the government has been trying to re-launch the enterprise. Given time, the 'Quality Mark' may become real.

If it fails – or even if it succeeds – it may prove necessary to extend the statutory controls to reduce the number of cowboy builders operating. The Building Act 1984 that enables Building Regulations may have to be amended to include quality of work, instead of just health and safety. Banks and Building Societies may have to be encouraged to look for quality from warranty-backed builders engaged in home improvements on mortgaged properties. The construction skills certification scheme may have to be widened to the domestic market and it would help if VAT- relief could be given to home improvement works, since a great many of us are persuaded to choose our builders on a 'cash-price' basis omitting that percentage. Unfortunately, at the same time the government has opened up building control to the private sector, licensing Approved Inspectors who now compete with local councils for the building control function.

It will, of course, be the client's choice, but allowing an Approved Inspector to operate as a controller of building work is likely to lead only to a reduction in standards. When the Inspector's living is dependent on keeping his customers happy, can he be truly independent?

Quotations and estimates

It is important to be aware of the status in law of a quotation and an estimate, because they are very different.
A **quotation** is a firm price which represents a contract between the parties. As such, it is legally binding.

- Having agreed a quotation, your builder must stick to it. If he or she does present you with a larger, final bill that has not been agreed upon, in law you are only obliged to pay the quotation price.
- If the quotation does not mention VAT, you may assume (in law) that it is VAT-inclusive. Should your builder add on VAT later to his bill, again you are only obliged to pay the original quotation sum. (If a builder is not VAT-registered, it is unlikely that he will have the facilities to engage in anything but minor works, since it is his annual turnover that qualifies him for registration – £54,000 in 2007.)
- Before you agree to any extras or alterations to the details of your extension while work is in progress, make sure that you agree the cost of them with your builder before instructing him to do them.
- Extras or variations should be agreed

in writing. You have no legal obligation to pay for them if you have not agreed to them. If you cannot agree upon a fixed amount for such a variation because it is unquantifiable by its nature – say, for example, because it involves investigation of concealed wiring or something else that is hidden – you might wish to agree a 'daywork rate' with your builder. This is an hourly labour rate, and you must be careful to monitor the time he has spent on the 'extra' work. The best way is to maintain a daywork sheet, which you can jointly sign each day, thus allowing you both to keep a check on the costs accruing. The hourly rate should be agreed beforehand. Of course the cost of materials and plant hire will be added to this labour charge, along with his overheads and profit, but your builder may wish to 'build' the latter into his hourly rate.

- Quotations should contain enough detail of specification or at least refer to the numbered and dated plans for the project as 'contract documents'. If nothing else, this is an indication that the builder has familiarised himself with the details of the scheme, giving confidence by his professionalism.

An **estimate**, on the other hand, is exactly that – a best guess. It allows the builder to present a higher or lower final bill. It is not legally binding unless it is supplemented with a written agreement stating that the price shown is a firm price. If your builder will only provide an estimate – and some will – try to agree in writing a 'maximum price' which will not be exceeded.

Contingency sums

It is usually wise to get an agreed contingency sum included with the estimate or quote, which will only be used to pay for unexpected extras should they occur. In this way, nasty surprises can be catered for, but care should be taken to ensure that the sum is only used for necessary work that was unforeseen when the job was priced. If it was not required, it will be deducted from the final bill when the job is complete. 5% of the estimate or quote would make a contingency sum for the average extension.

Provisional sums

When it is known that work on one particular element will be needed, but at the same time it is impossible to know how much or what work until it is carried out, a provisional sum is included. Again, this should be agreed as a round figure which should be capable of covering the actual cost. Once the work is complete and the true cost is known, the adjustments can be made to the final bill.

A contract may include several provisional sums for various elements of the work that are unquantifiable, for example: 'Allow the provisional sum of £500.00 for electrical work'.

Prime cost sums

PC sums, as they are usually labelled, are similar to provisional sums but relate only to the material element of the cost and not to the labour. They work in the same way as provisional sums, in that a round figure is agreed that will hopefully cover the amount needed, and the necessary adjustments are then made to correct the final bill. Often they relate to elements which the client has yet to decide upon.

Typical examples of PC sums might be: 'Allow the PC sum of £1500.00 for the supply only of kitchen units' or 'Allow the PC sum of £30.00 per sq m for the supply only of glazed wall tiles'.

Variation orders

VOs are written instructions from the client to the builder, authorising him to carry out additional work or omit work that was previously agreed. It is worth doing this even when there is no cost implication involved, so that disputes are avoided later. A book of variation orders can be kept and jointly signed by both parties against the description of the work and the cost implication. A copy should be kept by both parties, so a duplicate-type notebook with numbered pages is ideal for this purpose. If this system is diligently followed, there are rarely differences of opinion later on.

Finally, you might like to bear in mind that the cheapest price is not necessarily the best one. If you have appointed a builder who has drastically underpriced the job, it might be worth letting him out of the contract rather than risk the consequences of letting him tackle it. Many undesirable builders that have undercut the job because they are inept at estimating, can only minimise their losses by cutting corners, using cheap materials and generally trying to get away with anything that can be done quicker and cheaper! The resultant damage to your home extension may be costly in the end.

- Make sure that you get a receipt for all payments made to your builder.
- The safest method of payment is to use a credit card.

The Credit Protection Act gives you some protection, particularly in the case of deposits, should your builder go out of business before starting the work. If he doesn't have a credit card scheme, you might ask for a deposit indemnity. If it is a limited company, its directors should be able to provide it, and if it isn't limited, the proprietor should. You must remember that the indemnities will only work if you can locate these people personally, and this may not be easy if the firm has gone bust!

Contracts

A contract is a written agreement between you and your builder, and you can write one out yourself. Alternatively, standard forms can be used and professional builders may supply them. If not, contract forms can be obtained from: CIP Ltd, Federation House, 2309 Coventry Road, Sheldon, Birmingham B26 3PL.

The JCT80 Standard form is probably only appropriate for larger projects, but the JCT Standard form for Building Works of a Jobbing Character: 1990 Edition is likely to be more appropriate, and is available in three parts: JA/T/90 –

Tender and Agreement; JA/C/90 – Conditions of Contract; and JA/90/SPEC – A specimen of the above two forms. Another suitable standard form is 80/MW Minor Building Works 1980 Agreement.

The vast majority of extensions are built on simple agreements, but that doesn't mean to say that you can't apply your own conditions on the quotation. You may require the builder to protect your garden from undue damage during the work, that he doesn't start work until 9 a.m., that his workman do not have a radio playing on-site, etc.

Workmanship standards

Perhaps the most critical of all contracts or agreements is the standard of workmanship that will be employed on your extension. It will probably not surprise you to know that the Building Regulations are extremely ineffectual in this area – workmanship only has to be good enough for the building to perform its basic functional ability set out in the requirements that apply. A wall has to be horribly out of plumb before it becomes structurally unstable, and nobody in their right mind would want to pay for workmanship of this level.

So what to do? Well, there aren't many options available. The best at this stage is to refer to the British Standard (BS8000) for workmanship on building sites in the contract, and use the various parts of this standard as conditions of it. Alternatively, have your designer specify BS8000 on the plans, and have the plans referred to as a contract document. Like all British Standards, they are in themselves only advisory documents, but adopting them as contract conditions means that you will be able to enforce them. If the workmanship at any stage becomes unsatisfactory and can be said not to comply with these codes, your builder will be in breach of contract and you will be able to terminate your agreement. It would, of course, be civilised to give him at least one opportunity to correct the problem, but that may depend upon how appalling the work was.

Quality Assurance

This is something of a buzz phrase at present, and some builders offer it as an indication of their high standard of workmanship. But is it? BS5750: Part 1 is the same standard as ISO9001, and BS5750: Part 2 is the same standard as ISO9002. Either way, they are both about attaining the same standard repeatedly. The builder decides for himself what standard he can offer, and so long as he

keeps it up he keeps his Quality Assurance badge. Some builders are capable of maintaining a very bad standard of workmanship and are able to reproduce it faithfully over and over again, so presumably they would have no trouble with QA accreditation.

Payment

The Construction Act 1996 (aka the Housing Grants, Construction and Regeneration Act 1996) does not apply to the building of home extensions where the client is defined as a 'residential occupier'. Nevertheless, the code it invokes on matters of payment could be wisely employed in the contract or agreement between you and your builder. It includes the following points:

● It should be specified how much is to be paid and when it is to be paid,

---

FOR YOUR REFERENCE, THE 15 PARTS OF BS8000 ARE:

Part 1 – 1989 – Code of practice for excavation and filling.
Part 2 – 1990 – Code of practice for concrete work.
Part 3 – 1989 – Code of practice for masonry.
Part 4 – 1989 – Code of practice for waterproofing.
Part 5 – 1990 – Code of practice for carpentry, joinery and general fixings.
Part 6 – 1990 – Code of practice for slating and tiling of roofs and claddings.
Part 7 – 1990 – Code of practice for glazing.
Part 8 – 1989 – Code of practice for plasterboard partitions and dry-lining.
Part 9 – 1989 – Code of practice for cement sand floor screeds and concrete floor toppings.
Part 10 – 1989 – Code of practice for plastering and rendering.
Part 11 – 1989/1990 – Code of practice for wall and floor tiling.
Part 12 – 1989 – Code of practice for decorative wall coverings and painting.
Part 13 – 1989 – Code of practice for above-ground drainage and sanitary appliances.
Part 14 – 1989 – Code of practice for below-ground drainage.
Part 15 – 1990 – Code of practice for hot and cold water services (domestic scale).

Electrical installations should be conditioned as 'installed in accordance with IEE (Institute of Electrical Engineers) Regulations'.

the latter being best described as a stage in the works, rather than a time which might not be achieved. If, as the owner, it is your intention when this stage arrives to withhold payment, for example due to problems with the workmanship or materials used, you should notify the builder immediately in writing of the amount you are withholding and the reasons why.

- If you fail to do this but still withhold payment, the builder may give you no less than seven days' notice of his intention to stop work. This right to pull off ceases once payment is made, and the final completion date should be extended to allow for the time lost.
- In the case of most extension building, stage payments arranged at around monthly intervals would be appropriate.
- The final payment should be due within 30 days of practical completion.
- All payments should be made within 17 days of the date they are due (i.e. the billing date).

Contract time

The builder is being invited into your home, and you are at liberty to agree with him on the conditions of his employment. Plan carefully when the contract will start and how long it will last. Obviously there are no standards here, but you will need to ensure that your builder has free access to the 'site' at all times if he is to complete the work to schedule. Suddenly locking up and going off on holiday in the middle of the job is likely to lead to your builder finding alternative work which may not fit in with your return.

You can agree 'delay penalties' in the contract of so much per week. If the builder delays the work, the client can claim that it has taken longer than the agreed time and the builder can be penalised. But if the client has delayed the work, the builder, with his follow-up work adversely affected, can claim the delay penalty.

Facilities

In among all this, remember that builders are human and require the same facilities as you do whilst at work. How much of these facilities you are prepared to offer them from your home, and how much they bring with them, should be decided upon in the contract or agreement to avoid disputes later.

Electricity

In the 1980s, when all workmen seem to carry an arsenal of power tools, you were out of business if you didn't have somewhere to plug them in. The home-owner's electric supply was assumed to be available without question, if they wanted the job done. But now, thankfully, cordless power tools with up to 18V rechargeable batteries are here, and they wonder what they did before.

Water

Water is something that many people forget about. But around 200 litres of water will go into building even the most modest extension, and builders can't bring that many bottles of Evian with them.

An accessible outdoor tap is a wonderful thing to have when you're building. Having to run a hose from the kitchen sink might prove to be extremely inconvenient, so if you don't have an outdoor supply, ensure that the builders bring water butts that can be filled up at the start of the day.

Bathrooms

Here we get to a tricky subject. Clearly the builders have to go somewhere, but are you going to be at home all the time when they are building, and if not, are you going to leave the house open to them? You may be quite happy to do this, but if you aren't, it needs to be agreed that they will bring a portable site-loo with them. These little site huts contain chemical toilets similar to those in caravans, don't take up too much space, and can be hired.

Telephones

These shouldn't be an issue anymore. Most builders and tradesmen have mobile phones so they can be available to book further business while at work. If they don't, or if you live in a cellular-phone blackspot, access to your phone can be agreed and the phone bill can be itemised to assign any costs accordingly.

Snagging

A snagging list is the term given to all those niggly bits that need sorting out at the end of the job. Ideally, you should inspect the work at completion with the builder and point out anything that you consider needs attention – a crack that needs filling, paintwork that needs touching up, a door that needs easing,

etc. A copy of the list is then kept by both parties, and should not be added to. The work is then carried out, and final payment can be made once you are completely satisfied and once you are sure that the Building Control Officer is also completely satisfied.

If the contractor is providing you with a guarantee through his trade association, make sure that you possess it signed before releasing the final payment.

Disputes

If you do find yourself locked into a disagreement that cannot be resolved, or if either you or your builder default on the contract, a third party should be agreed upon to act as an arbitrator – this should be agreed at the start of the job, before communications have broken down, and the third party could be a surveyor or a trade association.

In instances where the work carried out is not up to standard and your builder is unwilling or unable to rectify it, you should advise him that you intend to have it independently inspected by both the Building Control Officer and a surveyor. This done, request a list of defective items from both parties. While the Building Control Officer will only be able to comment with regard to contraventions of the Building Regulations, their authority in these instances may help to at least get these points resolved. The privately employed surveyor should be one who is suitably qualified (e.g. RICS or MBEng) and who has no prior involvement in the project – in other words, not the designer of the extension. This is important because some of the problems with work may have derived from poor design in the first place. The surveyor's list is likely to be more comprehensive, since it may include areas of poor-quality workmanship and aspects of the work not covered by regulations.

Once a list of defects is produced by them both and everybody has a copy, a site meeting between all involved parties should be arranged, to discuss how the problems are to be resolved. If your builder is unwilling or unable to co-operate in this respect, you may be forced to take more formal action, ultimately through the courts. If this does become necessary, it will have helped your case considerably if the problems are well documented and you have given your builder every reasonable opportunity to rectify them. Photographs of the defects should be signed on the back and dated at the time of exposure. Courts dislike photos taken with digital cameras, since they are capable of being altered or 'enhanced'. If you are using a camera with an automatic date stamp, check that the time and date are correct when you take the pictures, or the camera is likely to be more of a hindrance than a help.

Try to adopt a civil and business-like manner to all your letters and phone calls, if for no other reason than because there are quite strict laws about malicious communication.

Deal with disputes early on – if left to fester, they only get worse.

Finance

While using a credit card may be the safest way to make a payment, it is not the best way to finance an extension, even if your card limit will take it. The interest rates on home-improvement loans are much more reasonable, the loans are widely available, and they are the most common way to finance an extension. There are two basic types: secured and unsecured.

Secured loans

These can be added to your existing mortgage, giving the lender the security of your home; consequently, most secured loans will require a valuation survey to be carried out. By law they are now advertised with the prerequisite statement about the consequences of defaulting on the loan – your home may be at risk. This security allows them to offer you the money at a lower interest rate than that of an unsecured loan. They may not be available in cases of negative equity or where the loan applied for is above a certain percentage of the property value. Before the loan is released, the lender may require sight of your plans and approval notices. The loan can usually be repaid over a period of up to 25 years, but a minimum borrowing amount is normally set.

Unsecured loans

These may be more suitable for smaller advances, where repayment will often be over a period of up to 5 years. Interest rates are higher because your home is not available as security, but the loan is more flexible and you won't carry the risk of losing your home should you default on it. In both cases, insurance is usually available to protect you against redundancy during the term of the loan.

Remortgage

It is not uncommon to finance home improvements by remortgaging; in recent times, transferring a mortgage from one building society or bank to another has proved to be a neat way of securing some extra cash. Financial cash incentives of up to several thousand pounds have been on offer to entice new customers, along with reduced or fixed-rate interest terms. These offers are available to the existing borrower, but not usually preferentially – in other words, you are treated as if you were a new customer. (Take care when considering this course of action, as there is sometimes a penalty for giving up your mortgage early.) Even though you may be not be increasing the capital amount of your mortgage, merely taking advantage of the new conditions, in the eyes of the Exchequer you are borrowing from scratch, and the current rules for tax apply.

If you are considering switching your mortgage to another lender to gain funds, seek advice from an Independent Mortgage Advisor who can tell you which bank or building society is offering the best deal and terms for you. And again, you will probably have to have a valuation survey carried out. It is certainly worth reading all the small print twice and discussing it through with the lender before engaging in such a transfer, as there are likely to be ties and conditions attached.

Local authority grants

When applying for a grant from your local authority, they will normally require at least two written estimates from reputable builders. The rules for the qualification and awarding of grants change quite often and are subject to the political and economic climate of the time. The current system is administered on a discretionary basis by each authority, and enquiries should always be made to your local authority grants section to establish the current situation. However, you will not get a grant for building an extension if:

● Your property is less than ten years old.
● Your property already meets the fitness standard and has the basic amenities – toilet, shower or bath, kitchen, etc.
● A cheaper way of providing the amenities, such as converting an existing bedroom into a bathroom, can be found.
● You are a council tenant (except in the case of disabled facilities grants).
● You just want to increase your living space, e.g. with a bedroom or lounge extension.
● The property is a second home or holiday cottage.
● You haven't been an owner or occupier of it for at least three years.

If your application is successful but government money is scarce, the amount of financial help you will receive may be determined by a means test. This is to ensure that the most help goes to those who are least able to pay for it themselves. Your local authority will give you some advice on how means testing is carried out and advise you on how much, if any, you will have to contribute.

Grants are usually awarded with conditions attached, e.g.:

- The work must be completed within 12 months.
- You must not change the contractor whose estimate was accepted.
- You must live in the property for at least five years after the work is complete.

Breach of the conditions applied could result in non-payment or refunding of the grant.

House renovation grants

Although this type of grant is mainly available for essential repair work, it could be available to build an extension where it is needed to bring the house up to the 'fitness standard'. If, for example, the property was very old and lacked the basic amenities of an indoor bathroom or toilet, the building of an extension might be grant-aided to include them. The fees for the design work and those payable to the council for planning and building control may be included within the grant aid.

Disabled facilities grants

An extension built solely to provide facilities for the registered disabled owner/occupier of a property may be financed in part or total by a disabled facilities grant; for example, a suitably equipped bathroom or shower room built onto the side of the house at ground level if the owner is unable to use the existing upstairs facilities.

These grants are administered by the local authority, as are renovation grants, but often involve occupational therapists from the health authority who may help in deciding what facilities should be provided. Some authorities have agencies with a drawing office that can provide the necessary design service as well. Their fees may be included within the grant aid. The majority of local authorities now have such home-improvement agencies set up to assist the elderly and disabled in these situations, often under the title of 'Care and Repair'.

Home energy scheme grants

These grants are only available for existing homes that require additional insulation, and to those qualifying as home-owners. They cannot be applied for in the case of new building work, extension or otherwise, where the insulation must be built in as work proceeds, even if you qualify as an eligible applicant.

Before you start work

Two days before work begins, notify your Building Control Officer of the start date. This is a statutory notice. You are required by law to give statutory notices to the officer at various stages throughout the job, and this is the first one. In practice they may not wish to visit at this stage, preferring to wait until the foundations are excavated, which requires another notice, but that doesn't mean that you need not notify them.

As with all matters of statute, it is an offence not to comply with them, and could result in prosecution in the courts. It is more likely that if you or your builder fail to notify them at the relevant stages and carry on regardless, you will be required to lay open and expose parts of the structure later. In the case of foundations and concrete floors, this tends to make a bit of a mess. **Make sure that you or your builder notify the officer for inspection.**

Building Regulation Approvals are accompanied by pre-printed postcards for this purpose, and also on occasion inspection schedules indicating at which stages the officer needs to be notified.

Incidentally, Building Control Officers and Planning Officers have rights of entry to your property at all times. They can't, however, force entry – if you did choose to obstruct them and stop them coming onto your property, they would have to apply for a warrant from the Magistrates Court and return later, usually accompanied by a uniformed police officer. You should also be aware that obstructing a Building Control Officer from entering is an offence in itself that may result in prosecution.

While we have the law book open, it follows that ultimately any contravention of the regulations that is not resolved may end up with you, the owner of the property, being prosecuted in court. Penalties are usually imposed in two parts, first as a fixed sum, and secondly as an increasing sum that grows according to the length of time the contravention remains afterwards.

In practice, of course, you and your builder will be given every assistance and advice possible to help you overcome contraventions amicably.

Section 36 of the Building Act 1984 requires you to remove or alter offending work within 28 days. You can apply to the courts for an extension of time to deal with the problems, or you can appeal against the notice, the latter being done by a qualified surveyor's report. In respect of Planning Consent, if you fail to obtain permission when it is needed and build your extension regardless, you will most likely be required to make an application retrospectively. If it is refused, you will probably be required to take it down or alter it in some way. Failure to apply for Building Regulations consent can also be rectified by applying for a 'regularisation certificate'. However, this usually involves laying open and exposing areas of construction, which can be extremely inconvenient; then again, it may prove less costly than a day at the local Magistrates Court or a thwarted house sale in years to come.

ID

It is important to check the identity of any unexpected visitor to your home. If you do get somebody who is minus credentials and you are too embarrassed to turn him or her away, telephone the council and seek confirmation. There have been plenty of successful robberies where intruders have gained access by masquerading as council officials.

In conclusion, try to remember that the majority of builders are trying to earn an honest living in return for quality work. Your home will be their place of work throughout the contract, and both parties must be sensitive to the needs of the other if the objective is to be met.

CHAPTER 4

Substructure

This chapter covers all below-ground building works up to damp-proof course (DPC) level, including site preparation, foundations, ground-floor slabs, suspended ground floors and below-ground drainage. Groundworkers are sometimes employed to execute this work in total, leaving the superstructure trades to follow.

Foundations

The principles involved in laying down foundations for a building are really quite simple. The object is to provide a solid and level base for the structure on subsoil which you can safely predict will **not**:

- Settle excessively due to inadequate bearing strength or underground works (mining).
- Be damaged by frost heave or sulphate attack.
- Be affected by ground movement due to seasonal changes, nearby trees or erosion and slope creep.

Foundations for new extensions often need to be deeper than those existing on the house – which may have been built some time ago – and the difference between the two may cause differential settlement (where the existing part of the house settles, and moves in response to the ground beneath it at a different rate to the extended part). At worst, this could lead to cracking in the external walls at the junction between the new and the old; to avoid this, flexible wall-tie methods should be

favoured, as opposed to the traditional brickwork bonding-in methods. Do not be tempted to partly underpin the shallow foundations of the house when digging deeper trenches alongside. To do so will only move back the position of any cracks further into the existing house, where flexible controls cannot be introduced. In most cases it is better to abut the old with the new and design in some provision for differential movement (see Chapter 5).

Conventional foundations

These are normally described as either strip or trench-fill.

Strip foundations are usually at least 600 mm wide and of a proportional thickness, but as an absolute minimum 150 mm thick. The exact thickness of concrete should suit brick/block courses, but would normally be between 225 mm and 300 mm thick.

On sloping sites it is important that the bottom of the trenches are cut level, and if the ground slopes naturally, that vertical steps are cut to maintain a level bottom. When concreting, steps should be overlapped by at least twice the height of the step or by 1 m (whichever is greater). Steps should be low in height and gradually change the level. Dramatic changes in the bearing depth will cause differential settlement, so the steps should not exceed in individual height the overall thickness of the concrete in general.

Trench-fill foundations are, as the name suggests, mass-concrete-filled to

CONCRETE

Ready-mix concrete for conventional foundations has a typical strength of 20N/mm2 (C20) and a mix ratio of something like 1:2:4. Full loads are usually 5 or 6 cu m. When poured into the trench, the concrete should be of a pudding-like consistency that needs raking or shovelling into position; it shouldn't be so wet that it can swim through the trench unaided. Ready-mix concrete is ordered **per cubic metre**, and so it is necessary to calculate the volume needed from the excavation measurements. As a rough guide, the table below is for trench-fill foundations in two widths and strip foundations in one width.

LENGTH OF TRENCH IN METRES

Trench-fill	5	10	15	20	25
450 mm wide	2	4	6	8	10 cu m
600 mm wide	2.6	5.2	7.3	10.5	13 cu m

Note: this table assumes a 1 m-deep excavation with trench-fill concrete 850 mm deep, leaving the top of the foundations 150 mm beneath ground; four courses of bricks would be needed to achieve normal DPC level.

LENGTH OF TRENCH IN METRES

Strip foundation	5	10	15	20	25
600 mm wide	1	2	3.1	4.1	5.1 cu m

Note: this table assumes a thickness of concrete for a strip foundation of 300 mm. In a 1 m-deep trench this would leave four courses of blocks and two courses of bricks to achieve normal DPC level at 150 mm above ground.

EXPERT DIY MIX FOR CONVENTIONAL FOUNDATION CONCRETE:

50 kg (0.033 cu m) of cement to
0.066 cu m of building sand to
0.132 cu m of coarse aggregate
(or 14 x 25 kg bags of cement to every 1 cu m of all-in ballast)

If you don't want to mix your own concrete or order ready-mix, which can be costly in less than full loads, some firms offer a 'we-mix-you-lay' service which falls between the two.

When ordering cement, the following figures may prove useful:
40 x 25 kg bags of cement = 1 metric tonne of cement
60 x 25 kg bags of cement = 1 cu m (approx.) of cement

All-in ballast is a pre-mixed selection of sand and aggregate. The volume mixes given for 1 m of all-in ballast take account of the fact that the sand element fills in the voids between the aggregate, making a 1:2:4 mix, for example, nearer to a 1:4 mix in practice.

High-alumina cement (HAC) must **not** be used in structural concrete (e.g. foundations, slabs, lintels, cills, etc.). It was tried in the 1960s, and we are still trying to repair the damage.

Do not concrete foundations before they have been inspected and passed by the Building Control Surveyor.

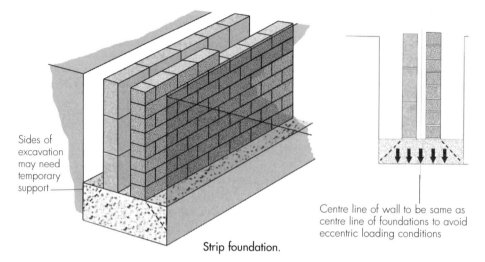

Sides of excavation may need temporary support

Centre line of wall to be same as centre line of foundations to avoid eccentric loading conditions

Strip foundation.

roughly 150 mm below the ground level. This is the most popular method in clay soils, where support can also be obtained from the sides of the trench as well as from the bottom. It can result in a reduced width for the foundation where the loading allows, and is often favoured because it avoids building below-ground brick/block walls in trenches that may be quite deep.

Before starting the excavation for foundations, make sure that you are aware of the position of any underground utilities and are legally entitled to begin work, having obtained all the necessary consents (see Chapter 2).

Special foundations

Foundation types such as raft, pad-and-beam or pile, are referred to as special foundations. They usually require a structural engineer's design, and are

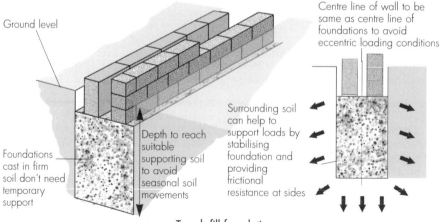

Ground level

Centre line of wall to be same as centre line of foundations to avoid eccentric loading conditions

Foundations cast in firm soil don't need temporary support

Depth to reach suitable supporting soil to avoid seasonal soil movements

Surrounding soil can help to support loads by stabilising foundation and providing frictional resistance at sides

Trench-fill foundation.

necessary to overcome a particular problem, whether it be filled ground, trees close by, desiccated clay or some other hindrance.

Raft foundations

These consist of a reinforced-concrete slab cast with a reinforced thickened edge around the perimeter. Often the slab reinforcement is pre-formed steel fabric mesh laid in sheets, and the concrete is a higher-strength grade than normal foundation concrete.

Raft foundations may be used for the following reasons:

- In soft ground, to spread the load from the extension, or in made-up ground, to bridge across weak areas in the soil.
- Where differential settlement is likely to be extreme.
- Where any mining subsidence is

likely to occur.

- Where the soil is susceptible to excessive shrinking and swelling. In this case the raft should be formed on top of selected non-cohesive fill material (such as clean reject stone), having reduced the natural ground level to a given depth.

If your existing house is built on a raft foundation, it would be appropriate, if not essential, for any extension to be similarly founded.

Pad-and-beam foundations

These consist of a series of mass-filled bases of concrete formed at whatever necessary depth and designed to carry reinforced ground-beam foundations, which span between them much as lintels do above ground. The pads are usually located at corners and at intervals on lengthy walls. They are

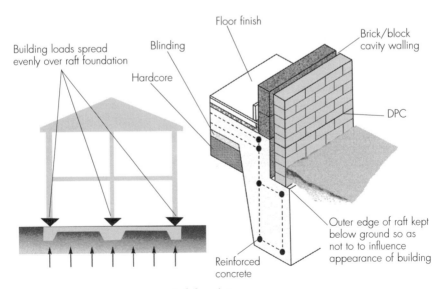

Building loads spread evenly over raft foundation

Floor finish

Blinding

Hardcore

Brick/block cavity walling

DPC

Outer edge of raft kept below ground so as not to to influence appearance of building

Reinforced concrete

Raft foundation.

FOUNDATION SELECTION TABLE

SUBSOIL TYPE	FOUNDATION OPTIONS	SUGGESTED WIDTH FOR SINGLE OR 2-STOREY
Rock requiring pneumatic pick for excavation	Trench-fill/strip	300 mm trench-fill/450 mm strip
Gravel/beach	Strip/raft	450–600 mm strip
Compact and contained clay (stiff)	All options	450 mm trench-fill 600 mm strip Raft or pad-and-beam (close to trees)
Sand/silt/clay (loose/soft)	Strip/raft	600–850 mm strip

designed on an area basis calculated by dividing the ground-bearing pressure by the load applied from each pad. Consequently, the pads will often vary in size. This type of construction may be used where deep foundations are required due to nearby trees. If heave is a problem, the ground beams may need protecting by being encased with specially treated polystyrene padding. This sacrificial compressible material will take up the heave (swelling) of the clay without damage to the concrete.

Polythene slip membranes can also be

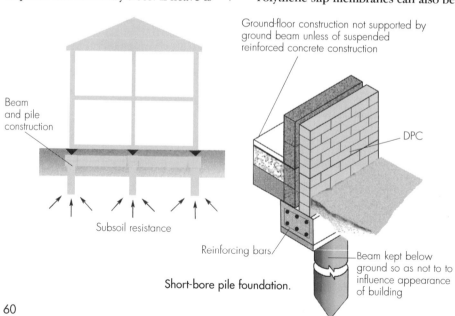

Beam and pile construction

Subsoil resistance

Short-bore pile foundation.

Ground-floor construction not supported by ground beam unless of suspended reinforced concrete construction

DPC

Reinforcing bars

Beam kept below ground so as not to influence appearance of building included. These can be achieved simply by lining the sides of a trench before concreting with 1200 g polythene, which will act to reduce the friction pressure between the ground and the concrete.

Pile foundations

These have become more common since the advent of mini-driven pile systems. The piles act to support reinforced ground beams in the same way as the pads do for the pad-and-beam system, but are more economical where excessive depths are required. Specialist contractors can design and install mini-steel-cased or pre-cast concrete piles, which are driven down in sections to a given depth measured by the resistance from the ground. The system can be quicker than digging and filling large pads, but can cause damage through ground vibration. It is suitable in clay soils, where trees exist or have been removed, or where nearby slopes or geological faults occur. Usually they must be either subjected to a load test or over-designed in terms of load capacity by a factor of three. Sonic tests can be carried out to check if they have been damaged (cracked) during installation, and if this is the case extra piles will be implanted near the failed one to compensate. They are often guaranteed against failure under load.

Archaeological areas

In some areas, planning conditions may be imposed which require all excavations over a certain depth to be inspected by archaeologists prior to concreting. The Ancient Monuments and Archaeological Act 1979 creates conditions where you may have to give six weeks' notice before any digging can be carried out on some sites, and where development may be delayed by a further 18 weeks to allow archaeologists to complete their investigations. If this applies to your site, contact should be made at an early stage.

FOUNDATIONS NEAR TREES TABLE

| TREE | DISTANCE FROM TREE TO EXTENSION IN METRES | | | | | | | |
	5m	8m	11m	14m	17m	20m	25m	30m
Oaks, willows, elms and poplars	3	2.8	2.6	2.4	2.2	2.0	1.5	1m
Ash, horse chestnut, lime, sycamore, walnut, maple and large conifers	2	1.8	1.5	1.1	1	1	1	1m
Beech, birch, hawthorn, holly, magnolia and fruit trees (apple, cherry, pear, plum, etc.)	1.4	1.2	1	1	1	1	1	1m

Measure the distance to the tree from the extension and read off the depth of foundations in shrinkable clay soils. In the case of hedgerows, it would be appropriate to base the depth on the worst-case species to be found in the hedgerow.

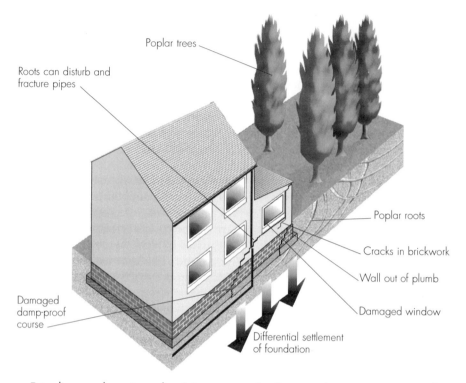

Extending your home towards existing trees can be disastrous if precautions are not taken.

Notwithstanding the above, all fossils, antiquities and objects of value should remain or become the property of the site owner. When involved on such digs, archaeologists normally carry out their work with meticulous care and often leave the trenches in perfect condition when they are finished.

Since the hot summer of 1976, general practice has been to extend the formation depth of traditional foundations in shrinkable subsoil to at least 1 m below ground level. Clay is very susceptible to volumetric changes, even when trees are not nearby. Where trees do exist, the depth will depend

upon the species and the distance to it. The table on page 61 does not cover all species, but will act as a guide for the most common. Clearly some of the depths shown would warrant investigating alternative foundation types – pad-and-beam or raft may be more appropriate.

This table is only a rough guide which has been calibrated to suggest depths up to a maximum of 3 m deep and tree distances no closer than 5 m. Outside these parameters, an alternative 'special foundation' would be more appropriate. Precautions should be taken not to damage the roots or branches of the tree, which may destabilise it. Cutting through a live root of 50 mm diameter or bigger is not advisable, and the foundation should be designed to bridge over roots, allowing plenty of space for future growth without exerting pressure on them. Tree roots, in turn, can exert considerable pressure on lightweight structures, such as single-storey extensions, and during growth they may cause structural damage. If you are building close to a tree, seek the advice of a registered arboriculturist.

Note that the tree may be young at present, but foundation depths must be based on its mature height when it is fully grown.

Cutting down a tree in shrinkable clay subsoil will not help, because the ground is likely to become waterlogged and swell to an extent which can cause damage to foundations. This effect is known as heave. It is the reverse of shrinkage, but the resultant damage can be just as bad.

Even a basement boiler room under a house can dry out clay subsoil, causing shrinkage and subsidence.

Shrinkable clays

Most of these are found in the south and south-east of England, but you can check against the Geological Survey map for your area; most reference libraries have them. Alternatively, if you take a sample of the clay fresh from the ground and roll it between your forefinger and thumb, highly shrinkable or 'plastic' clay will roll into a long thin shape without crumbling or breaking apart.

Underpinning can be an expensive business, and after several dry summers and many subsidence claims, some insurance companies that provide buildings cover have inflated their premiums for properties located in areas of highly shrinkable clay. This may have been done somewhat indiscriminately by postcode areas. If you feel unfairly affected, you may wish to notify them of the precautions you have installed against subsoil movement.

Health and safety

Some projects are notifiable to the Health and Safety Executive under the Construction (Design and Management) Regulations 1994 – known as the CDM Regulations. Where the project is 'notifiable' to the HSE – if it lasts for more than 30 days or will involve more than 500 person-days of work – the builder is required, when digging over 2 m deep, to provide protection to prevent people from falling in, i.e. a fence or barrier placed around trenches. Even where the project is not notifiable, it is sensible to ensure that all trenches are suitably protected by laying substantial boards over them or guarding them. Bear in mind that a board might encourage a visitor to walk over it; should it fail and they are injured, you may be as liable to action under civil law as if you had not protected them at all.

Adding a first-floor extension or loft conversion

A first-floor extension has the benefit of avoiding groundwork altogether if it is built on top of the existing single-storey structure, but this doesn't mean that the foundations are not considered. The existing foundations may be of indefinite

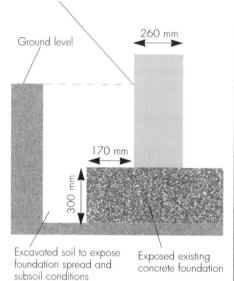

Existing wall measured at 260 mm thickness assumed to be central on foundation so (170 x 2) + 260 = 600 mm wide foundation

Ground level

260 mm

170 mm

300 mm

Excavated soil to expose foundation spread and subsoil conditions

Exposed existing concrete foundation

Example of existing foundation check.

quality, and imposing the extra weight of a new storey on them may be all that is needed to cause subsidence.

Without a doubt, one of the first things you should do before embarking on a new extension of this kind is to expose the existing foundations by digging a few trial holes down alongside them, to check their suitability. If you later find out that they are unsatisfactory and will need to be underpinned, the cost of doing so may render the project unviable. So what is acceptable? That depends on three things:

- The extra weight that will be imposed.
- The quality, thickness and spread of the foundation.

● The nature of the subsoil.
And four if you have trees very near in shrinkable soil, as these will undoubtedly be the cause of problems in the near future.

A example of the kind of assessment to be made is as follows:
A typical first-floor extension may add around 30 kn (3 tonnes) per metre to the line load along the foundation. Exposing the edge of the foundation reveals it to be 1 m deep below ground level, with concrete 300 mm thick and projecting 170 mm from the wall face. The wall is known to be 260 mm thick, and so, if assumed to be centrally placed on the foundation, the foundation must be 600 mm wide.

30 kn/m divided by 0.6 m = 50 kn per sq m of load is the net increase in bearing pressure to the ground.

To find out whether the exposed subsoil will cope with this, consult your structural designer and local Building Control Officer and invite them to inspect the trial holes and advise you. **In addition to checking out the foundations, existing lintels and beams that are subjected to increased load should also be checked.**

Ground-floor slabs
Ground-bearing slabs
Once the foundations have been concreted and the substructure walls built up to DPC level, the preparation for the floor slab can begin. This will consist of a hardcore base, at least 100 mm thick, blinding, a damp-proof membrane (usually 1200 g polythene)

10 Expert Points

THE FOLLOWING TEN EXPERT POINTS WILL HELP YOU TO ACHIEVE A GOOD OVERSITE:

1 SOIL STRIP
Ensure that the topsoil and vegetation are stripped off and that you begin from subsoil level.

2 MATERIAL
Ensure that you use acceptable material for hardcore (see the table on page 66).

3 MATERIAL SIZE
Ensure that the hardcore material is no larger than 100 mm (half-brick) units.

4 LEVELS
Ensure that you have correctly calculated the depth of construction through to finished floor level, and that your oversite level is correct.

5 DEPTH
Ensure that the oversite covers at least 150 mm in thickness. Ensure that the hardcore, if deeper than 150 mm, does not exceed 600 mm in total thickness. On sloping sites where part of the make-up may exceed 600 mm deep, it may be acceptable to use lean-mix concrete in layers with the hardcore to make up the difference.

6 COMPACTION
Ensure that the hardcore is compacted in layers no more than 225 mm thick and is preferably mechanically compacted with a plate compactor. Where a stone-type fill is used, take care that you do not push out the external walls.

7 BLINDING
Ensure that the hardcore is blinded with fine material, such as sand, to a maximum thickness of 20 mm. Do not lay the blinding material too thick. It is only intended to protect the polythene damp-proof membrane from being punctured by sharp edges of hardcore.

8 DAMP-PROOF MEMBRANE (DPM)
Lap and tape down polythene if it is cut for the DPM. Ensure that the DPM is dressed up over the outside walls so it can be lapped with the DPC later. Polythene DPMs can help to protect the concrete slab from sulphate attack. Sulphates may be contained in some fill material, such as brick rubble.

9 INSULATION
Use the correct depth and type of insulation graded for floors, not walls! Phenolic (or polyurethane) is often used in 80 mm thickness. To fit it, cut the insulation into strips and stand it up the sides of walls to the slab depth when insulating below the concrete slab so that the slab is fully encased.

Some larger extensions over 100 sq m may require less insulation when the perimeter over area (P/A) ratio is calculated since most heat loss occurs around the edges of floors.

10 CRACK AVOIDANCE
Make sure that you are not forming the hardcore on filled ground, or where subsoil heave will cause problems. Your foundations and the precautions taken for them will need to be reflected in the slab design. Even on good subsoil, the addition of a lightweight fabric reinforcement such as A142 is beneficial to avoiding settlement cracks; it can also be used in garage extensions where extra-thick concrete slabs (over 150 mm) are used. In very large slabs movement joints, such as fibrous material strips, should be used to allow some expansion to occur without damaging the slab.

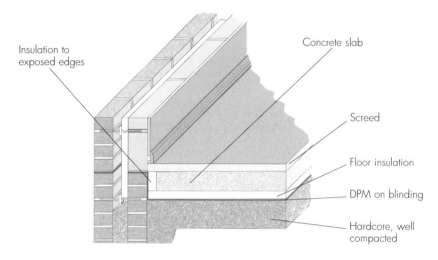

Insulation to exposed edges

Concrete slab

Screed

Floor insulation

DPM on blinding

Hardcore, well compacted

Typical concrete ground-floor construction.

and in most cases insulation boards. The concrete slab is then formed at least 100 mm thick on top of this lot.

With all this 'make-up' it is important to ensure that the top of the slab is formed at the correct level, particularly if you want your new extension floor to be level with your existing floor.

Floor slab settlement is the most common of the major defects associated with new construction. If the preparation is not right, floor slabs easily settle and crack up.

This preparation is subject to a one-

OVERSITE MATERIAL

USE:
Clean broken bricks, concrete, tiles only for hardcore, reject or crushed stone (washed), road-base aggregate.

AVOID:
Colliery shale, soft insulating broken blocks, poor-quality demolition rubble*, loose chalk (types 1 and 2).

*Note: there are sound environmental reasons for re-using demolition hardcore in oversite preparations, but it is essential that it is hand-picked and 'clean'. Be prepared to spend some time sifting the rubbish out.

Note also that sulphates in hardcore or in subsoil can attack concrete. Where this is likely, use sulphate-resisting cement in place of ordinary Portland cement.

Polythene DPMs will also help to resist sulphate attack.

DIY CONCRETE MIX FOR GROUND-BEARING SLABS:
50 kg (0.033 cu m) of cement to 0.1 cu m of building sand to 0.2 cu m of coarse aggregate (or 10 x 25 kg bags of cement to every cubic metre of all-in ballast)

SPAN BETWEEN FOUNDATION-BEARING WALLS	MESH SIZE	CONCRETE GRADE	SLAB THICKNESS
up to 2.4 m	B385	C35	130 mm
2.4–3.0 m	B785	C35	130 mm
3.0–3.7 m	B1131	C35	150 mm
3.7–4.3 m	B1131	C35	180 mm
4.3–4.9 m	B1131	C35	200 mm
4.9–5.5 m	B1131	C35	230 mm

This table is only a guide and allows for one standard-height (2.4 m) partition, cement sand floor screed and the self weight of the concrete slab itself. A structural engineer may be required to prepare a bespoke calculated design in accordance with BS8110: 1985.

● Note that 'B'-type mesh has main bars running one way and lesser secondary bars running the other, and is laid in rectangles. It is critically important to place it with the main bars running with the span shown in the tables.

● Where more than one sheet of mesh is used, joints must be overlapped by at least 400 mm and tied together with tying wire.
● The mesh should be seated in position on preformed stools to achieve the correct cover to the bottom of the slab.

EXPERT DIY CONCRETE MIX FOR SUSPENDED IN-SITU SLABS:
50 kg of cement to
0.08 cu m of building sand to
0.13 cu m of coarse aggregate
or 8.5 bags x 50 kg of cement to every cubic metre of all-in ballast

SIZE OF JOISTS (MM)	100 X 50	125 X 50	150 X 50	175 X 50
Maximum span of joists (m)	up to 1.9	1.9–2.5	2.5–3	3–3.5

SIZE OF JOISTS (MM)	200 X 50	225 X 50
Maximum span of joists (m)	3.5–4.1	4.1–4.6

The maximum span for timber joists of regular size is 5.25 m for C24-grade timber, using 225 x 75 mm section joists spaced at 400 mm centres. Beyond this span, sleeper walls should be built from internal foundations to provide intermediate support. These walls must be perforated with air bricks to allow a cross-flow of air beneath the floor. Where different load conditions apply (e.g. where partitions are supported by the floor), a bespoke calculated design by a structural engineer may be required in accordance with BS5268: Part 2: 1996 – for example, where internal partitions are proposed to be built off the floor structure.

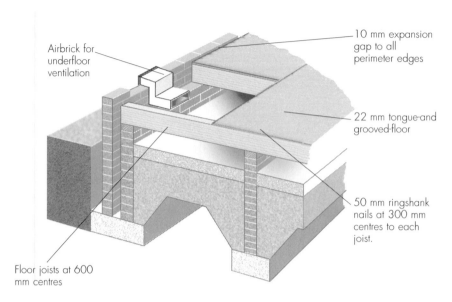

Airbrick for underfloor ventilation

10 mm expansion gap to all perimeter edges

22 mm tongue-and grooved-floor

50 mm ringshank nails at 300 mm centres to each joist.

Floor joists at 600 mm centres

Suspended timber floor.

day Statutory Notice of Inspection to the Building Control Surveyor, who will need to inspect the work before the concrete is poured.

Suspended ground floors

Where suspended ground floors are proposed, the load-bearing walls of the extension are used to support the floor structure instead of the ground. Consequently, extra weight is transferred to the foundations, and this should be borne in mind when their width is being determined.

Generally speaking, all suspended-floor methods work up to a span of about 5.5 m – if you have dimensions greater than this between your external load-bearing walls, it is likely that you will need to provide extra load-bearing walls internally to break up the span.

In the case of made-up ground (filled sites) or clay heave, you will need to use a suspended ground-floor structure, of which there are three basic types: suspended in-situ concrete slabs, suspended timber ground floors, and precast concrete beams with block infill.

Suspended in-situ concrete slabs

These slabs have steel reinforcement in the bottom part which is supported from the bearing walls and spans between them. This would normally require a structural engineer's design to calculate the grade of steel and thickness of concrete to be used. The reinforcement is typically available in prefabricated mesh format of various grades, and the concrete required is of a higher strength than normal, and is often set to a greater thickness.

On page 65 are some typical specifications for a few given spans between foundation-bearing walls. They assume a maximum 63 mm-thick cement/sand floor screed finish with domestic floor loads, and a 40 mm depth of cover between the reinforcement and the underside of the concrete.

Suspended timber ground floor

This is basically the same construction as a timber first floor would be, using timber joists to span between load-bearing walls. The difference comes from the need to ensure that the floor is damp-proofed and properly ventilated. Consequently, it is essential to provide the following:

- A concrete ground-covering slab, around 75 mm thick, on polythene, to prevent growth and damp.
- At least 125 mm of air space beneath the floor joists and ground.
- A good cross-flow of air beneath the floor joists and the ground, equal to at least 550 sq mm of air per 1 m run of wall.
- DPCs beneath timber plates on which the joists will be sat and fixed.
- On sloping sites, a drain to allow water to run out at the bottom.

Timber joists will, of course, only span so far, depending on their size and spacing. The table on page 67 is a guide, based on:

- C16 (aka SC3 or GS grade) timber joists spaced at 400 mm centres.
- Standard flooring-grade chipboard,

22 mm thick, and domestic floor loads.

Timber is also commonly available in 63 mm and 75 mm widths.

Ordering structural timber

There are specific requirements for timber used in construction, particularly in the case of structural members.

Grading

There are many strength grades for timber, ranging from the weakest softwood to the strongest hardwood. C16 and C24 are the common grades used for structural members, such as those in load-bearing situations like floor joists and rafters. It is now a requirement of the Building Regulations that structural timber is DRY-graded. This means that its moisture content is limited to a maximum of 24%. In the past, wet timber has been the cause of much shrinkage in homes when they are occupied and heated. This shrinkage can, at worst, cause distortion and structural displacement, and at the very least cracking of finishings.

Every piece of structural timber must be stamp-marked to say what stress grade it is, among other information to say whether it is DRY (air-dried slowly) or KN (kiln-dried). You should quote that DRY grading is required when ordering the timber.

Preservatives

These should be requested on ordering. Treatment is carried out under pressure/vacuum and affords protection against fungal and insect attack. This is essential in areas known to suffer with house long-horn beetle (*Hylotrupes bajulus L*), such as parts of Surrey, Berkshire and Hampshire. All timber preservatives contain harmful chemicals, and any on-site treatment of timber, whether inside or outside, should be done with extreme care and while wearing protective clothing.

Selection

This should be done before accepting the delivery. Check for splits, shakes, knots and any bent or warped timbers, and reject anything unsuitable before signing the delivery ticket or paying.

Environmental issues

If these are of importance to you, you will want to see that any timber you buy has been marked with the FSC (Forest Stewardship Council) trademark. This means that the timber has been cut from sustainable managed forests that have been certified by the organisation throughout the world. The FSC trademark is reproduced below.

FSC

Struts

Solid noggins or herringbone strutting should be used between floor joists to provide lateral restraint as follows:

● for joist spans up to 2.5 m not required
● for joist spans between 2.5 and 4.5 m one row of struts at mid-centre
● for joist spans over 4.5 m two rows of struts at one-third centres

Insulation

Phenolic foam insulation boards can be suspended between joists on side battens as a single sheet of 100 mm thickness, or two layers of 50 mm thickness, to achieve the minimum standard for a ground or exposed floor. 150 mm will bring it up to a similar standard achieved by roof insulation.

Services

Timber suspended floors come out on top when it comes to housing services. Central heating pipes can be easily notched into the top of the joists above the insulation. Electrical cables can be fed through drilled holes in the centre of the joists. Waste pipes and drain pipes can pass through the void beneath the joists and be clipped for support to their underside. (See also Chapter 6.)

Precast concrete beams with block infill

This system is perhaps the most costly for an extension. Precast concrete T-shape floor joists are purchased from a specialist company and blocks are laid flat in between them to form the floor. A cement slurry is required over the top before the insulation or screed can be laid. This system is also available using expanded polystyrene blocks in lieu of concrete blocks, for a dry floating floor finish with good insulation qualities.

Ventilation to the underside (void) of the floor may be required, particularly if you have gas-supply pipes running there. Usually, the ground is treated with a layer of polythene weighted down with

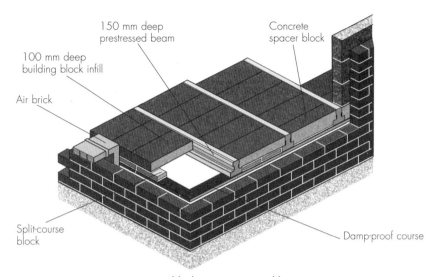

150 mm deep
prestressed beam

Concrete
spacer block

100 mm deep
building block infill

Air brick

Split-course
block

Damp-proof course

Concrete spacer blocks on pre-stressed beams.

sand to prevent growth, but obviously this system is not prone to the decaying weakness of timber. Manufacturers will mark up a plan showing the beam positions and specifying the correct beam sizes when securing an order.

Below-ground drainage

Before leaving the groundwork and starting on the superstructure, it is often advisable to install below-ground drainage for foul or surface water.

Foul drains

These carry dirty water from WCs, baths, basins, washing machines and sinks, and connect either to a main sewer or to a septic tank or cesspool. The most common form of drainage material these days is PVC-U (plastic), which is versatile and easy to install and keep clean. It is laid on a bed of fine gravel or pea-shingle and covered with more of the same. Ideally it should be laid with a fall

of at least 1:40, but manufacturers will often state much less. Check the gradients of pipes before backfilling, using a spirit level rather than by eye.

By far the biggest failure of drainage comes from badly made joints. Water-test all drainage for your own satisfaction before backfilling, to ensure that it is watertight. Expanding bungs or airbags can be bought or hired from plumbing and drainage merchants. Place one at the bottom of the run, preferably at the last manhole, tie a piece of string to it and secure it so it isn't washed away, and fill the pipework with water. Check the water level regularly at a gulley or manhole at the top of the run to see if the level has dropped. If it holds its level perfectly for at least ten minutes you can assume it is satisfactory. Beware of air bubbles trapped in the pipes. Do not attempt a water test where the fall of the drainage exceeds 2 m overall, as the head of pressure may be too great. Note that the Building Control Officer may be required to witness the test, either now or when the building work is completed; it is a Statutory Notice of Inspection.

Building over drains

Where they pass through or beneath the structure of the extension, drains require protection. In walls, prestressed concrete lintels are often employed to bridge over drains, but the resultant hole around the drainpipe should be filled to prevent rodents from getting under the house. If the floor slab is not suspended, lightweight reinforcing mesh (e.g. A142 grade) can be employed in the concrete to spread the weight away from the drainpipe.

Building over public sewers

This will require special protection

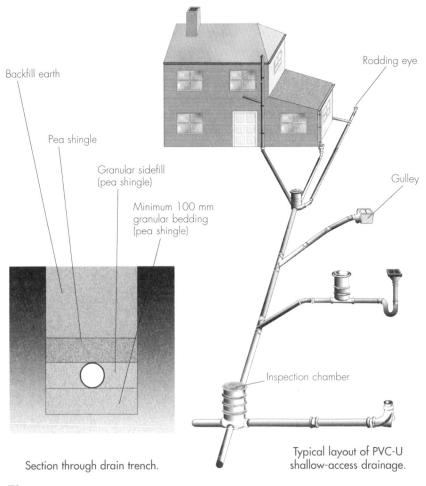

Backfill earth

Pea shingle

Granular sidefill (pea shingle)

Minimum 100 mm granular bedding (pea shingle)

Rodding eye

Gulley

Inspection chamber

Section through drain trench.

Typical layout of PVC-U shallow-access drainage.

measures agreed with the water authority who own the sewer. They may require you to enter into a contract of agreement, but increasingly they are prepared to issue details of the protection they require on the understanding that you will adopt them as work proceeds.

Internal manholes are best avoided if possible, but where this can't be done, the covers to them must be double-sealed and screwed or bolted down to prevent foul smells from leaking out into the house. You cannot bury them – they must remain accessible. Covers that are recessed and will take a screed infill to look less obtrusive and maintain the floor finish are available, but it is best to avoid internal manholes, even if this means re-routing existing drainage.

Drains near trees

There is every reason to avoid placing drains near trees. First, the excavation itself can, if deep enough and close enough to the tree, destabilise it. Second, the roots of trees can be ruthless when searching for water and can break drainage pipes, and third, removed trees can result in heave of clay subsoil, causing drains to be displaced. If you have no choice but to run your drainage near to trees, precautions should be taken to protect them both:

● If you think you will expose roots, dig the drainage trenches by hand.
● Do not cut through roots greater than 50 mm in diameter. Line drains so they run over or above them.
● Encase the drains with concrete, using flexible jointing material in the concrete at the position of all pipe

joints to maintain the flexibility of the system.

● Consider forming a root barrier between the drains and trees if there is sufficient space to do so. A root barrier is a deep and narrow trench excavated and filled with concrete to form an obstruction for the roots below ground. If it is not formed properly, roots may eventually breach the barrier. Use the foundation guide table (see page 61) for advice on the appropriate depth for the barrier in relation to the tree, and make sure that the barrier is formed up to finished ground level, otherwise the roots will simply go over the top.

Drainage gulleys

External gulley pots for kitchen sinks, etc. can now be purchased with built-in rodding access. It is well worth investing in a 'roddable' type back-inlet gulley, as this will make clearing any future blockages that much easier.

Rainwater downpipes are often connected directly into below-ground drainage with pipe-size adaptors, but should they become blocked with leaves or other matter, it can be very difficult to clean them out. Gulleys positioned at the bottom of downpipes can overcome this problem, but the downpipes should discharge below the grating level.

Where you are connecting surface water into a combined drain (one which takes both foul water and surface water), it is essential that trapped gulleys are used to prevent foul air from venting out of the rainwater pipes.

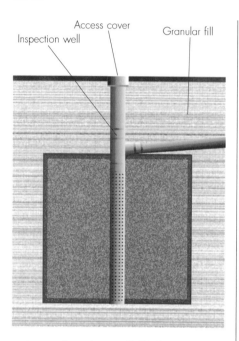

Inspection well · Access cover · Granular fill

Section through a small, filled soakaway with perforated inspection well extending to base of soakaway, providing access to discharge drain outlet.

Rainwater drainage

Soakaways

In many areas water authorities discourage surface water (rainwater) from being directed into foul drainage, which is already overladen. Wherever possible, and particularly in water-catchment areas (aquifer zones), soakaways which take the surface water down into the subsoil at a safe distance away from buildings should be used; the recommended minimum distance is currently 5 m. Soakaways for domestic extensions should be of suitable capacity for the run-off area, and are often formed by pits filled with hardcore (such as brick rubble – not sponge-like aerated concrete blocks!), capped with a polythene or geotextile sheet above the pipe inlet level. Careful consideration of the subsoil and its percolation abilities should be made before digging the soakaway. In heavy clay soil, a deep, trench-style soakaway with a perforated pipe run off may work better than a cubic pit. Always oversize soakaways, as they are prone to silt up in time, thus reducing their effectiveness. Precast concrete manhole rings are also used for large soakaways – these can be perforated with holes and filled and backfilled with large stone-type material.

If you intend to connect your surface water to a septic tank, take account of the tank's capacity to accept the load in addition to the foul water, and particularly the irrigation drainage from the tank, since it is this that will determine its disposal. A percolation test should be carried out on the subsoil to check its rate of porosity.

If you are interested in conserving rainwater for use in the garden, storage tanks from which the water may be pumped in a drought, could be used in the ground. Unless these tanks are going to be excessively large, it would be wise to install an overflow to a soakaway. There are some more adventurous products around for storing rainwater, filtering it and pumping it back into the house for re-use. I can't see how they could be used for anything other than WCs, though, and because of water bylaws and the need to separate potable water from any likely contamination, these rainwater systems require an entire plumbing system separate to the standard mains-water one.

If you intend to connect your rainwater drainage to a public foul sewer which is not combined, you should first obtain the agreement of the water authority controlling the sewer.

In respect of foul-water treatment by septic tanks, their installation should be approved by the Environment Agency (in England and Wales) in addition to the local Building Control Authority, since they may wish to avoid foul-water percolation in water-catchment areas (aquifer zones).

Connecting new drainage to existing is always best done with a manhole, since the new pipes can be introduced at invert level and accessed for testing separately from the existing ones. If you wish to connect new pipework by jointing it directly to existing, make sure that you use proprietary connectors that are compatible with the pipe diameters and materials.

Old pitch-fibre pipes are often squashed out of shape and are thus difficult to connect to. A recently introduced type of connector is formed of durable rubber with adjustable metal rings that can be tightened to secure the joint. These can be used where more specific adaptors aren't available. Test all connections before backfilling.

Damp-proof courses (DPC)

In order to protect the extension against rising damp, a DPC must be built in at least 150 mm above the outside finished ground level. Ideally, it should be at the same level as the existing house DPC, thus forming a continuous barrier. Corners and any other joints are fully lapped, and the DPC should also overlap

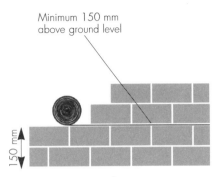

Minimum 150 mm above ground level

150 mm

Damp-proof course.

with the DPM (damp-proof membrane) used under the floor, again to form a continuous barrier. Where timber-frame structure or suspended-timber floor structure is used, the DPC is positioned directly beneath the soleplates supporting the structures, keeping the timber dry.

Where unusual ground conditions prevail and the floor structure will be below the outside ground level, tanking with an appropriate material may be required to ensure adequate damp-proofing – see the diagram above.

The type of damp-proofing membrane required will depend upon the soil conditions, whether active water pressure is anticipated, and the height of the wall between the floor slab and the outside ground level. All these factors will determine the construction of the retaining external wall. Both, if not detailed on the approved plans, should be agreed with the Building Control Surveyor before work commences.

DPCs are subject to a one-day Statutory Notice to the Building Control Surveyor before being covered.

CHAPTER 5

Superstructure

The term superstructure covers all
structural elements of the building
above ground level. Traditionally, that
means everything above the construction
of the ground-floor level and the DPC,
both of which were covered in some
depth in the last chapter.

Walls

In England and Wales the principal
method of wall construction is masonry,
predominantly cavity-wall masonry,
although the cavity is often totally filled
with insulation to meet the
requirements for energy conservation.

Timber-frame construction still only
represents about 8% of English and
Welsh housing. In Scotland timber frame
is considerably more prevalent, with
45% of the share, but this is nothing
compared to Australia, North America
and Scandinavia, where it represents at
least 90%. The reasons for this lie more
within tradition than climate – even in
Japan, with a temperate climate similar
to Britain's, 50% of homes are built in
timber-frame construction.

In general, it is advisable to build
your extension in a similar construction
to that of the existing house. To change
to another form will only increase the
risks of differential movement between
the two, which can even result in
unnecessary cracking.

Masonry construction

Cavity walls
The idea of building a wall in two
separate leaves for improved weather
resistance first appeared at the end of
the 19th century. It proved successful:
driving rain might have been able to
penetrate the outer brick leaf, but it
couldn't bridge the air cavity to get at
the inner leaf. Until the 1980s the clear
cavity wall prevailed in Britain, but the
trend to insulate cavities took hold with
the increasing need and standards for
energy conservation in new building
work. Since then standards have
increased again and again, and now,
approaching a new century, the clear
cavity wall is virtually extinct.

At present, total-fill insulation is the
norm, bringing with it more onerous
standards of workmanship for
bricklayers than ever before. If water is
to be kept out of the insulated cavity
wall, the insulation must be built in
more carefully than most would care
to admit.

When the insulated cavity wall fails
and the inner leaf gets wet, the finger of
accusation swings wildly about and
invariably settles on the workmanship of
the bricklayer. Because of this risk and
the fact that it is magnified in areas of
severe exposure, many builders and
designers shy away from total-fill
insulation and strive to achieve at least a
residual air cavity with partial-fill
insulation or, better still, provide a
weatherproof cladding, like cement
rendering or weatherboarding, on the
outer leaf to protect it against the
vagaries of the elements.

Solid walls
Solid brick walls are extinct in new
buildings today. To meet the current
requirements for energy conservation,

external walls must achieve a 'U' value maximum of 0.30 (watts per metre squared by degrees Kelvin). This is a measure of thermal transmission through an element of structure, showing how much heat can pass through it – the higher the U-value figure the more heat is escaping, and consequently the worse it is. It is no longer possible to build with energy efficiency in mind using solid brickwork alone. Even a solid brick wall that is 440 mm thick will still only achieve a U value of 1.33, letting in four times as much heat as is currently acceptable.

Modern technology allows us to have U values down to around 0.25 in cavity walls, but in solid walls even a 215 mm-thick insulating block may require extra insulation in the finishings to achieve this value. These lightweight insulating blocks have been around since the mid-1980s and have proved popular with bricklayers, but not so popular with home-owners. They have a very low compressive strength, and trying to fix something heavy like a cupboard or shelf to them subsequently has proved extremely difficult. If you are using them, dry-lining the internal finishings instead of plastering will give you a fighting chance of getting fixings to stay in the wall, as well as covering the inevitable shrinkage cracks.

In terms of speed, solid-wall construction must have the upper hand, but of course this requires time to be spent on external finishings. The cost of lightweight blocks is now considerably less than when they were first available, making solid walling a cost-effective option nowadays.

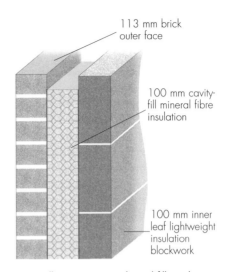

113 mm brick outer face

100 mm cavity-fill mineral fibre insulation

100 mm inner leaf lightweight insulation blockwork

Cavity wall construction with total fill insulation.

The only risk to water penetration through a properly clad solid wall seems to come from allowing water to lay against it – for example, laying a concrete path up tight against a solid wall without providing an impervious damp-proof membrane between the two is likely to cause a problem. You may have noticed that in rendered walls the wall is painted with a black bituminous paint band around the bottom, and the render is finished above ground level with a bell-shape to kick the water off as it runs down the wall. These features are not there for decoration.

Timber frames

Cavity construction in timber frames invariably means providing a timber-frame inner leaf as the structural element and a brick or block outer leaf as a rain shield.

The insulation within timber-frame structures is perfectly located between the timber studs of the framework, and because of this it can be considerably thick and still maintain a clear cavity, earning timber-frame properties their reputation for energy efficiency. The greatest risks come from condensation forming within the structure, but modern materials have reduced this problem to acceptable levels. With the construction lending itself to 'system building', where manufacturers produce a design-and-supply package with the option of erecting it as well, the timber-frame extension can be structurally built in a 'one-stop-shop'. On the other hand, it isn't exactly science, and some 'specially trained erectors' have a habit of crashing in, sending hammers and nails flying for a day or two, and crashing out before you know what's hit you. On the whole, I think you would be wise to have your timber-frame extension built with a touch more care and time, not to say designed with a less frugal attention to materials.

Many countries prefer a more substantial timber section for the framework than in the UK – 50 x 150 mm is the norm in Scandinavia, and 50 x 100 mm in Britain. Either way, the frame still needs to be braced, either with diagonal timbers between the vertical studs or by lining it with plywood sheathing. The latter is preferable, since it provides a diaphragm-like structure which is highly resistant to racking movement under wind loads. In both methods, the walling is made up in manageable panels on the ground and erected into position on site.

The soleplates of timber-frame walls

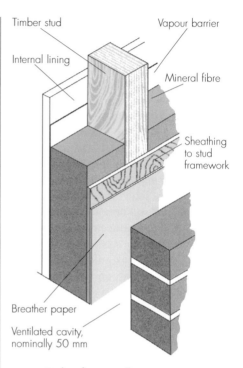

Timber-frame wall construction.

need securing down without penetrating the DPC. To achieve this, special anchor plates allow the plate to be fixed to the ground-floor structure rather than the wall substructure.

Sheathing is normally covered with a breather membrane (building paper), which adds some weather resistance behind the cladding. It is usually stapled to the sheathing and needs to be well lapped at joints and repaired after it gets torn or damaged, as it usually will.

Internally, the plasterboard finishing is fixed over a vapour-control layer (polythene) to restrict condensation within the structure from coming through into the house. 'Warm-wall' construction, where the insulation goes on the outside of the sheathing, does not need a vapour-control layer.

Like breather membranes, vapour-control layers are stapled to the stud frame, with joints well lapped and damage repaired immediately after the insulation has been installed between the studs.

Single-leaf timber-frame construction

By omitting the outer masonry leaf and, instead, providing a weather-resistant cladding to the frame, you have single-leaf timber construction. It may not appeal to a lot of people in Britain since it too closely resembles the garden shed,

but it is an option.

One major drawback of this method is fire resistance. If the timber frame walls are within 6 m of the site boundary, they may need some additional fire resistance – see 'Fire Spread and Unprotected Areas' later in this section.

Soon after completing the erection of the timber frame, the roof should be pitched and covered and the windows glazed. Do not allow the frame to stand exposed to the elements for too long. External finishes, such as cladding and weatherboarding, are covered in Chapter 7.

10 Expert Points

HERE ARE TEN EXPERT POINTS FOR TIMBER-FRAME CONSTRUCTION:

1 LEVEL FOUNDATIONS
Check that foundations have been accurately set out, within plus or minus 10 mm per 6 m length of wall.

2 LEVEL FLOORS AND SUB-WALLS
Check that floors and walls below baseplates (soleplates) are level to plus or minus 6 mm in 6 m.

3 LEVEL BASEPLATES
Take great care in levelling beneath baseplates on a mortar bed and DPC.

4 ANCHOR BASEPLATES
Secure these using special baseplate angle fixings, not by bolting through the plate and DPC.

5 VERTICAL WALLS
Do not allow the wall panels to be moved out of plumb to accept incorrectly made trusses or beams.

6 GAPS
Avoid gaps between wall panels and poor nailing between panels.

7 UPPER-STOREY PANELS
Check that the upper-floor wall panels are nailed securely to floor joists, and that they are packed out beneath properly between the joists.

8 SPLIT TIMBER
Discard split timber caused by nailing too close to the edge of timbers.

9 DAMP-PROOFING
Make sure that the outer breather membrane overlaps the sole plate and the DPC beneath it is lapped up inside the plate to protect it from wet floor finishes.

10 TIMBER GRADING
All timber should be regularised, bear a stress-grade stamp, and be marked DRY or KD to show low moisture content. External wall timbers should also be vacuum- or pressure-pre-treated with preservative.

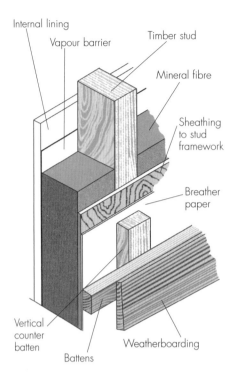

Internal lining
Vapour barrier
Timber stud
Mineral fibre
Sheathing to stud framework
Breather paper
Vertical counter batten
Battens
Weatherboarding

Typical single-leaf timber-frame wall construction.

The construction illustrated above shows how single-leaf timber walls can be built to meet current standards where no unprotected area restrictions are in existence.

Insect attack

We in the UK are extremely fortunate that our indigenous insects are, for the most part, well-behaved, and are easily killed if they aren't. In many other countries of the world, insects destroy more buildings than fire and flood put together. Often the insect responsible is one of the 2000 species of termite (*Isoptera*), some of which are wood-borers. Only two termite species are resident in Europe and are confined to the warmer Mediterranean regions at that, extending as far north as Bordeaux in France. One of these, *Reticuliformes lucifugus*, is, alas, one of the species that tunnels into timber, living in the excavated chambers and feeding on the wood. Termites' role in nature is to break up fallen timber and return it to the soil, but unfortunately for us they are unable to tell the difference between a dead tree in a wood and four-by-two in somebody's roof.

A colony of termites was discovered in a house in the West Country in the spring of 1998, where they had been accidentally introduced from abroad via a holiday packing trunk. The case was highly publicised, and with good reason, but this was, however, an isolated incident, and the advice to the public and the building industry is that prevention is not required. In any case, one hard winter should render any

USING TIMBER PRESERVATIVE

If you are preservative-treating timber on site, the timber should not be used until it has thoroughly dried out; the preservative may otherwise corrode fixings. Be aware that the vast majority of timber preservative is environmentally unfriendly. It is designed to kill fungus and insect life, and will do an equally fatal job on other creatures. It contains toxic substances, and when applying it you need to use protective clothing and maintain a high standard of personal hygiene.

From July 2004, the use of Copper Chromated Arsenic (CCA) timber preservative is illegal in homes.

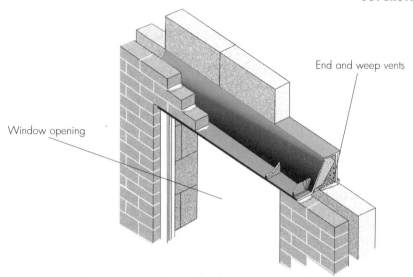

End and weep vents

Window opening

Isometric view of typical lintel showing stop end and weep vents

termite colony extinct.

If you do discover termites (recognisable to many as white ants) in your house, contact your local council's Environmental Health Department, who will advise and assist you with extermination; otherwise, preventative treatments are not necessary. Mind you, with scientific predictions that the climate in Britain will become steadily warmer over the next century, that advice may have to change in the future.

Our worst offender is a juvenile delinquent in comparison with termites – the deathwatch beetle (*Xestobium rufovillosum*), which tends to prefer old damp timber, another reason why you should be careful about building old oak beams into your home. It does, however, have one endearing feature – it lets you know it's there by banging its head against the tunnels it digs in the wood. Apparently the male does this to attract a mate, but it has the advantage (for us)

of working equally well in enticing pest-control men.

Lintels

In spite of the vast range of lintels that are available to the building industry, only a handful of types are commonly used. Most steel lintel companies produce at least 50 lintel types for use in as many different situations, but if you visited 50 small building sites you would be lucky to meet more than three or four different lintels.

It seems to be a question of availability mixed with ignorance. Builders' merchants know that builders ask for the same standard lintels time and time again, and so they stock them and nothing else. If you do ask for something else out of the catalogue, you are likely to be met with a look of incomprehension and an order form. The end result is that people continue to use the same lintels, often the wrong ones for the situation, because they are all that is easily available. The only way to break this circle is to prepare a lintel schedule before you dig the foundations, and to obtain some quotes, followed, if necessary, with some early orders at the merchants.

Lintels should not be cut down in length to adapt them. Apart from negating the manufacturer's guarantee, you will cut through their galvanising protection by doing this, thus leaving the end exposed to corrosion.

The prestressed concrete lintel is perhaps the most misused of all. Commonly available in 63 x 100 mm section to suit a cavity-wall leaf, it is widely used to carry loads it was never designed for. It is, in fact, only suitable for small openings, such as internal doorways up to around 1.25 m wide. Deeper PCC lintels for higher loads and greater spans are made, but it usually proves harder to obtain them.

It is worth remembering that lintels are designed to carry uniformly distributed loads. Where point loads are placed on them, from the bearing ends of other beams for example, they should be checked out by a structural engineer. Some lintel companies provide a structural design and specifying service for their customers free of charge.

Windows

It isn't unusual for home-owners to experience some conflict with Planning and Building Control authorities over the size and position of windows and doors. Of all the elements of your new extension, these are likely to be the most contentious. Siting them so they

do not overlook a neighbouring property, sizing them so that they do not represent a fire risk across a boundary, sizing them again so that they do not represent an unacceptable heat loss, choosing frames that reflect the existing home's fenestration detail, repositioning them so that they do not compromise the structural stability of a wall or corner... and so on.

You may be forgiven for thinking that what you wanted, and where you wanted it, has somehow gone out the window (so to speak). The only advice I can give you is to try and be flexible and, where possible, consider the opening casement rather than the fanlight. In the event of a fire you may need to escape from a window, only to discover that it is near-on impossible to break the glass of a sealed, double-glazed unit. The minimum opening size that most people can climb through is 850 mm high by 500 mm wide – bear in mind that scissor hinges in PVC-U windows bring the casement in when open, thus reducing the clear opening size.

Safety glazing

Every year hundreds of people are injured in accidents involving glass. The injuries sustained can be serious, and even fatal, with the hands and wrists being most vulnerable. Low-level glazing presents a particularly high risk, especially to children. To help reduce the number of injuries, in 1992 the Building Regulations were extended to include safety-glass requirements in critical locations. Shortly afterwards, the Glass and Glazing Federation (GGF) introduced its own code of practice to glaziers and other glass suppliers on the same detail.

Glass in critical locations means that glazing within 800 mm of floor level in a window or in doors and sidelights will need to be safety glass. It shouldn't be possible to purchase any other kind of glass for these situations, but occasionally a window is installed at a lower level than anticipated, so check your cill heights before ordering. Safety glass can be toughened, laminated, annealed in small panes or tempered, depending upon its position. Laminated is the most secure, since it has the ability to resist intruders as well. It does this by laminating the two panes of a double-glazed unit together with a clear-plastic interlayer which cannot be easily penetrated. The glass will crack on impact like a car windscreen, but without any sharp or protruding edges. Toughened glass, on the other hand, shatters into small pieces, but also hangs together. It can, however, be knocked through afterwards, making it less suitable from a security point of view.

A low (less than 800 mm from floor level) upstairs window may need to be fixed rather than openable in any case, to protect people from falling out, especially children.

Ventilation

As the Roman poet Ovid wrote in 1BC, 'Languor seizes the body from bad ventilation' – actually he wrote, '*Aere non certo corpora languor habet*', but it still wasn't a bad piece of forward thinking, considering it was nearly 2000 years before sealed, glazed units were invented.

Good ventilation is more important now than it has ever been. We live in hermetically sealed times, and yet we still introduce gas and other fuels into our homes for heating and cooking. Older properties tend to be conveniently riddled with draughts, but with the modern extension we must design to seal out draughts and introduce controllable ventilation in different forms. The first of these is rapid ventilation, which should equal at least 1/20 (1/30 in Scotland) of the room's floor area in openable area, and this means openable windows and doors.

In addition to being able to open the windows, we must also introduce a permanent amount of background

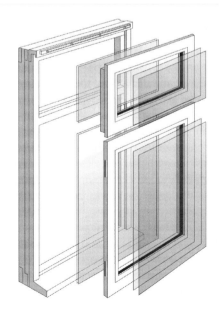

Exploded detail of a typical off-the-shelf double-glazed window.

ventilation which can trickle through all the time. Trickle vents tend to be about 10 mm deep, and are ideally positioned in the heads of window and door frames, where they are less of an unwanted draught. All new habitable rooms should have trickle vents serving them, preferably from windows on opposing walls to maintain some air movement across the room. An alternative is the crack ventilation on the window's casements which allows them to be secured marginally open. This is becoming more popular, but security is an issue on ground-floor windows.

No daylight requirements exist in England and Wales under the Building Regulations, but 10% of the floor area is considered the minimum acceptable amount under the fitness standards for homes. In Scotland a minimum area of 15% is currently required by the Scottish Standards to the Building Regulations. In either case the figure is often considered too low by the average person – leading to a maximum of 25% of the extension area (in glazed elements) limiting the amount of heat loss from windows to ensure energy conservation. Double-glazing with wide argon gas-filled cavities and low-emittance coatings are the standard, and not easily improved upon. This also improves sound insulation. The only way to meet the two separate rules is to increase the insulation in other elements of your extension or existing home as a trade-off and provide SAP (standard assessment procedure) calculations to justify the extra glazing.

If noise is a real problem – your extension is close to a busy road or you live near an airport or football ground –

the best sound insulation comes from triple-glazing: windows which provide three layers of glass sandwiched together by two sealed cavities. To get the best out of these, the casements should offer a good fit to the frames, preventing sound from leaking in around the edges.

Rapid mechanical ventilation is covered in Chapter 6.

Bay windows

Bays are a popular choice, since they admit a greater amount of daylight for the same structural opening as a conventional window. They have had something of a bad press lately, due to the ignorance of the 'replacement PVC-U window industry'. By their very nature, bay windows contain posts in the corners to support the roof above them; when these posts have been removed to accept the replacement window, the support has not been replaced, leaving the window to fail under the load.

Since it is possible to build up your own bay window in the extension by using ordinary windows, make sure that structural support exists in the form of corner posts and lintels to support the bay roof. The usual amount of reinforcing that goes into a PVC-U window frame is not sufficient to support anything but itself.

Doors and security

Doors are a constant source of amazement to me. The British door, it has to be said, is perhaps the lowest quality of door in the Western world; it is often cheap and nasty, and is probably responsible for a large number of house break-ins. This may be partly due to the fact that there is not – and never has been – a British Standard for door construction. There is one for windows, which sets out tests for water-tightness, etc., but strangely enough, doors in this country have never been required to be anything in particular.

Standard external timber doors are usually 44 mm thick and 838 mm wide. If you are fitting a new one, the first thing you should do when it arrives on site is leave it alone for two or three days. Just stand it roughly in the position where it is due to be hung, so that it gets acclimatised.

If you are planning to hang the door yourself rather than employ a carpenter, cut off the horns level and plane the edges trim carefully. Use a long plane rather than a short one, and check frequently that you are keeping the door edges square. It is sometimes necessary for the leading edge of the door to need bevelling before it will close smoothly. Do not plane off more than 6 mm from the top and sides and 10 mm from the bottom rail, and remember that any door should be reduced in size equally from both sides, rather than taking it all off one side.

The door should be varnished or painted soon after it has been installed, to prevent it from absorbing moisture and swelling. Some woodstains carry a guarantee against peeling and cracking for several years after treatment, so invest in a good-quality finish to upgrade your timber door.

Security is as old as time. *'Cavendi nulla est dimittenda occasio*, wrote Publilius Syrus in around 43BC – 'No opportunity for security should be let slip'. Although history is unclear as to whether this maxim was intended for door locks, it makes a good one for them.

Security-wise, patio doors and French windows tend to fare worst – some can be easily lifted off their runners, and most need extra locks. Glazing should always be done internally. There is little point in fitting locks to a window or door if all the intruder has to do to get in is prise off the glazing beads and remove the glass.

The easiest door locks to use tend to be mortise types with a lever handle on the inside, linking a deadbolt and a latchbolt without you needing a key; from the outside, a key operates the deadbolt and the latchbolt with the handle operation. The Building Research Establishment has tested various locking mechanisms, and this type was found to be the easiest for people, especially the elderly, to use. Over 93% of the pensioner test group could open the doors with these locks in under 2 seconds, making them a safe option as well as a secure one. For best security, a minimum five-lever mechanism deadlock is ideal for external doors.

The problem with fitting mortise locks on their own is if you forget to lock them on your way out. Adding an automatic deadlocking cylinder rim lock overcomes this problem, although these tend not to be the most architecturally attractive items of ironmongery.

Sliding patio doors need to be fitted with special locks at the top and bottom to prevent the doors from being lifted off the runners.

All external doors should be fitted

with a pair of hinge bolts below the top and above the bottom hinges. These will spread the load on the hinge side of the door, thus resisting forced entry. Most PVC-U external doors now come with a five-point espagnolette locking system with a deadbolt as standard, which is fine.

According to police statistics, 64% of all burglaries are through the rear of the house, but still 28% are through the front. Most of those are through insecure doors and windows, so, having fitted the locks, remember to use them. Check your insurance policy to see if British Standard locks are required. Using locks that don't comply to BS3621 might leave you more vulnerable than you think.

Cat flaps

Be extra careful about your choice of locks if you intend to install a cat flap in the door. Those door locks that need a key to open them from the inside are likely to be best in this situation, provided that you remember to remove the key from the lock when you lock up. You should also ensure that the cat flap is installed as low as possible in the door (with extra deadbolts fitted high up), to prevent a long arm from reaching through and manipulating them (the locks, that is, not the cat).

Fire spread and unprotected areas

An unprotected area (UPA) is any part of the building that does not have the fire resistance of other parts, such as external walls. Since the Great Fire of London in 1666, building regulations have sought to control fire spread between buildings.

Conventional windows and doors are unprotected and afford little fire resistance. If they are located on a wall within 6 m of the boundary, there will be restrictions on their total size. These areas are accumulative, and you may need to take account of the windows and doors already in existence on the house wall that is to be extended.

External fire doors can be obtained, but the vast majority are for internal use only. Windows can be glazed with fire-resisting glass, but at great cost, and since fireproof glass comes in a wide variety of standards of fire resistance, it is essential that you agree with your Building Control Surveyor beforehand on the exact product you intend to use. Bear in mind also that the frame itself is part of the window, and the glass requires special fixings if the fireproof glazing is to stay there during a fire.

Timber cladding of elevations constitutes half an unprotected area if the wall behind it is fire-resisting (e.g. brickwork or blockwork). This means that you are allowed twice the area in boarding that you would be allowed in the case of windows or doors, but

THE TABLE BELOW SHOWS MAXIMUM PERMITTED UNPROTECTED AREAS (UPA) FOR HOMES UP TO 24 M LONG:

Distance to boundary	UPA max
Less than 1 m	1 m²
1 m	5.6 m²
2 m	12 m²
3 m	18 m²
4 m	24 m²
5 m	30 m²
6 m	no limit

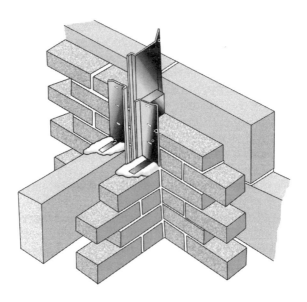

Vertical damp-proof course shown fitted between two profiles.

remember that it must all be totalled up to come within the allowable limit of so many square metres in area.

If the boundary to your property is positioned somewhere that cannot be built on in the future, a public highway or river for example, the boundary can be notionally taken as the centre line of the road or river.

Tying-in and abutments

In spite of all your best efforts in using compatible designs and materials, you may still have to accept the fact that your extension is a new addition to the structure of your house and may settle at a different rate to it. Perhaps you were required to have foundations much deeper than the original ones, to comply with the current Building Regulations – if this is the case, it is reasonable to

assume that some movement will occur at the joint between the new and the old walls.

Brickwork profiles can be used as an alternative to bonding in the brickwork. They accommodate up to about 10 mm of movement. Essentially they comprise steel plates that are expansion-bolted to the existing wall, one for each leaf of the cavity wall, with ties that are built into the new mortar joints.

If you are securing these plates to a cavity wall, the cavity should be cut into between the profiles, using a skill saw, and a vertical DPC should be fed into the slot to prevent rain from bridging across from the outer leaf of brickwork. The edge of the DPC should be returned behind the outer leaf profile which, when tightened up, should help to keep it in position. Equally, the cavity should be cut open to maintain it, but this may weaken the bolt fixing of the profiles and hence the DPC.

The downside of these profiles is that the end result has the appearance of a straight vertical joint in the wall; this may not look so bad when walls abut at right angles, but it can look pretty dreadful when you're extending a wall line straight out. In these situations, I would tooth-in the brickwork or try to locate a rainwater downpipe over the joint to conceal it.

Before deciding on profiles or toothing-in, you ought to check that the bricks you intend to use are available in the same size as the existing bricks.

Bricks

The quality of facing brickwork will influence the appearance of your extension more than anything else. You can start off on the right track by choosing the right brick. Brick choice in the UK has never been greater, partly because we are importing more continental bricks these days, but also because we are producing our own in even greater variety than previously.

There are a number of brick-supply specialists who have libraries that their customers can visit to match their bricks. If you can't find one near you, a sales rep may be willing to visit your house and match one for you; alternatively, you are going to need to collect some catalogues. The only problem with the latter is that brick colours are often subtle and photographs in catalogues do not always reproduce them reliably.

Bricks in extreme exposure zones should be frost-resistant (FR) and contain a low-soluble salt content. In addition to this, sulphate-resistant cement should be used in the mortar.

Choosing a bricklayer

In the housing boom of the 1980s, when it wasn't possible to build new homes fast enough – but everyone tried – bricklayers were highly sought after, and some developed enormous egos to prove it. Competitions were held to see who could lay the most bricks in an hour, and many of them carried this statistic around with them like a golfer's handicap. Nobody seemed to worry too much if the walls weren't quite straight or the corners weren't quite square – it was enough that they were being asked to put mortar between the courses.

And so bricklayers became simply that, layers of bricks, and this explains the point, which is that some brickies are not prepared to mess around with all the sundry items of brickwork, like cutting open existing cavities, bedding wall plates, fixing restraint straps, etc. This, they feel, is always somebody else's job, and if you are employing individual tradesmen to build your extension, you need to watch out for this type. On an extension there are a lot of sundry items, and a brickie who isn't prepared to see to them will prove to be an inconvenience, if not a liability. Make sure that brickies appreciate all that is expected of them when they take the job on. In the late 1990s this hasn't been so much of a problem, and few tradesmen now expect to be waited on hand and foot on small domestic jobs.

Brickwork

As mentioned earlier, apart from matching the colour, the sizing of many bricks has changed in the last 15 years, from imperial to metric. This might not seem like a big problem to the home-owner, but it is to the bricklayer if he is to line in with the existing courses. Brickwork with irregular mortar joints is unattractive, if nothing else.

Uniformity of brick size tends to be a bit of a bugbear with bricklayers; it is not so much a problem with wire-cut and mass-produced bricks, but hand-made ones can be irregular to the extreme. An experienced bricklayer will be able to discard unsuitable bricks and work within certain tolerances with others. Not so many bricks are produced with frogs these days, but where they are, the norm in cavity walls is to lay them with the 'frogged face' upwards but in solid brick walls, laying them with the 'frogged face' down is traditionally thought to improve the bond.

A variety of mortar joints can be finished by pointing, and at the end of each day's bricklaying the brickwork should be cleaned off and joints pointed up before the mortar hardens. Special pointing tools are available if you want to do this job yourself, but a rounded smooth piece of wood or metal can achieve the same effect. Like grouting between tiles, it is time-consuming but possibly therapeutic.

Bricklaying ought to be suspended in extremely cold weather (below 2 °C) and protected overnight against frost. If you must continue work, anti-freezing agents can be added to the mortar. Plasticising additives are often favoured by bricklayers in any case, since they keep the mortar smooth and workable.

The mix of cement and sand for mortar is influenced by the strength of the brick. An average mix would be 1 part of cement to 6 parts of sand plus whatever proportion of plasticiser is recommended by the manufacturer. In historic buildings, the need to match in with a lime mortar may necessitate a 1:1:6 mix (cement:lime:sand), which is as near as possible to Roman cement.

If you are mixing your own, remember that cement mortar shouldn't be re-wetted after mixing, and it will need discarding after 2 hours, so don't mix up too much in one go.

Bricklaying sand must be kept clean, and to this end it is now available from merchants in large reusable bags of 1 tonne weight. If you must buy it loose, keep the pile well covered with sheeting or every cat in the neighbourhood will think it's a public toilet.

Colouring agents can be added to the mortar, for example to achieve a strong contrast with the brick colour. Black mortar joints look particularly striking against red bricks.

Stability

External walls are not only subject to vertical loads from the floors and roof; they must also resist wind loads side-on. This means that, like a beam, they have a given maximum span in relation to their thickness. The span for any wall is the distance between the opposing load-bearing walls or other points of buttressing support. An approximate rule of thumb for this maximum span is 50 times the effective thickness of the wall. In the case of a cavity wall, the effective thickness is found by adding together the thickness of both individual leaves and then multiplying the sum by 2/3, e.g.:

$$0.112 \text{ m} + 0.100 \text{ m} = (0.212 \times 2/3) = 0.14133 \times 50 = 7.067 \text{ m}$$

In a small extension the external walls may be the only buttressing walls you have, and so it is important that their strength isn't compromised by window and door openings near to the corners. At least 550 mm of wall should be maintained from the corner to the opening. If this proves unacceptable to your design, you may have to consider

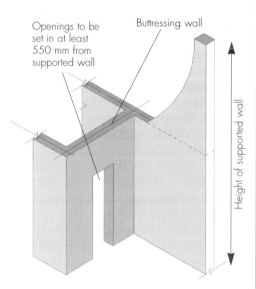

Openings to be set in at least 550 mm from supported wall

Buttressing wall

Height of supported wall

The length of the buttressing wall should be at least ⅙ of the overall height of the supported wall.

building in a metal wind post to the cavity wall closure, to provide the buttress effect.

When your ground-floor level is much higher than the outside ground level, a retaining wall situation exists. As a rule of thumb, the height difference between the two should not be more than four times the thickness of the wall. If it is, the combined dead and live loads may push on the wall, and in these situations it should be designed to resist this.

The UK has a wide variety of weather conditions. In the far north of Scotland, wind, rain and sub-zero temperatures are more common than in the south-east of England, and these factors combine to determine the design of many elements of a building.

The first thing that has to be said about weather is that it isn't predictable and never does as it should. The British Standard for wind loading gives the north-western coast of Scotland as a much higher wind speed than the south-east of England, and yet who was it that got the hurricane in 1987? In their defence the British Standards Institute would say, ah well, this is average wind speed we're talking about, not once every 200 years. In any case, the figure for the Western Isles is about 16 metres per second (35 mph) faster than it is for London, and the highest wind speeds have been recorded in the Shetlands at around 177 mph.

The UK also has an index of exposure to driving rain (the sort that comes in sideways) based upon the location. Again, the western half of Scotland fares worst, although there are little pockets of severe exposure in many areas, particularly those within 8 km of the sea and estuaries. The index is a combination of the wind speed and the annual rainfall in the area. Added onto this are areas where frost has occurred on more than 100 days a year. (In addition to being a valuable asset to designing your extension, the exposure index atlas is a useful thing to have when planning your holidays.)

Wall ties

The installation of materials and fixing components in brickwork calls for a high standard of workmanship. Nowadays most of these fixings are galvanised or stainless steel, to prevent them from corroding. Alas, there are some insulation materials (urea formaldehyde, for example) and mortar additives that have recently been discovered to react with the galvanised parts of wall ties, reducing their life expectancy dramatically. When wall ties fail, they do so quietly and without drawing attention to themselves – until, that is, the wind sucks out the outer leaf and deposits it on the ground quite suddenly. At this stage people will fall over themselves and the rubble at their feet to tell you that you had wall-tie failure. Stainless-steel wall ties and fixings should be utilised wherever possible, to reduce the risk of corrosion.

Wall ties act to join together the two leaves of a cavity wall, sharing lateral loads from the outer to the inner. Stainless steel ties that last much longer are required and accommodate the standard 100 mm wide cavity. Butterfly-wire wall ties are rarely suitable now, especially in exposed areas where they don't offer the

strength of other types, like the flat-twisted and double-triangle ones, and consequently shouldn't be used in these areas. Neither are they suitable where the cavity exceeds 75 mm width, regardless of the location. The ends should be fully bedded in the joints, not simply touching them.

Wall ties are made to suit a given cavity width, so if you do make any last-minute changes to the width of cavity in your walls, you may well have to change the wall-tie specification to suit.

Cavity-wall insulation and exposure

As a student in 1987, I based my professional thesis on the problems with cavity-wall insulation, and I still see the same problems today. The main problem is one of rain penetration. When the first total-fill insulation products were introduced to this country, approval in the form of a BBA certificate was sought from the British Board of Agrément to endorse them. Part of the testing procedures related to their resistance to water penetration, because it is a an established fact that driving rain can get through the outer brick leaf, and it is therefore critical that it doesn not get through the next layer, the insulation.

The manufacturers claimed that the orientation of the fibres in these mineral-fibre insulants encouraged the rain to run off, and they demonstrated this fact at many a trade fair by floating bits of the insulant in trays of water. Look, they said, it floats, we could let this stay in there all day and still it wouldn't soak up the water. The tests proved satisfactory, the

Installing blown cavity-wall insulation into traditional brick/block cavity wall.

certificates were issued, and all over the country mineral-fibre and glassfibre insulation was built in or pumped into the cavity walls of our homes.

Alas, some of those walls were more exposed to driving rain than others (and yet the certificates claimed that they were suitable for severe exposure as well), and it wasn't long before I and many other Building Control Officers around the country were pulling wringing-wet handfuls of the insulant out of cavity walls. As usual in the aftermath of disaster, the accusations swung wildly about – the insulation people blamed the bricklayers, the bricklayers blamed the insulation, the owners blamed the builders, the build-ers blamed the architects, and so on.

The end result was that the walls had to be cut open (the houses were occupied by then), and the affected insulation was removed and left out for

several months until the walls were dry. The brickwork had to be treated with a silicone coating to increase its rain resistance, and the cavities were reinsulated much later, to the owners' understandable annoyance.

As a result of instances like this, some new home warranty insurers insisted that total-fill insulation be avoided altogether. Exposure to the elements is a very localised thing, which can vary from one house to the next. Trees, hedges and neighbouring buildings can all contribute to providing shelter for a house, giving each its own micro-climate, and from a national insurer's point of view, a blanket restriction must have seemed to be the easiest way of tackling the problem.

Time moved on, and it became known that home-owners in general had little faith (not surprisingly) in the insulation installers' own guarantees. So in April 1995 the industry launched a rescue bid on its reputation and set up the Cavity Insulation Guarantee Agency (CIGA) as an independent guarantor who, for a very small premium, will certify the work and materials of 'approved installers' injecting cavity insulation into walls.

If you have total-fill insulation in your extension walls, it would be worth your while to explore the possibility of having it injected in before plastering by an 'approved installer' and taking out a CIGA 25-year warranty. Although at present you may have to do the whole house to qualify for the insurance, I understand that pressure is upon them to expand the scheme into new building work. The ever-increasing standards of thermal insulation make it difficult to avoid, and if you must use total-fill insulation in an exposed area, I would strongly advise you to finish the outer walls with rendering, weatherboarding or vertical tiling (see Chapter 7). If you are unable to do this, given a 100 mm cavity, you could use a 50 mm partial-fill high-performance insulation board, such as polyurethane foam, which, being thinner, will allow you to retain a clear 50 mm cavity for rain resistance.

Lateral-restraint straps

External walls of any length need supporting at roof level, and those that are more than 3 m long need extra support at floor and ceiling levels as well. This support comes from tying in the wall to these other elements of structure, and the contemporary technique for doing this is lateral-restraint strapping.

When they were first introduced, these galvanised metal straps invoked some natural speculation: at 30 mm wide and 5 mm thick they didn't look substantial enough to hold a wall in place, but they proved their worth in October 1987. With gable-end walls shifting all over the south of England under the force of the hurricane, it was those with properly fitted straps that stood firm.

These straps will only act to transfer lateral forces (wind load) effectively if they are suitably positioned and well fixed to both elements of structure. The rules for ensuring that they work are as follows:

● Straps should be positioned at maximum 2 m spacings. Set the first one so that it is positioned at least half a brick in (100 mm) from the end bearing of the first timber.

● The turned-down end of the strap should be built into the masonry wall, not screw-fixed to it later. With the strap bedded in this fashion, it isn't necessary to provide any other fixing to the wall.

● The length of the strap should be sufficient to cross at least three joists or rafters. Straps should be fixed to each joist with No. 10 woodscrews 50 mm long or by twisted-drive nails 65 mm long. Care should be taken to nail more than once to each of the three timbers.

● Sometimes forgotten, but essential to the arrangement, are the timber noggins which must be fixed between the joists or rafters underneath the straps. So long as they are at least half the depth of the joist or rafter, and no less than 38 mm thick, they will be fine. In reality, it is often easier to use the natural offcuts from the timbers themselves to do this job. Remember to start the noggins by packing out off the wall with the first one.

Provided that the above points are followed, straps can be positioned above or below joists or rafters. It is acceptable to rebate them in so that finishings can cover them flush.

Occasionally, an opening in the floor or roof, such as that for a stairwell, may mean that straps can't go in at the 2 m interval. In these cases it is usually acceptable for one strap to be located at

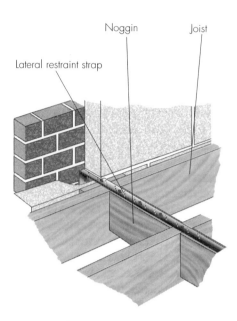

Lateral restraint strap

Noggin   Joist

When fitting a lateral-restraint strap, remember that it will only be fully effective if it is fixed into the masonry wall, not screwed to it as an afterthought.

each edge of the opening to compensate, provided that the opening is no more than 3 m long.

Where the joists do not run parallel with the wall but are at right angles to it, an option to the strap becomes available in the form of the restraint-type joist hanger. Using this type of hanger to support the joists with their hook-over tongues is an acceptable alternative to the twisted-type lateral-restraint straps otherwise needed.

If you are employing concrete suspended floor slabs instead of timber, straps may not be needed at all, so long as you have the floor structure adequately bearing on the walls (normally this would be the case with

the inner leaf of the cavity wall totally supporting the concrete slab). Precast concrete beam and block-infill floors should be treated as timber floors, with straps built in under the floor finish.

Internal walls of any length need supporting at the top of each storey.

Internal walls

Non-load-bearing walls or partitions can be built from timber studwork, metal studwork or masonry. They are usually 100 mm thick, although metal-stud partitions may be thinner.

On the ground floor, blockwork partitions are usually the cheapest to build and offer some sound insulation between rooms. At first-floor level, it isn't advisable to build blockwork off the timber joists, even if they are doubled-up and strong enough to take the weight. The timber shrinkage and deflection may result in cracking to the wall above or, worse, dislodging it. Some insurance companies offering warranties will not accept this arrangement, requiring timber studwork which can be nailed to floor joists via the soleplate at the base and nailed to ceiling joists via the headplate at the top. The partition is less than half the weight of blockwork and can be insulated to some degree for sound insulation.

Party walls

Sometimes known as separating walls, these are the walls which separate individual dwellings.

If you and your neighbour are extending homes together, the wall you build between you will be a party wall, and as such it requires two special properties. The first is an hour's fire resistance – not a problem with masonry – and the second is sound insulation, always a problem afterwards. Good sound insulation between homes is hard to come by. It doesn't help when you consider that newly built properties that have met the minimum standards of the regulations, all too often become the battlefield for noise complaints and neighbour wars. The regulations don't seem to impose a high enough standard for much of the public's liking.

Perhaps in building your joint extension you would like to exceed the minimum standards, to the benefit of both you and your neighbour. Noise is a form of pollution, one which generates a lot of complaints. It is defined as unwanted sound, and sound comes in two ways, either airborne or impact. Airborne examples are speech, screaming and hi-fi speakers. Impact examples are footsteps, children running and pianos being moved (although I accept that the latter could conceivably fall into both categories!).

Airborne sound creates vibrations in the air which spread out like ripples on a pond and set up vibrations in walls and things. The most effective way to insulate against airborne sound is to put something in the way of it – the heavier the better. A wall built of dense concrete blocks is better than a wall built of common bricks, and a wall built of common bricks is better than a wall built of straw.... This density insulation is a result of something else you may have heard of known as the 'mass law'. Doubling the mass of a wall will reduce the sound transmission through it by one quarter.

Impact sound, on the other hand, relies more on physical separation, creating a space – a continuity gap in construction, but since it only applies to floors the best way to achieve impact sound insulation is to provide a 'floating floor' which insulates the floor decking from the joists. A decent carpet on a thick underlay will do the same job.

A wall that combines density of materials with air separation is probably the best solution. Start with two individual leaves of dense concrete blockwork built as a cavity wall. Provided that the cavity is kept clear, and you don't stuff insulation into it, the cavity will act as a barrier that prevents airborne sound from tracking across. You will also need to make sure that your floor joists run parallel with the wall, instead of being sat on it, which will cause impact sound to vibrate through. Dry-lining both sides with plasterboard stuck on dabs will also help, but if you really don't want to hear from your neighbours ever again, adding a layer of dense mineral-fibre sound insulation suspended behind the plasterboarding will do the job.

The edges of the dry-lining need to be sealed with acoustic sealant to block air paths, and you need to consider where your windows are going to go in the adjoining outside wall. It may seem odd, but the nearer they are to the party wall the better – the reason for this is because the shorter the length of wall between them, the less chance there is of it vibrating with low-frequency sound, an effect known as flanking transmission. The new wall may need to be tested by a registered acoustic engineer to prove that it meets the airborne sound insulation requirement. They test using specialist equipment just before completion and a certificate of compliance issued. Check with your building control officer if it is required as it is not always possible to do it without testing the existing party wall.

Conservatories and sun lounges

It may not surprise you to know that the government, in making legislation for conservatories, has always had a totally different definition of what they are to the rest of the country. In 1985 conservatories were exempted from the Building Regulations, and to date they remain exempt, provided that they meet certain criteria about which you agree with your local Building Control Officer.

The *Oxford English Dictionary* (1993) defines a conservatory as 'a greenhouse for raising tender plants,' and in particular 'one attached to and communicating with a house' – and this seems to have been the Department of the Environment's view when they exempted them from the regulations. However, you may have noticed that they aren't being sold with this definition in mind; on the contrary, many are being flamboyantly marketed as a cheap way to extend the living area of your home, with glossy adverts showing them luxuriously fitted and furnished, perhaps – but only perhaps – with a potted plant in the corner. Some middle ground must be found.

It would go against all the current energy-conservation measures in place today if we opened up all conservatory

extensions to the house, making them open-plan additions to a room and thus needing to be heated all year round. With a glass or plastic roof and a myriad of windows, your fuel bill would in any case be expensive. So it makes sense to separate them from the rest of the house with a draught-sealed door, and also to isolate any radiators in there by fitting them with thermostatic radiator valves. These can be set to a frost setting in the winter, just enough to keep any plants from harm. The pipes to the radiators should be insulated, and are best run in access ducts through the floor.

Double-glazed or triple-walled polycarbonate roof sheets give some insulation, but they still let out 16 times more heat per square metre than a normal roof. Having said that, they can also absorb heat from the sun, and in the spring and autumn they provide a useful source of warmth that can be allowed and helped to circulate around the rest of the home.

From a structural point of view, conservatories are lightweight and need holding down (as opposed to holding up) to resist wind uplift or clay heave (soil uplift). Most domestic conservatories are quite compact, with end panels providing their wind-resistant buttressing, but, like walls, if they become too lengthy they are going to need stiffening in the middle with a wind post, frame or even a brick pier. Suppliers of PVC-U conservatories should be aware of the size limitations of their standard design, but with the industry being an extension of the replacement windows one, it is always worth checking.

The effect of wind uplift can be made worse when some of the windows or doors are open, with the wind pressure pushing up the roof from the inside as well. This pressure can be relieved by introducing roof vents. A ventilated ridge can be designed-in to achieve this, and it will also help to relieve some of the tremendous heat that can build up on summer days. A south-facing conservatory is often a bad idea: temperatures can become phenomenally high inside, causing the plastic roof sheets to warp out of shape and the furnishings to cook. Roof blinds are essential in this situation.

Once conservatories exceed 30 sq m floor area they require a Building Regulations application. They may also need one if you intend to open-plan it with the house or if it is built above ground level – for example, on top of a single-storey extension.

All critical-location glazing (low-level windows and doors) should be safety-glazed, preferably with toughened glass (see 'Windows and Doors'). If you are fabricating your own using standard windows, aim for cill heights of at least 800 mm above the floor finish.

Most conservatories are formed on a concrete slab base of no particular strength, and this is fine so long as the subsoil is not subject to movement through the seasons. Unfortunately, much of it may be, clay in particular, and a lightweight structure like this could offer little resistance to clay heave. Clay

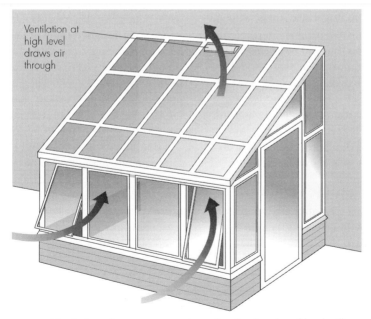

Ventilation at high level draws air through

Ventilation of your conservatory at low-level and roof-level will not only reduce heat in summer but also force wind uplift.

tends to heave when it becomes waterlogged in winter or after trees have been removed, and it may therefore be necessary to form a more structural foundation that will take account of this movement. You may in any case be solely responsible for the base. Castellated anti-heave boards can be used around foundations to combat heave – if left to the salesperson or his or her surveyor, this matter may well go overlooked.

Sun lounges are usually regarded as conservatories with solid roofing instead of clear or translucent roofing. The preformed ones have a solid PVC-UE roof, which is moderately insulated but still a long way short of current standards for roof insulation. What separates a sun lounge from a normal extension is glazing, with windows around the length of all the walls. They may still be exempt from Building Regulations if separated as conservatories, but you must check with your local authority Building Control Office before making plans.

Above all else, it should be remembered that conservatories and sun lounges are for seasonal use only, and do not carry the design requirements of an extension for year-round habitable use.

Integral garage structure

Garages being what they are, people often choose to construct them to a lesser standard than the rest of the home, which for the most part is fine, but there are limits as to how far you can go when the garage is attached to the house.

Half-brick walls are fine when there is nothing but roof structure to support,

but even then they need buttressing piers to stiffen them up against the wind. These piers should be spaced at maximum 3 m centres starting from the corners and are normally one-brick size. Unfortunately garage doors, given their size and nature, need thicker walls on either side of the opening; usually 215 mm brickwork is used on the door wall to strengthen it.

Apart from wind, one other lateral load is applicable to garages, vehicle impact. One and a half tonnes of car arriving at just above a foot off the ground into a pier can do a lot of damage. It only becomes a problem when the design of the garage makes this accident more likely or more devastating. For example, locating a slender brick pier that holds up the floor above and between two garage doors will create a risk. The pier should be structurally designed to resist impact or be protected. Sadly, the only advice the design engineer will find is currently in British Standard BS6399, which is based upon public car park design, allowing for a car velocity of around 22 metres per second (61 km/h or 38 mph).

I don't know about you, but I am fortunate enough not to know anybody who drives into their own garage or drive at that speed. You may wish to invite your engineer to agree a more reasonable impact speed with the Building Control authority.

Scaffolding

Without a doubt scaffolding is not something for the DIY enthusiast, although this doesn't stop some from trying. If the requirements of all the health and safety legislation around today relate to nothing else, they relate to scaffolding. The erection of a temporary working platform, which may at times support a considerable weight, is something that requires a specialist who is qualified and licensed. Even so, it is advisable to quote that you want scaffolding erected in accordance with BS5973. This may turn out to be your defence if an accident occurs and a tradesman employed by you is injured due to the scaffolding's collapse.

You should request a handover certificate once the scaffolding is up. This is a guarantee that it has been erected properly and is now your responsibility. Because it may become damaged during the building work, it should be checked at least once every seven days. Look to make sure that handrails and kick boards are all in place, that poles and baseplates haven't sunk into soft ground, that ladders are still tied in position, and that scaffold boards are in position.

Over half of all accidents on building sites are falls; consequently, any scaffold or trestle over 2 m high should be protected by edge guarding. If people are likely to be passing underneath the scaffolding, metal grids can be installed to protect them from damage by falling bricks and debris.

Professional scaffolders have one drawback: they have a tendency to arrive on site with all the grace and timidity of a herd of stampeding elephants, and you would be well advised not to book them in on a Sunday morning and to keep anything remotely valuable – garden gnomes, potted plants, cats, etc. –

indoors when they are expected. If there will be other tradesmen on site at the time, their arrival should be forewarned in the same way that hurricanes are (in some countries).

To scaffolders, taking down their scaffolding is unprofitable – the only benefit being that they can move it elsewhere to put it up again – and consequently some may send only one person along to dismantle and drop it. Make sure you ask for at least two people to take it down so that the job can be done carefully without the need to drop poles to the ground. Remember that as a home-owner you have a responsibility for ensuring the health and safety of people lawfully visiting your home.

Make sure that the people using your scaffold tie the top of the ladders to it and do not remove any protection, such as handrails, without replacing it. It is often necessary to temporarily remove protection to get large materials up, like trusses.

Should you need it, the trade body for scaffolders in the UK is the Scaffold Contractors Federation.

Roof structure

The first roofs to be constructed in Britain were put up by a bunch of local builders called the Saxons. They were quite good with timber and built their huts by pitching rafters together, wigwam-style, on the ground. They did, however, notice a problem with this method – headroom. It was OK directly under the apex, but at the edges of the hut, with the eaves at ground level, something had to be done. They could of course have chosen to build walls and sit the roof on top of them, but obviously they anticipated the problems with timber-frame construction long before Barratt Homes did, because they chose to dig out the floor instead. Even so, the basic form of roof construction didn't change much until the advent of the roof truss.

Trussed-rafter roofs

Roof trusses have been with us since the 1960s, and yet many people still remain sceptical of their strength. The timber sections used are remarkably slim compared to those required in a cut-and-pitch roof, and the punched metal nail plates which hold them together seem even more fragile. Trusses have the disadvantage of creating a largely inaccessible roof space due to the web of diagonal members involved.

The stability of the trussed-rafter roof relies upon other elements than just the individual trusses themselves. To form a roof that is stable under wind-loading, the trusses must be braced with extra timbers running across them longitudinally and diagonally. Even the tiling battens across trusses help to brace them against the wind. If wind bracing is omitted or improperly installed, the stability of the roof will be compromised. Your trussed-rafter manufacturers will be able to provide you with information regarding the position of wind braces in addition to supplying the structural design calculations for the trusses themselves, but they are unlikely to do either until a firm order has been placed.

Before trusses can be ordered the

manufacturer needs some information from you, and it is worth checking this information twice before sending it. The consequences of making a mistake here could prove to be expensive.

The key to the strength of roof trusses is in the connector plates, and the fact that these plates are individually available throws up the risk of somebody knocking up their own trusses at the bottom of the garden. This is not a good idea: trusses are computer-designed, and are manufactured in a controlled environment.

I am not suggesting that all trusses cannot be made up on site; some can, but the system is a different one and utilises much larger timber sections with some heavy bolting of connections. The end result may look like a truss in shape, but it feels and weighs like a cut-and-pitch roof.

TRADA (the Timber Research and Development Association) produces standard details for the site fabrication of these trusses, given a certain span and pitch. They are designed to go in at much larger spacings than conventional trusses, with cut-and-pitch construction in-fixing between them.

The only benefits I can think of for constructing a roof in this way are that you are a carpenter with plenty of time on your hands, and labour charges don't apply; or your roof span is so great as to make a cut-and-pitch roof impractical, and you are loathe to use manufactured roof trusses because they appear so flimsy.

Because of their nature, trusses require careful handling. When storing manufactured trusses on site, they should be stacked clear off the ground on bearers and sheltered from the effects of sun and rain.

Give some thought to how these trusses are going to be lifted into position. If they are not too large, at least three men will be able to manhandle them, but larger trusses will need mechanical handling. To give you some idea of weights, a single fink truss of 30° pitch with a span of 7.7 m will weigh 35 kg. An attic truss for providing an accessible space in the roof of the same span will weigh 110 kg. There may be less members in the latter, but the

design demands much larger sections of timber, particularly in the ceiling ties, thus making it much heavier.

Truss clips are metal plates used to secure trusses to wall plates, because the truss timbers are easily damaged by skew-nailing. Square-twisted sheradised nails are used in the holes provided in these clips. Their improved withdrawal strength makes them the ideal tool for this application.

There are drawbacks with manufactured trusses which increase with the level of complexity in the roof design. Invariably, truss manufacturers

10 Expert Points

HERE ARE TEN EXPERT POINTS THAT SHOULD ALWAYS BE INCLUDED WITH YOUR TRUSS ORDER:

1 SPAN
The span measured over wall plates – not the clear span between walls but that which includes the wall-plate bearings.

2 PITCH
If you are aligning with an existing roof, it may be easier to calculate the pitch by measuring the height of the roof from within your loft space. Specialised spirit levels, which can be placed along the rafter to measure the angle, are also available, and make this job a relatively easy one.

3 OVERHANGS
Make sure that you include in your order the type and size of any overhangs that will be required.

4 ROOF TILES, ETC.
The type or weights of all roof coverings must be considered.

5 WATER TANKS
The size and desired position of any water tanks to be housed in the roof.

6 WIND-LOAD INFORMATION
The height and location of the building.

7 BEARINGS
The details and positions of the supports for the roof (although the suppliers may not design these supports).

8 TRIMMINGS AROUND OPENINGS
The positions and sizes of any openings for chimneys, loft hatches, skylights or dormer windows, etc.

9 ACCESSORIES
You will have to confirm if you will need their straps and clips, or gable ladders and wind-bracing timber, or whether you will be supplying your own.

10 PRESERVATIVE
You will need to request whether or not you wish the timber to be pressure-treated with preservative.

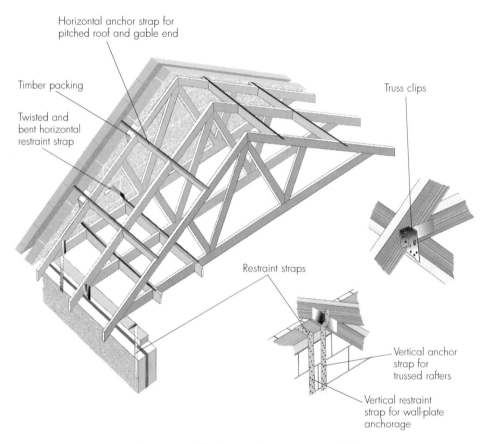

Horizontal anchor strap for pitched roof and gable end

Timber packing

Twisted and bent horizontal restraint strap

Truss clips

Restraint straps

Vertical anchor strap for trussed rafters

Vertical restraint strap for wall-plate anchorage

Truss clips are used for fixing timber trusses to wallplates.
They avoid the damage that can be caused by skew nailing.

will mark up the plans with areas of hatched-out construction labelled 'Support by GC' or some such cryptic message, meaning 'This is a fiddly bit that requires a carpenter with a bundle of wood to sort out, rather than us'. If you're not careful, a complex roof can end up with as much 'Support by GC' as trusses, making the truss option an uneconomical one. Check before you order just how much of the roof

structure they are actually providing.

Where the extension's trussed roof joins with the existing roof side-on to form a T-shape intersection, timber layboards are nailed up the existing rafters to support diminishing valley trusses. Where the existing roof is not formed of manufactured trusses and the extension's roof is fairly small, it might prove more economical to use loose (infill) timbers to cut and pitch the intersection, instead of reducing trusses.

Vertical-restraint straps and other fixings

Vertical-restraint straps for anchoring down the wall plate are half the thickness of lateral-restraint straps, but are formed of the same 30 x 5 mm-section galvanised steel. Their task is to secure the roof against the effects of wind uplift, although in the case of heavy roof coverings, such as dense concrete tiles, the self weight alone will do this without the straps.

Too many builders seem to regard restraint straps as decoration only, and leave them poorly fixed or not fixed at all. In the case of lateral-restraint straps, they need to be built into the cavity wall's inner skin at rafter, ceiling and first-floor level, and are thus the responsibility of the bricklayer and are covered in the 'Walls' section of this chapter. With them in position, the carpenter can then screw them to the timbers and provide the noggins

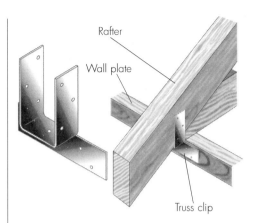

Use truss clips to secure trussed rafters to wall plates.

beneath, but vertical straps should be plugged and screwed to the wall. Fixing these metal straps onto soft blockwork walls can be a problem, as ordinary nailing will simply pull out – square-twisted 'drive' nails may bite in a lot better, but it may even prove necessary to employ some special fixings. All vertical-restraint straps should be spaced

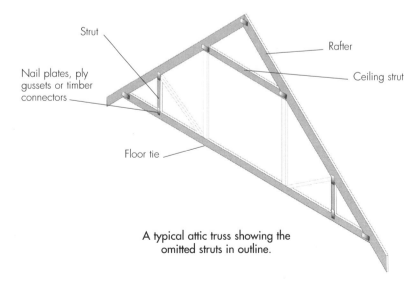

A typical attic truss showing the omitted struts in outline.

at maximum 2 m centres.

Joist hangars, like straps, need to be built into the walls as they are constructed. It is not acceptable to rake out old mortar joints and feed in joist hangars later. Where joists do have to be supported from an existing wall, face-fix joist hangars are available, requiring expansion wall bolts to fix them. Alternatively, a timber wall plate can be bolted along the face of the wall at the appropriate level, with restraint-type joist hangars secured over the plate to take the joists. I would recommend the latter as the most acceptable method, but care should be taken to use enough expansion bolts on the plate for the load proposed. Placing M10 bolts at maximum 300 mm centres along the plate will cater for most situations.

Straddle hangars are available for supporting timber joists on either side of a beam or wall, to ensure a continuity of construction and levels.

Nails

Nails fall into three basic groups – wire nails, cut nails and improved nails. Improved nails have their own little section in the British Standard for the Structural Use of Timber. Examples are square-grooved and square-twisted

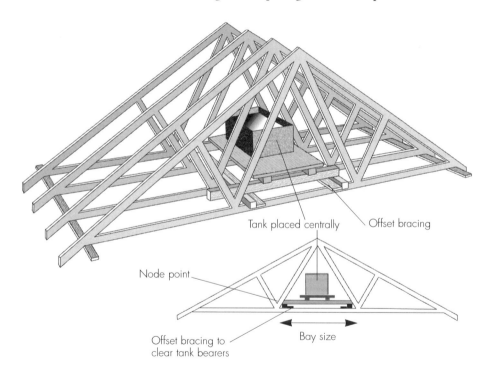

Water tanks should be placed centrally in roof spaces.

shank nails (commonly known as drive nails) and annular ring-shanked nails. These nails bite hard into wood and are harder to pull out. To be slightly more scientific about it, the grooved and twisted shank nails have a withdrawal load about one and a quarter times that of ordinary round wire nails, and the annular ring-shanked nails about one and a half times. Woodscrews, by the way, have a withdrawal load about four times greater. For this reason, improved nails are recommended for securing structural fixings, such as truss shoes, joist hangers and framing anchors.

A good indication of a builder's quality is to see what nails he has used on structural fixings. To a cowboy a nail is a nail, and since plasterboard nails are the cheapest, it isn't uncommon to see them being used for everything.

Water-tank supports

As you can appreciate, there is a considerable weight in cold-water tanks, and the arrangements that support them must therefore spread the load out across several ceiling joists. Trussed-rafter manufacturers can design-in tank loads for you and provide standardised information on where to position them and how to construct the stands.

In general, tanks are best placed centrally in a trussed roof. Timber bearers should be spread over at least three ceiling joists if the tank capacity does not exceed 230 l (50 gallons), or over at least four if it is up to 300 l (66 gallons). If chipboard is used for the deck, it should be flooring-grade and moisture-resistant, but exterior-grade plywood is the ideal material.

When you are thinking about where to locate a water tank, bear in mind two things: first, how accessible it will be for maintenance, and second, that a litre of water weighs a kilogram – thus a standard domestic tank weighs nearly a quarter of a tonne! Therefore, if there are any internal load-bearing walls available, use them.

Cut-and-pitch roofs

Using the table on page 107, it is possible to design a simple roof without the services of a structural engineer, but the more complicated the roof structure becomes, the greater becomes your need for a structural design. It is never a good idea to substitute a carpenter for a structural engineer.

Carpenters will almost always be prepared to design even the most complex of roofs, based on their experience, but will almost never have the expertise to provide the structural calculations to justify it. It is not considered sufficient that they built one 20 years ago in the same way, and it is still standing today; current structural standards have evolved considerably and continue to do so. For this same reason, it is essential not to assume that you can copy the existing house roof structure in the extension. Nine times out of ten it will be outdated and unacceptable.

There are still carpenters around who believe that everything can be formed out of 'four by two' (50 x 100 mm sections of timber) if you use enough of it. This is not the case, and hasn't been since the early 1960s – 50 x 100 mm joists will span less than 2 m, and rafters not much further. Propping up rafters with four-by-two struts onto the ceiling joists will only place point loads on those joists, making the situation worse. Unless you are forming a very small roof, give a wide berth to carpenters who speak of four by two!

Moisture content of timber

Timber is probably the only material which can actually alter the shape of a building after it is built. It can twist, creep, split and shake all over the place, without the slightest regard for design or appearance. This is almost always due to its moisture content. Timber that is 'green' becomes seasoned at a much accelerated rate in the centrally-heated environment of the house. For this reason, structural timber now has to be kiln-dried with a moisture content of less than 24% (see Chapter 4).

In 1985 my wife and I moved into our starter home on a new estate. Like most, it soon suffered a drying-out process so severe we could have used it as a clubhouse for Alcoholics Anonymous: the floor joists shrank back from the walls as if they had a bad case of halitosis, the staircase strings cracked and split, and a gap opened up between the kitchen wall and the ceiling so wide we could have used it as a serving hatch. In old cottages this is called character, but in new homes it is called shrinkage.

The only way to avoid this kind of drying out is to use kiln-dried timber. If this becomes a problem in historic buildings, where old oak beams are required and you can't bear the thought of them just being planted on superficially, then you must choose aged, dry, well-seasoned oak and not

something that has been recently dragged out of a farm pond.

Carpenters and joiners

There are carpenters and there are joiners. Some say the difference between the two is that carpenters work outdoors and joiners work indoors, and there is some credibility with this analysis, but it is of the elementary kind.

It could be more a matter of natural persuasion. In boom times, anyone who could saw a lump of wood in half and then nail it back together could call himself a carpenter – and many did, finding work on housing sites, not only putting trusses on houses but nailing the wind-bracing to them as well. In leaner times these chippies are less prolific, and only the better craftsmen, who can cut and pitch a roof with both skill and speed, are left trading. Having said that, the carpenter's work is structural and the best way to test the quality of it is to give it a good kick (I don't recommend this method on tank stands) to see if it moves. Opposing skew nailing and good jointing will hold firm.

Joiners tend to concern themselves more with the finished appearance of their work – staircases, mouldings and yes, even kitchen units – and many of them regard carpenters in much the same way as vegetarians regard butchers. Joiners like things to fit together neatly, working with much more care and at a slower, 'all the time in the world' speed. They certainly never appreciate people kicking their work.

Of course I am generalising here – it is possible to find the universal carpenter/joiner who can meet all your needs using only the one bag of tools. But if you want to be sure, the acid test is to get them to hang a door.

Hanging doors is the equivalent of palmistry in this business; it tells you everything you need to know. I am not suggesting that you hover over him or her while they do this. Let the job be done (keeping an eye on the time taken), and afterwards take a good look at the workmanship. Look at the hinges to see how snugly they fit into the chiselled-out recesses. Look at the gap around the door to see how well it sits in the frame, and so on. All of us use doors all the time, so trust me when I say you're going to know a well-hung one when you see it.

RAFTERS

Rafter size

(C16 or SC3 grade)	Max. span (measured along rafter between supports)			
Angle	Roof pitches from		Roof pitches from	
	22.5°–30°		31°–45°	
Spacings	400 mm	600 mm	400 mm	600 mm
50 x 100 mm	2.45 m	2.14 m	2.53 m	2.21 m
50 x 125 mm	3.05 m	2.67 m	3.15 m	2.76 m
50 x 150 mm	3.65 m	3.20 m	3.76 m	3.30 m

Ceiling joists

Size of joist (C16 OR SC3 grade)	Max. span (measured between supports)	
	at 400 mm spacings	at 600 mm spacings
50 x 100 mm	1.84 m	1.73 m
50 x 125 mm	2.47 m	2.31 m
50 x 150 mm	3.11 m	2.90 m
50 x 175 mm	3.72 m	3.44 m
50 x 200 mm	4.37 m	4.04 m

Flat-roof joists

(C16 or SC3 grade)	Max. spans (measured between supports)	
	at 400 mm spacings	at 600 mm spacings
50 x 125 mm	2.53 m	2.37 m
50 x 150 mm	3.19 m	2.97 m
50 x 175 mm	3.81 m	3.47 m
50 x 200 mm*	4.48 m	3.97 m
50 x 225 mm	5.09 m	4.47 m

* If you are using glassfibre insulation only between joists, you will need at least 50 x 200 mm joists to allow for 150 mm insulation plus a 50 mm air gap.

All the above maximum spans are given for standard C16 grade (SC3/GS) timber. These figures may be increased by 3–5 % when using C24 grade (SC4/SS) timber.

These figures are based upon the standard snow load of 0.75 kn/sq m, which basically equates to about two feet of snow laying on the roof. If you live in a region where this is frequently exceeded, step up a section size on the table. Snow also has a habit of building up in valleys between pitched roofs, and a structural design may be needed to take account of this.

A customised structural design by calculation may further increase these spans.

Roofing

Perhaps more than in any other area of building, roofing has its cowboys. Indeed it even has its villains, con men who find the roof-repair business an easy way to relieve the vulnerable of their money. I like to think that the latter would not attempt to roof a new extension; they seem to prefer carrying around a handful of tiles, a bucket of muck, and being away from a job within a few hours before anyone realises they've been done. It is amazing just how many 'roofing repair specialists' appear after gales have hit – anyone with ladder and a bucket is in business.

Even if we eliminate these villains and opportunists, the roofing business still seems to have more resident cowboys than any other area. Maybe it's something to do with their work being up there, away from close scrutiny. Often the only time a customer finds out that the work is bad is when the roof begins to leak, by which time they are paid and long gone.

In an effort to clean up the roofing business, the National Federation of Roofing Contractors was founded. Trade members are offered training and qualifications as well as technical support and advice. But without a doubt, the most valuable product that a member of the NFRC can offer you is an independent guarantee. For most domestic home extensions, a modest fixed rate payment will buy the home-owner 'Defective Workmanship' insurance, which will require the NFRC contractor to repair or renew defective work for ten years from the date of its completion. It also ensures that if your contractor goes out of business during the warranty period, another NFRC contractor is appointed to make good the work.

For a slightly higher fee, a 'Defective Workmanship plus Material Failure' insurance is also available.

One drawback exists with both of these policies – they require that the contractor uses new materials. This might not seem like a problem if you live in a relatively modern house, but in many areas of the country, authentic secondhand tiles and slates may be required to blend in with the environment and not just in listed buildings or Conservation Areas. It does, however, highlight the risk in using 'seconds' as opposed to new materials; many of the latter also come with free material guarantees, some of up to 20 years, offered by the manufacturers.

It would be pleasing to report that you will find hundreds of NFRC contractors in your local Yellow Pages, but I couldn't find one in my home town, nor in the town where I work – in fact, in working my way through several large towns in Kent, it was some time before I could find half a dozen from the Directory of Members. Given how many roofing contractors there are in business, the NFRC members must represent a very tiny percentage of the overall market. If membership of such an organisation like this is left to be voluntary, the future doesn't look like improving to any great degree.

Pitched roof coverings
Slates
Natural slate is still available in this

country, some imported from Spain and other European countries, and some of it still produced from Welsh mines. If you don't actually need 500-million-year-old slate dug from the hillsides of Blaenau Ffestiniog, you can now purchase artificial-resin slates which look surprisingly authentic. Whatever you decide, most slates are available in a variety of sizes, so it should be possible to match them in with existing courses.

The roof pitch will have some bearing on the amount of end lap you need for each slate. For example, a 560 x 305 mm slate, known traditionally as a 'small duchess' – for some reason, Welsh slate sizes all have traditional names of titled ladies – will need a minimum end lap of 65 mm at 45° pitch, but at 20° pitch you will need twice as much end lap. The lower the roof pitch, the more risk of wind uplift on the slates, allowing driven rain to penetrate, and so the amount of lap is increased to counteract this effect. This applies to tiles as well, whether they be plain or concrete interlocking.

Tiles

Clay peg tiles may still be handmade in some areas where traditional buildings prevail, but if they still look too new against an old north-facing roof you can speed up the weathering-in process by spraying liquid fertiliser onto the finished roof.

As with bricks, new tiles tend to come pre-randomised these days so that they can be laid direct from the pallet without your roofer having to mix them on site, although an experienced roofer will still keep an eye on the colours and shades to ensure that large monotone patches don't occur.

With an extension, some existing roof tiles may need to be removed to cut the new roof into the existing one. These tiles are often reused for economy, but beware of where you fix them – they are extremely likely to be less than a perfect match, and if put together in one position they can create a great square of colour shade on the roof.

In trussed-rafter roofs, batten joints should be staggered and not all cut to butt-joints on one truss. Even tile battens add to the lateral stability.

Slates and tiles are meant to be pre-mixed these days, the same as bricks, and consequently they can be laid direct from the pallet.

Fixing tiles

The fixing of roof tiles varies dramatically depending upon many factors, such as the roof pitch, the location, the degree of exposure and the weight of the tiles. In some instances every tile will need nailing (for example, wherever a roof pitch of 45° occurs), but in others only the perimeter tiles will need nailing, and all the others will simply interlock together and rely upon their dead weight and shallow roof pitch to remain weather-resistant. The fixing specification for your extension roof tiles will therefore be unique to your situation, and guidance should be sought from the tile manufacturer; do not rely on anyone else to tell you what fixings you require.

Close-boarded roofing

If you are forced into having a much

10 Expert Points

THIS LIST OF TEN EXPERT POINTS TO ACHIEVING A QUALITY ROOF FOR YOUR EXTENSION INCLUDES NFRC MEMBERSHIP, BUT CURRENTLY YOU MAY HAVE TO PLACE EMPHASIS ON THE OTHER NINE POINTS:

1 INVITATION TO QUOTE

Invite at least three roofers to visit your property and provide a quotation. If you have full plans drawn up, they should be able to give you a fixed quote rather than an estimate. If you don't have the plans but the roof structure is already formed, the same should apply.

2 VARY MATERIALS

Invite them to suggest a variety of materials which would be suitable, and to quote on them individually.

3 APPROVAL OF MATERIALS

It is important to bear in mind any planning requirements the local authority may have. Often a condition will be placed on your consent, requiring you to submit a sample of the material for their approval before starting the work. A reputable contractor should be able to provide you with free samples for this purpose. If not, merchants will do so.

4 MATERIAL GUARANTEES

Find out what guarantees are available for the materials. For example, some elastomeric roofing felts now available for flat roofs come with a manufacturer's 20-year guarantee.

5 WORKMANSHIP GUARANTEES

All material guarantees require that the product is laid in accordance with the manufacturer's recommendations, so they are worthless unless your roofing contractor lays them correctly. Ask your roofer what 'independent' guarantees he can offer for his workmanship.

6 VIEWING PREVIOUS JOBS

Unless he is a member of a trade body, it is unlikely that a roofer can offer any worthwhile guarantees for workmanship. Ask to view some of his previous jobs in the locality, and look for neat mortar bedding of ridge tiles and verges, which are an indication of a good roofer. If, on the other hand, they are messy, with mortar splashes on the tiles, etc., look for another roofer. In addition, ask if you may contact any of the roofer's previous customers.

7 INSURANCE

Ensure that the roofer has an adequate level of insurance and safety cover. Since roof work is overhead, the risk of injury to third parties or neighbouring property is perhaps greater than in other trades. £1,000,000 is appropriate cover.

8 CHECK QUALITY OF MATERIALS

If you are using secondhand materials, insist that they are hand-selected to sort out any cracked or broken tiles or slates.

9 MATERIALS INFORMATION

If you are using new tiles or slates, obtain a copy of the manufacturer's technical leaflet from their sales department. It may contain a lot of superfluous information, but it will tell you some very important facts about using the product, such as the minimum pitch (angle of rafters) it can be laid at for weather resistance, the gauge (spacing of the batten rows) required for the correct lap of each row, and what special tiles are available for eaves and verges. All these things can be checked easily before a single tile is laid.

10 NFRC MEMBERSHIP

Try to find a member of the National Federation of Roofing Contractors at the right price – remember, that doesn't necessarily mean the cheapest price – and use them and their insurance warranty.

lower roof pitch, or if you are located in an area of severe exposure to the elements, it may be worthwhile considering a close-boarded roof. This means covering the rafters with softwood boarding or ply sheathing before felting, battening and tiling, providing an extra layer of weather resistance. It will undoubtedly add to the roof strength against wind, as well as improving its weather resistance.

This type of roofing was quite popular in the 1920s and 1930s, but it is noticeable that properties of this era have often needed to have the boards removed or replaced due to rot. If you are going to close-board your new roof, it is advisable to counter-batten it before felting. This involves nailing vertical softwood battens at least 12 mm thick down the slope of the roof along the line of the rafters; the underlay felt then goes over, followed by the tile battens and the tiles. In effect, you are creating an air void above the boards to prevent the build-up of condensation on them. It is equally important to ensure that the roof void itself is properly cross-ventilated beneath the boards, that the boards are treated with preservative, and that you allow for their weight in calculating the load to the roof. Trussed-rafter manufacturers will need to be informed of this extra dead load, which would not normally be included.

Cold-roof construction

This has been the conventional construction method since we started insulating our roofs, installing the insulation between the ceiling joists and allowing the roof space above it to remain cold. Unfortunately, with current requirements for energy conservation being what they are, insulation thickness is considerably increased and the temperature difference between the warm house below and the cold roof void can be extreme, to say the least. The warm, moist air in the house rises as vapour, which can permeate through the ceilings and insulation and, on reaching the cold air of the loft, condense into moisture. So what is wrong with a little condensation in the attic? Well, it could eventually rot the timbers, it could corrode the metal fixings that anchor and hold the roof timbers together, ultimately causing them to fail, and it could degrade the insulation, but perhaps most frightening of all is that it could cause a short circuit in the electrical wiring.

It's not as if we're really talking about a 'little' condensation here, either. New houses are particularly vulnerable to condensation, with an estimated water content the equivalent of 65 baths being used in their construction. Extensions of, say, 12 sq m still contain at least 3 bathfuls of water. Even when the house dries out, we ourselves generate moisture at an impressive rate: according to the British Standards Institute, the normal behaviour of a family of five produces over 22 l (about two and a half buckets) of water per day.

A good cross-flow of air is needed from the eaves on one side of the roof to the other, or if this is too far (more than 10 m), from the eaves to ridge on both sides. There are manufacturers who specialise in producing roof vents for every conceivable situation. The

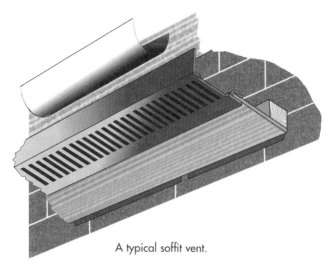

A typical soffit vent.

majority are installed at fascia or soffit level, but tile and slate vents are available along with ridge tile vents. They vary considerably in design, so you may need to shop around.

Air bricks can be built into gable ends to help to ventilate very small pitched roofs, but generally they do not let in anywhere near enough air for the average roof. Those terracotta clay air bricks of 230 x 75 mm have, for example, less than 15% of their area in holes, and you would need at least 25 to ventilate one side of a 6 m-long roof to current requirements. Your gable ends would be so full of holes that you'd be able to grate cheese on them; they also let in insects, such as wasps, to nest in your roof, whereas proprietary roof vents incorporate insect mesh to keep them out. Again, avoid using air bricks for roof ventilation!

Perforated tiling felt may help to dissipate condensation, but it can't always be relied upon to do so without the usual roof vents being installed. It

does depend upon the type of tiles and construction being used.

Of course in severe exposure areas, this free flow of air might represent a sub-zero gale fresh from the Russian Steppes which could freeze even insulated water pipes, so it might be worth considering warm-roof construction as an alternative.

Warm-roof construction

Where the insulation layer is provided on top of the roof structure, rafters or flat-roof joists, directly beneath the coverings, this is termed warm roofing. The roof space below is therefore left to be heated by the rise of warm air from the house. On the face of it, this might not seem ideal from an economical point of view, but having a warm dry attic is going to protect your Christmas decorations as well as your water pipes. When warm roofing was first introduced to Britain in the late 1980s, it was sold on the basis that you didn't need to ventilate the roof void at all since the risk of condensation had been removed; the current view is that some degree of ventilation is still required.

There is still the risk that warm, moist air will condense, either on the cold face of the insulation or on the cold roof coverings above, where it may freeze and rapidly thaw to moisture. To prevent this moisture getting back into the roof void, high-performance roofing felts, which allow water vapour through to escape but prevent condensed water itself from getting back in, have been developed. These felts are an expensive alternative to the traditional 'type 1F' underslating felt, but they have the added advantage of being much tougher, and they do not tear so easily.

One other essential precaution when using warm roofing is to create an extra air gap between the tiles and the insulant. This is done by counter-battening – a method of fixing rows of softwood battens down the roof slope, following the rafter lines in pitched roofs, before felting and fixing the tiling batten across laterally (see also 'Close-boarded roofing').

Insulation material for warm roofing tends to be more expensive than conventional glassfibre quilt, since it is required to be denser and thinner. Polyurethane foam boards and the like are often used, as they can support the weight of roof coverings easily between joists and rafters, in addition to offering

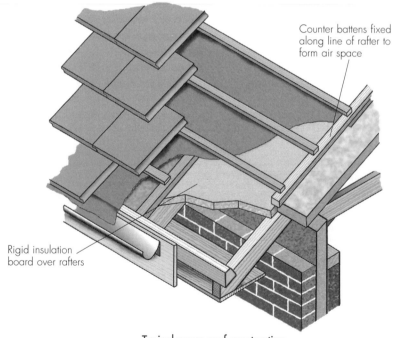

Counter battens fixed along line of rafter to form air space

Rigid insulation board over rafters

Typical warm-roof construction.

a high thermal conductivity, thus making them a good insulant. With so many varieties of insulation board on the market it is easy to assume that one product will do for every situation, but this is not the case. Make sure that you use the right material for the right use.

If you are constructing a room in the extension roof, solely providing insulation between the rafters constitutes a cold roof, which requires leaving a good air space above (at least 50 mm) and cross-venting it. Often this makes it necessary to provide deeper rafters or to counter-batten them to make them deeper.

Flat-roof construction

Flat roofs have had a bad press for some time now, with a shortness of life sometimes as little as five years, and often no more than ten. They are subjected to a lot of thermal movement compared to other parts of the building. They lay there all day, soaking up the sunshine, then suddenly the day ends and the temperature falls with the night, causing thermal movement. Because of this, the flat roof covering needs to be protected with a solar reflective covering – most often white mineral chippings which are bedded in hot bitumen, but solar reflective paints of bright silver finish are an alternative. Caution should be taken in selecting a paint, as some of them do not have very good resistance to fire spread, largely because they are solvent-based and may not be suitable within 6 m of a boundary. Look for an FAA, FAB or FAC fire-spread rating. Flat roofs these days should last a lot longer, and the cases where they don't are

invariably attributed to bad workmanship, although I believe that the materials and the very concept of flat-roof design ought to carry some of the blame as well.

By definition, anything less than 10° in pitch is a flat roof, but this hasn't stopped a lot of roofers actually laying them flat or with flat spots. To be fair, in the 1960s there was a school of thought that suggested that bitumen and asphalt had to be kept moist to prolong their life, and therefore the roof should be laid flat so water wouldn't run off it – I like to think that history has proved them wrong. Flat roofs should be laid to falls (a slope of 1:60 is advisable) by nailing tapered softwood furrings on the joists before boarding. The time to get out your spirit level and check it is when the deck sheeting (usually 18 mm or 25 mm plywood) is laid before felting.

In the last three decades traditional flat roofing has consisted of three layers of bitumen-based felt, hot-bonded to each other with bitumen tar and finished with mineral chippings also bedded in hot bitumen. Invariably the chippings, there to reflect the sun's heat and protect the felt, soon become loose and dislodged. The sun cooks the felt in summer and it freezes in winter, poor jointing around wall edges and pipes cracks away, and before you know it the roof needs repairing. The only types of felt recommended by the BRE are the glassfibre and polyester ones.

Flat roofs on single-storey extensions often provide a nice working platform for burglars to reach first-floor windows (frequently left less secure than those at ground level), and flat roofs on two-storey extensions are sometimes outlawed by planning authorities because they look so dreadful.

If you must have a flat roof, my advice can only be to take full advantage of the latest technology in roofing membranes. Elastomeric membranes and glassfibre coverings are now available with insurance-backed guarantees of 25 years. The new high-performance felts have better elasticity, better ageing properties and can be laid at lower temperatures, as well as being stronger and more resistant to tearing and puncturing, and they don't need to be covered with chippings or solar-reflective paint.

With any kind of flat roofing, the joint and edges are the weak points, so if you can avoid soil vent pipes penetrating the roof, do so. Abutments of flat roofs with walls should be formed so that the roof covering is dressed at least 150 mm up the wall, and the corner is rounded out with an angle fillet and a lead flashing

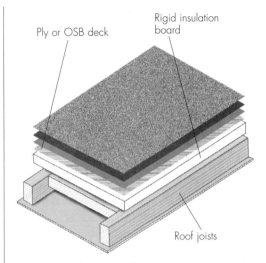

Typical warm-roof construction.

dressed over the joint. Bitumen felt stuck to the wall by itself is not sufficient, but is surprisingly common.

Warm roofing has tended to be more popular with flat roofs than pitched.

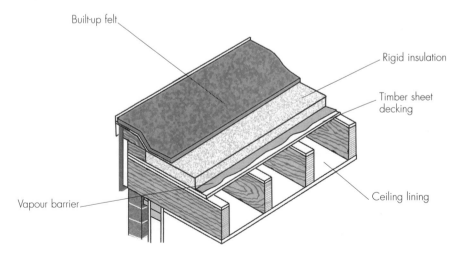

Another typical warm roof.

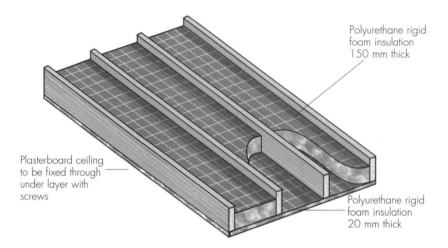

Polyurethane rigid
foam insulation
150 mm thick

Plasterboard ceiling
to be fixed through
under layer with
screws

Polyurethane rigid
foam insulation
20 mm thick

Typical cold flat roof construction with insulation between and beneath the joists.

This is usually because the need to level in the roof with an existing one doesn't often arise, and hence they can afford to be built up higher, but also because providing ventilation of the cold void in flat roofs can be tricky when they butt up against the house wall.

It is even possible to buy flat-roof decking, consisting of ply boarding prelaminated to the insulation, to speed up the construction process.

Cold-roof construction of flat roofs requires a good cross-vented air gap (at least 50 mm) above the insulation layer, and when this is added to the insulation thickness with the material laid between the joists, the required depth can often determine the size of the roof joists in excess of the structural requirements.

There are other traditional materials that can be utilised for flat roofing; these include lead (see below), zinc and copper sheeting, in addition to the ubiquitous asphalt.

Leadwork

There is nothing like lead for longevity: it lasts well over a hundred years, is extremely malleable, and can easily be cut and fashioned to fit the contours of roofs. Lead is coded according to weight, ranging from Code 3 to Code 8, based on weight in pounds per superficial foot. Code 4 is the minimum weight for flashings, and Code 5 the minimum for flat-roof coverings and valley gutters.

> WORKING WITH TAR AND BITUMEN
> Tar and bitumen are associated with skin cancer, therefore it is essential to wear protective gloves and clothing when working with them. While this is common practice amongst flat-roofers, other bitumen-based products, such as DPCs, are not usually treated with the same respect, and in consequence some manufacturers have withdrawn them from the market.

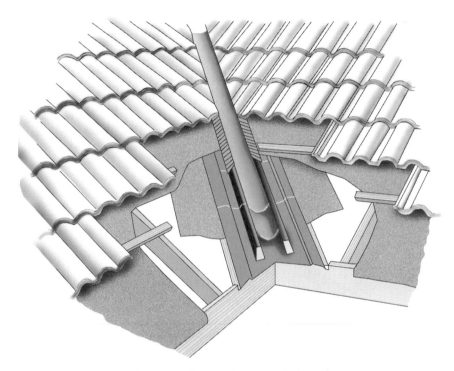

GRP bedded valley trough with interlocking tiles.

If your roof construction involves forming a box gutter at the intersection of the pitched roof and the external wall, or a tapered valley gutter between two pitched roofs, there are some standards required which are often unfortunately overlooked.

First, box and tapered gutters must be laid in bays along their length, with drips (steps) between each bay. Code 5 lead demands bays of 2 m length and a maximum width (girth) of 800 mm. These drips form the lap joints. Pitched valley gutters should be laid in maximum strips of 1.5 m with normal laps of at least 150 mm, or 225 mm for shallow roofs of less than 30° pitch.

Second, lay the lead on valley boards to at least a 1:80 fall; and third, never nail down the sides of lead gutters, because this restricts thermal movement and causes them to crack. Never lay sarking felt beneath the lead, as this will cause it to stick to the boards. Finally, don't use improved, galvanised-steel or aluminium nails up here; copper or stainless-steel clout nails should be used to fix lead.

Although leadwork is invariably found solely at roof level these days, it has always been the role of the plumber, not the roofer, on building sites. I can't

117

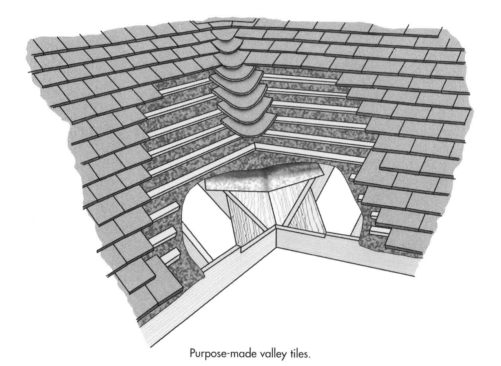

Purpose-made valley tiles.

explain why this is, but the fact might help you in finding a skilled leadworker.

Having promoted lead to the hilt, I must admit that there is a much easier way to form a pitched valley gutter. GRP preformed gutters have recently become available; they are cheaper than lead, much quicker to fix, and don't necessitate you wearing gloves when you handle them.

False-hip roofs

Before you consider the flat roof as your only option, there is one other resort – the false-hip (or false-pitch) roof. This is

essentially a combination of the two, flat in the middle with a mono-pitch around the edge to improve the appearance.

False-hip roofs need a lot of structural consideration before they are built. The vertical stud frame at the back of the mono-pitch needs to be supported, and the flat-roof joists may not be able to carry this weight. In such cases, structural beams need to be designed-in at this position.

Apart from the additional expense of designing and constructing this type of roof, there is also the added problem of draining it of rainwater. If this isn't

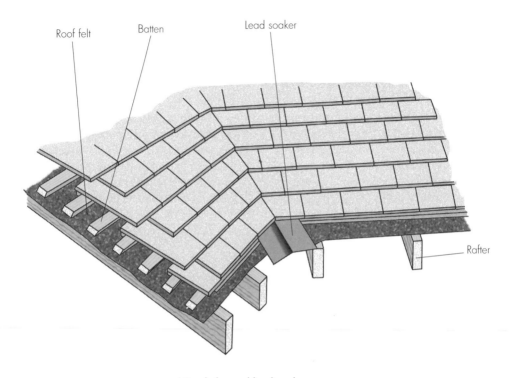

Roof felt   Batten   Lead soaker   Rafter

Mitred tiles and lead soaker.

properly dealt with, the inner flat bit is likely to become a swimming pool. To avoid this, it is a good idea to lay the flat-roof deck with a slightly greater fall than you might have done for a conventional roof.

There are two ways of draining it, depending on the position of the flat deck. A section or two of the mono-pitch ridge can be omitted to form a lead saddle for draining the roof deck, but this requires carefully creating cross-falls on the flat roof if the water is to be drained over these saddles and not pool against other parts of the ridge. This can

only be done with the flat deck located at ridge level.

The other option is to construct the flat deck at ceiling (eaves) level and provide secret gutters concealed within the structure with rainwater outlets in the flat deck.

The danger here is that the outlets will become blocked with falling leaves, etc., and as a consequence, protective cowls will need to be fitted to cover the outlets. Even with these, some careful and regular inspection and maintenance is needed to check that the roof is draining properly.

CHAPTER 6

Internal Work

Breaking through

There comes a point when any extension must be opened up to the rest of the house. You need to agree with your builder when this is going to happen and how it is going to happen. Many good builders have upset their customers needlessly by breaking through without giving ample notice to their customers or properly protecting their furnishings.

There are easy ways of doing this and there are hard ways. You could insist that the job is done carefully by hand, without mechanical tools. Your builder is going to need to know this in advance of his quotation, since the work will be time-consuming. If you leave it undecided, the builders will undoubtedly go for the fastest method, which usually involves a disc power cutter (skill saw) and a phenomenal amount of dust.

It may be acceptable for you to reach a compromise between the two. Once the extension is roofed, a disc cutter could be used to cut the opening almost, but not quite, through the wall from the outside (extension side). This will generate a lot of dust within the extension, so the windows and doors will need to be open, but none inside the house.

Once the extension is secure, windows and doors are fitted, glazed and made lockable. The workmen can then move to the inside of the house and can finish off the job with the minimum of mess by breaking the final veneer of the wall, using hand tools

such as a hammer and bolster, the debris being removed out through the extension. With some consideration, it is amazing how tidily this can be done, but I would still recommend that the room's furnishings be covered with dust-sheets and the floor coverings well protected.

This job is made a lot easier if the opening is cut from beneath an original window opening, leaving the original lintel above it undisturbed. However, not everyone will be this fortunate, and a new beam or lintel may have to be installed, either due to the extra weight from the extension roof or floor or because the opening needs to be widened. If this is the case, temporary support must be set up to take the weight from above before the work can begin. Adjustable props are normally used to do this, with timber (scaffold) boards at the ends to distribute the support evenly. The number of props needed will be determined by the load they are required to carry.

It is important that the props are not overtightened once in position. You are not trying to jack up the floor or roof here, merely to stop it from dropping once the opening is cut. If the props are overtightened the ceiling finishes will, at the least, be damaged, but there is always the possibility that structural timbers will be displaced. Hopefully, your builders will be well experienced at this task and will carry it out without any problem, but for peace of mind, it is worth discussing with them and perhaps even being there when it is done.

When lintels are being installed like this, they may need dry packing to the supported wall to ensure that it is bearing evenly upon them. You don't want to have to wait for the wall to drop for it to come into contact with the lintel. This means that the temporary support will have to remain in position for a few days while the cement-mortar dry packing hardens.

Some consideration may need to be given to the end bearings of the new lintel or beam, which may mean installing padstones under the ends to spread the load to the wall. This will depend on the structural design, and it is impossible to make generalised assumptions here. If the padstone design allows it, you may find it easier to use a precast concrete lintel (63 x 100 mm in section) to act as a spreader padstone. These lintels are easier to install than casting in in-situ concrete padstones. Alternatively, engineering bricks or dense concrete blocks are often used for padstones.

Never break through until the roof is weathered in and the extension is secure, with windows and doors fitted, glazed and lockable. If you do need a cavity tray at the abutment, make sure that it is installed before breaking through (see Chapter 7).

Integral garages

If your extension includes a garage, this will demand a certain amount of isolation from the habitable parts of the house in two matters, fire spread and thermal insulation.

Fire spread

Because of the inherent risks that come from storing a car in your home, an integral garage must be separated by its construction to at least a half-hour's fire resistance. To prevent oil and fuel spillage from spreading into the house, the finished garage floor should be lower than the house floor by at least 100 mm. It may be possible to achieve this difference purely by the house-floor finishings if insulation and screed are present, otherwise you are more than likely going to have to cast the concrete garage floor slab lower than the rest or sloping away from the house floor. This can only be avoided if you have a great enough depth of finishes in the habitable part to increase the level sufficiently – an 80 mm thick insulation layer and 63 mm screed on top will achieve this, but a masonry sill is necessary.

Although this work is included under internal work, it obviously benefits from

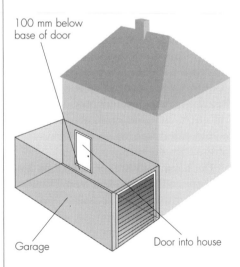

100 mm below base of door

Garage

Door into house

The wall and any floor between the house and the garage must have 30 minutes of fire resistance. The door into the house should be at least 100 mm above the level of the garage floor.

some earlier thought at the groundwork stage, since you may need to form the garage slab lower. To overcome a mistake in this area, people often consider using a raised threshold on the door between the garage and house, but a normal timber threshold may not suffice, and you may need to cast a concrete threshold step and raise the door to match.

The door itself should be to at least an FD30 standard (Fire Door – 30 minutes) and should be fitted with a self-closing device. Fire doors are coded to reflect their standard, and a wide variety of standards exist. Since they look the same as any other door, the industry identifies them by building in a colour-coded core to the back edge of the door. FD30 doors are coded by a white core with a blue circle inside it.

It is no longer necessary to have one of those bulky overhead closures that you see in offices; discreet door closures that are rebated into the closed edge of the door have been available for some time. Because of differential air pressure, these closure mechanisms sometimes need to be adjusted before the door will close properly on the latch.

The frame itself should be suitable for the door and fitted with at least 25 mm thick door stops, thicker than normal internal door stops, which are screwed in position. Alternatively, intumescent strips and smoke seals can be rebated in around the frame.

Intumescent strips expand under fire and effectively seal the gap between door and frame, preventing smoke from getting around (although not under) the door. The disadvantage with these is that

if activated by fire, they seal the door shut by rapidly expanding, a bit like expanding foam fixative, and make it impossible for anyone to use the door to escape – however, a general consensus of opinion holds that if you are still in the garage when that temperature is reached at the door, you are probably already dead (this type of seal is designed to prevent fire from spreading to another part of the house rather than anything else).

Smoke seals do an excellent job on garage doors because they also help to prevent exhaust fumes from entering the house. If you are a driver you will know that even a can of petrol can give off fumes, but warm petrol in a heated engine is worse (benzine in fuel is known to cause cancer). Smoke from a fire can be cold and could be busy leaking around the door before the temperature gets up high enough to activate the intumescent strip.

A cold smoke seal looks a lot like a caterpillar-style draught excluder and does two jobs for the price of one on a garage door, but it is also possible to buy both intumescent and cold smoke seals in one strip.

While you couldn't fit a smoke alarm in the garage (the exhaust fumes would set it off constantly), you could install a heat detector. These are also suitable for kitchens and activate once a preset temperature is reached, usually between 54° and 62°C.

A masonry wall separating the garage and house will easily achieve the fire standard, provided that it is fire-stopped at the abutments of the roof or fire-resisting ceiling. This is normally achieved with mineral-fibre strips which are packed into position.

If you propose to use a timber-stud wall, it will need to be lined on both sides with sufficient plasterboard (or cement-fibre board) to achieve the fire resistance. The drawback with this method comes from the need to cover the joints between the boards, either by using two layers and staggering them, or by wet-plastering the surface.

If you have a room above the garage, the ceiling finish may be needed to protect the floor to at least 30 minutes' fire resistance. Again, plasterboard or cement-fibre board can be used, but the problem of joints reoccurs.

If you have the patience and are economically minded, you can cut off strips of boards the width of the timber floor joists above and tack them onto the joist undersides before covering with a single-sheet boarding that will be jointed over the strips. This can only be done economically by the serious DIY enthusiast, since it will be time-consuming, to say the least; it is much quicker to double-layer the boards or wet-plaster the ceiling.

Lintels over garage doors and windows may support a floor above, and in this instance they should also be fire-protected.

Effective fire protection becomes a particular problem if there are no other finishes to your garage walls, which is often the case. The most effective solution for this is to screw and bond cement-fibre board or plasterboard onto the exposed parts of the lintel as neatly as you can, or wet-plaster it with cement and sand render.

Energy conservation and thermal insulation

There is no need to insulate the floor of a garage, unless it is to be a heated garage or there is a room below. If you are heating the garage, you ought to think about how you are going to insulate the garage doors and the draughty edges around them, as well as the walls. You might be able to find a good-fitting roller-shutter door that carries some insulation in it, but most standard garage doors prove to be a source of great heat loss.

Assuming that you are not so passionate about your car's comfort, only the walls between the garage and house will need to be insulated. Here, the standards are no longer reduced from those required for the home's external walls, with the integral garage now being regarded as a fully ventilated space. But you may wish to give some thought to your own geographic location and micro-climate before settling for less insulation here. The same goes for any floors above the garage which will need insulating. This can easily be done in the case of timber floors by lagging between the joists with glassfibre quilt.

Because heating boilers are often less than attractive and sometimes noisy, integral garages can make good homes for them. If you propose to locate your boiler here, the primary pipework (the pipes which carry hot water from the boiler) should be insulated. Rigid-foam pipe insulation is used to make a snug fit, but bends in the pipes and joints in the insulation need a bit of care and plenty of duct tape. If your garage is too well-ventilated or in a cold location (Scotland, for example), you ought to insulate all pipes, even cold-water ones.

For convenience you may want to have the timer controls separated and located in the home somewhere (such as the hot-water cylinder cupboard), not in the garage next to the boiler.

Electrical installation

The construction of a new extension is the perfect opportunity to have things just how you want them, and this opportunity is nowhere more appreciated than in the case of the electrical installation. One of the most common complaints by the owners of

10 Expert Points

HERE ARE TEN EXPERT POINTS TO HELP YOU DESIGN AN INTEGRAL GARAGE:

1 ACCESS INTO THE GARAGE
Consider locating the internal fire door between garage and house within a well-ventilated and less-occupied part of the house, such as a utility room or lobby.

2 FIRE DOOR
Check that the internal door is at least an FD30 standard by the identification core (white core with a blue circle inside).

3 FIRE-DOOR FRAME
Check that 25 mm-thick door stops are screwed in position on the frame, or that intumescent strips and seals are used.

4 DOORSTEP
Make sure that you have allowed for at least a 100 mm-high step up from the garage floor level into the house.

5 HOUSE/GARAGE WALL INSULATION
Check with your Building Control Officer that the wall between the house and the garage will provide enough thermal insulation.

Often extra-thick insulating blocks are found to be the easiest and cheapest method, but standard blocks or bricks will need insulation added on. This can be done by framing out the wall with timber battens, insulating between them and finishing by plasterboarding over the top.

6 WALL STRENGTH
Consider the wall thickness on either side of the garage piers. A half-brick thickness (112 mm) is not strong enough, while 215 mm or cavity-wall thicknesses are fine.

7 ROOMS ABOVE THE GARAGE
If there is a floor above the garage, it will need to be separated with thermal insulation and 30 minutes' fire resistance. Check your options with ceiling finishes.

8 LINTEL FIRE PROTECTION
Where a room occurs above the garage, steel lintels above openings need fire protection, so check your options. Where they only support the roof, this isn't essential.

9 BOILERS
Boilers located in garages should preferably be the wall-hung, balanced-flue type, and should be positioned high enough to avoid car impact. The pipework should be well insulated and the timer controls located other than in the garage.

10 CAR IMPACT DAMAGE
Isolated piers that support a floor above the garage should be avoided. Where this can't be done (e.g. with a brick pier between a pair of garage doors in a double garage), they should be built extra strong to resist accidental vehicle impact, or protected against vehicle impact.

enough power points – now you have the chance to put in sockets where you want them, rather than where the developer thought they should go.

Why bother with installing single-socket outlets when doubles are only marginally more expensive? Position lights on walls as well as ceilings, put switches where they are most convenient, install outdoor lights. It really is worth giving a lot of thought to the layout; don't leave it up to the designer. If you are using an electrician registered under the Government's 'CPS – Competent Person Scheme – and you should – he or she will advise you beforehand if your proposed layout breaks any regulations.

The ring main is the circuit which supplies current to the socket outlets. Ring circuits are restricted to 100 sq m, but any number of socket outlets can be provided within this. A modern house is likely to have two ring circuits already, which are identifiable from the fuse box by two red 30-amp fuse cartridges.

Electrical work is not an area for the DIY enthusiast – deaths have occurred as a result of live wires being mistakenly earthed to the water main (and thus the kitchen sink). In England and Wales, the controls on electrical work offer a choice of two routes. The first is to employ electricians who are registered with the CPS and able to self-certify their own work. This is the favoured option. The second, through either DIY or a non-CPS registered electrician, is to submit the work for approval under the Building Regulations (part P). This means approval of the design, installation, testing and certification; all of which could mean you have to pay the

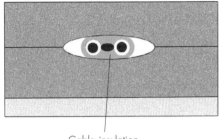

Cable insulation fully enclosed within insulation.

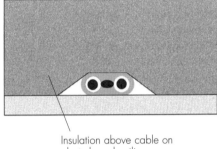

Insulation above cable on plasterboard ceiling.

Building Control Service an additional fee to check it. Electrical Safety was introduced to the Building Regulations for the first time on 1 January, 2005.

There are several bodies that have registered on behalf of their members under the Competent Person Scheme. Of those the ECA (Electrical Contractors Association) and the NIC EIC (National Inspection Council for Electrical Installation Contracting) are the principle organisations.

Electrical cables that run in, or by, thermal insulation material can become dangerously overheated. To reduce this risk (which may occur where wiring runs under ceiling insulation in roof voids or through wall insulation in timber-frame walls), the cable should be derated. This

125

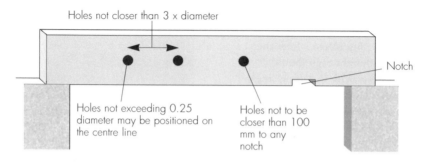

Holes not closer than 3 x diameter

Notch

Holes not exceeding 0.25 diameter may be positioned on the centre line

Holes not to be closer than 100 mm to any notch

Limits for drilling floor joists for electrical cables.

means reducing the current capacity of the cable, by 50% when fully surrounded by insulation, and by 25% when it is on one side only.

Electrics and timber structure

When fixing socket outlets and switches to timber-stud walls, noggins should always be provided between the studs to support the boxes. Don't allow your electrician to cut away at load-bearing studs in timber-framed walls to house the boxes.

If any tear holes exist in the timber frame's vapour barrier after the electrical first fixing, these should be sealed up with impermeable adhesive tape before they are covered.

Electrical first fixing is the stage when all cables are routed around and boxes fixed in. The second fix is after the wall, floor and ceiling finishings have been installed, and covers to power sockets, ceiling roses, etc. are installed.

Drilling joists for cables

As part of the first fix, electricians usually need to run their cables through floors, and this is normally done by drilling holes in the timber joists to feed them

through. Because it is possible to weaken the joists by doing this, holes must never exceed one quarter of the depth of the joist in diameter, and should be drilled through the joist centre. It is also necessary to locate them between one quarter and around one third of the span measured in from the wall bearing. Holes should not be drilled closer together than three times the largest diameter. The diagram above gives rough guidelines for this procedure.

Electrics and masonry structure

If the masonry walls of the extension are to have channels (known as chases) cut in them for the cable trunking, the depth of these chases must be limited to one quarter of the wall thickness when they run vertically, and one sixth when they run horizontally. In the instance of a cavity wall, this relates to the internal leaf thickness by itself. If you are using hollow or cellular blocks in the wall construction, avoid cutting out chases altogether.

These days it is rare for chases to be needed at all; plastic cable covers are pinned to the walls to run the cables through before being plastered over.

Extractor fans

Mechanical extractor fans are needed wherever high degrees of humidity occur, such as in kitchens, bathrooms and utility rooms. Rapid ventilation is needed to remove it.

It has become traditional to have extractor fans that are switched on with the light in bathrooms, but unless the room is windowless, the fan should be operated independently. The reason for this is that unless you make a habit of bathing only during the hours of darkness, the fan will not be operating every time it is needed. A better solution is to install a humidity-sensor fan, which cuts in automatically when high humidity is present, whether the light is on or off.

In bathrooms, fans should be connected to an isolator switch so that the supply can be switched off, allowing them to be safely worked on. This has become necessary in recent years because of the trend in wiring them up to the light.

Fans will only operate effectively over a certain length of duct which is proportional to the extract rate and power. A standard 15-litre-per-second bathroom fan will only remove air through a very short duct before it becomes ineffective.

Humidity levels between 70 and 100% RH facilitate mould growth. Humidistats on fans should thus be set to operate at no higher than 70%.

Axial fans are usually found at the cheaper, lower-performance end of the market, but are sufficient for bathrooms, where they can be mounted on an external wall and just sleeved through the wall. If any length of ducting is required to reach the outside air, a higher extraction rate or a centrifugal fan should be used.

Ducting of fans reduces their performance. A 4 m long duct reduces performance by 25%. Flat ducting reduces airflow more than flexible round ducts, so kitchen-extractor hob fans connected to flat unit-top ducts need to be of sufficient power to compensate for this.

Where open-flued appliances are used in kitchens, such as boilers without balanced flues, combustion air is required to serve them. If this air is removed by an overenthusiastic extractor fan, the consequences could be disastrous. To prevent this, you need to ensure that sufficient fresh air is introduced to meet all the ventilation needs, without robbing one to pay another. In addition, a reduced-rate fan of 20-litres-per-second maximum output should be installed (directly over the cooker will be most effective).

Solid-fuel appliances, such as woodburners and Agas, require a lot of combustion air, and are not at all compatible with extractor fans.

Generally speaking, extractor fans from reputable companies more than meet the rated outputs necessary to comply with Building Regulations, and the above situation is the only time when you need to exercise caution.

In bathrooms, fans should be sited away from water spray and out of the reach of people using the bath or shower. Extra-safe, low-voltage fans are available for bathrooms.

Fans should always be located on the

opposite side of the room to the window or windows.

Condensation traps should be used where any part of the ducting is higher than the fan itself, particularly where the duct runs through a cold roof void. Warm, moist air being sucked out of the room will easily condense on the colder duct walls, causing water to run back into the fan and shorting it out. A condensation trap in the duct, positioned as close as possible to the fan, will protect it. Horizontal ducting that slopes away from the fan will do the same job.

There are basically two kinds of louvred shutter for the wall venting of fans: gravity-return flaps and electrically powered flaps. The first can be the cause of much irritation, particularly in exposed locations where the wind blowing across the surface of the louvres can rattle them all night long. The solution is thermo-electrically operated shutters which close to a fixed-shut position and won't be rattled by any amount of wind.

Charcoal-filter-pad extractor hobs do not meet the requirements of the Building Regulations for rapid ventilation; externally vented fans are required in these situations.

Although extractor fans are commonly used, they can be noisy and inefficient from an energy point of view. The alternative really needs applying to the whole house rather than to the extension by itself, but since it may be

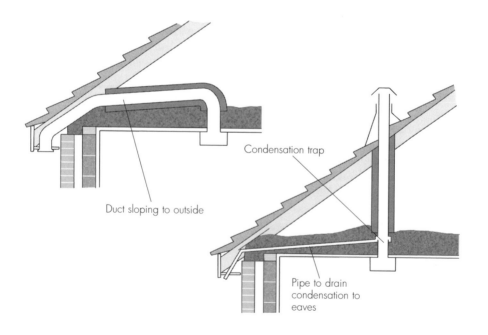

Condensation trap

Duct sloping to outside

Pipe to drain condensation to eaves

Insulating a horizontal extract duct and a vertical extract duct.

the way forward it is worth mentioning.

Passive-ventilation systems or heat-recovery systems can be installed in place of extractor fans. Passive stack vents allow warm, moist air to rise naturally into the colder loft space, with or without a central fan up there to help draw it. Heat exchangers located in the roof space transfer most of the heat from this stale air and reintroduce fresh, warm air into the dry, habitable rooms, thus saving on fuel costs as well as ventilating the home. The exchanger runs an adjustable-speed fan permanently to recycle the air, trickle-fed during the night, normal during the day, and faster during cooking or bathing times to rapidly reduce humidity. If you suffer from hay fever or the effects of air pollution, the benefits of not having the windows open will also be an advantage.

Smoke alarms

The majority of fire deaths in the UK have occurred in the home, around 700 every year, with ten times more than that injured. And the biggest threat in a fire comes from smoke, not flames. The combination of these two facts has led to mains-powered smoke alarms being necessary in extensions now as well as new homes. In hallways and landings they can be installed within 7.5 m of the entrance to any room and still generally heard within, but it is better to extend the protection to the rooms themselves where fires are at risk of starting. Smoke is silent and can engulf a home in minutes – smoke alarms save lives, and building them in makes a great deal of sense.

For most of us, smoke alarms are an afterthought, and we trundle off to the DIY store for a handful of battery-operated types. These are cheap and they work, but they're going to cost you a fortune in batteries over the years. A mains-powered alarm wired in now will pay for itself quite soon, and it doesn't necessarily need wiring to a separate fused circuit. Providing the alarms have a battery back-up that takes over if the power fails, it is usually acceptable to wire them in with the lighting circuit This battery back-up will last long enough for you to discover that there is a fault in the electrical circuit if your lights aren't working.

Smoke alarms can operate as stand-alone units or be interconnected so that if one goes off, they all go off. They should be sited on ceilings at least 300 mm away from light fittings (so that they are not obstructed by lampshades) or walls, as the corners of rooms tend to be smoke-free zones in a fire.

If alarms do go off accidentally when you're burning the toast, the fuse at the distribution board can be temporarily removed to switch them off, or the smoke can be fanned away from the unit. False alarms like this can be avoided by locating them away from heaters, cooking areas, heating-duct outlets, bathrooms and garages. It isn't just smoke which can set them off – steam, condensation and fumes can do it as well.

Another important thing to consider when siting smoke alarms is how easy they will be to get at for cleaning and maintenance – don't fix them up over the stairs unless you have a circus background! Some are designed to be fixed vertically to walls, and it is best to locate them between 150 and 300 mm down from the ceiling. Most smoke detectors come with a protective dust cover which should be kept on after installation, until all the building work is finished and the extension is occupied.

Because smoke alarms cannot be installed in kitchens, garages or boiler rooms, heat alarms are available for these areas. The domestic fixed-temperature models are activated by a temperature of around 54°–62°C. I am advised that about 46% of all domestic fires start in the kitchen, so installing a heat alarm into a new kitchen extension would clearly be beneficial.

Carbon-monoxide alarms

Carbon monoxide (CO) is a deadly gas. It is invisible, you can't smell it, you can't taste it, and it has a fondness for the haemoglobin of our bloodstream. Once breathed in, it displaces the oxygen in our blood which we rely on to stay alive, thus suffocating us from the inside out. Carbon monoxide can be released into your home's atmosphere by poorly maintained appliances such as gas ovens, gas- and oil-fired boilers, blocked chimney flues and even exhaust fumes creeping in from integral garages. According to the UK National Poisons Unit, CO is the biggest cause of death by accidental poisoning in the home, with an estimated 200 fatalities a year.

Prevention is better than detection, and making sure your appliances are properly maintained is the best solution, but as a back-up to this, a CO alarm could be wired into your new extension. Since you are perhaps at the greatest risk when asleep, installing one near to

the bedrooms is ideal, and to be doubly safe, an extra one could be installed downstairs in the living area. There are no legislative requirements for you to install a CO alarm, and they are nowhere near as cheap as smoke alarms, but if they save one life, then clearly they are worth every penny.

Internal finishings
Floors

Concrete ground floors can be insulated above the structure at the internal finishing stage. Floor-grade insulation can be laid to a finished slab and covered with either polythene and floorboarding or cement and sand screed. With boarding, the timber should be glued at the joints with PVA glue and the boards set back from the wall edges by 12 mm to allow for movement. The wall finish and skirting will cover this. It is important that the insulation is laid flat to accept the boards. Screed finishing on insulation should be at least 65 mm thick and reinforced with galvanised chicken wire to prevent cracking. A polythene sheeting should again be used if the insulation is the mineral-fibre type, to prevent the screed from soaking into it.

In the case of timber boarding to a suspended-timber floor, the spacings of the joists can determine the thickness of the boarding. With joists at 400 mm spacings, 18 mm-thick chipboard floor-grade boarding can be used, but at up to 600 mm spacings, 22 mm-thick boarding becomes necessary. I would recommend that you always use the latter, and to avoid creaking floors, screw and glue the boarding down, rather than simply nailing it in place.

It is now possible to decorate timber-boarded floors as well as concrete ones with ceramic floor tiling, thanks to modern waterproof adhesives and thinner tiles, but remember that timber can shrink after installation.

Parquet or woodblock flooring is not suitable for bathrooms or kitchens, where it will get wet.

Ceilings

Like walls, ceiling finishes need to have some restriction to the spread of fire across the surface. This is easily achieved by using plasterboard, but if you do want to steer away from a plastered or artexed ceiling, you should look towards achieving a Class 1 fire-spread rating. Timber boarding by itself won't have this, and a painted fire-retarding solution will need to be applied to it; in a clear finish, it can be applied over stain. Unfortunately, these fire-retarding solutions are pretty toxic and require a controlled environment in their application with plenty of ventilation; they are also jolly expensive. Small rooms, such as cloakroom WCs, will not present a problem from fire spread, and untreated timber may be acceptable here.

If the timber boarding is the only finish to a first-floor structure, it will also need fire resistance – a separate thing to the spread of fire on surfaces. In two-storey construction a modified half hour is all that is required; in three-storey homes, a full half hour. Again, paints can now do this, but since they require maintenance, fire resistance is best afforded by plasterboard. Because of this need for floor structures to have fire

resistance, first-floor extensions built on top of single-storey parts of the house may need new finishes to the existing ceilings below. Because they aren't considered part of the new extension, this sometimes gets overlooked by builders and home-owners alike.

No fire resistance is required by regulation in the UK to roofs, i.e. ceilings to roofs need only restrict the spread of fire over the surface. For some reason, it has always been acceptable for roofs to burn down so long as floors and walls don't.

Artex or plastic paint has no fire-resisting attributes, so make sure that the plasterboard type and thickness is sufficient for the fire resistance you need. Plaster-skimming of ceilings does add to fire resistance.

Plasterboard is commonly available in two thicknesses: 9.5 mm and 12.7 mm. Where joists occur at 400 mm centres either thickness is suitable, but where they occur at 600 mm centres, as in roof trusses, then the thicker board must be used to cope with the extra span.

Foil-backed plasterboard should be used when boarding against a cold roof void to provide a vapour check, although pinning up some polythene before tacking the boards will do this job much better.

Plasterboard is produced in 2.4 x 1.2 m sheets and is thus suited to joists at 400 mm or 600 mm centres; if you have varied this spacing for structural reasons, now is payback time because the boards are all going to have to be cut to suit. Boards should be staggered when fixed to avoid straight joints the length of the room. If you are artexing over them, the long, straight joint will remain visible.

Beams

When it comes to providing structural fire resistance most people are aware that steel beams (commonly referred to as RSJs) need protection. Steel behaves badly in a fire, twisting, sagging and buckling. In the case of a two-storey house, a steel beam supporting the floor or walls over an opening will usually be clad with two layers of plasterboard and a plaster finish.

If you feel, however, that this lacks imagination, be aware that boxing it out in veneer strips of Parana pine will do nothing to protect it from fire. It will be necessary to treat any wood veneer with intumescent paint, which can be bought as a clear finish, to retard the charring rate of the timber and hence achieve the minimum half-hour fire resistance – untreated softwood chars at the rate of about 20 mm in 30 minutes. For the conceptual minimalists among you who believe that bare-steel beams make an interesting focal point in any room, the intumescent paint people provide a full range of violent primary colours that will really show bolt connections and fillet weld at their best.

Loft conversions

Loft conversions in two-storey houses are looked upon as third-floor extensions in fire-safety terms, and consequently structural fire precautions have to be introduced to the property. The theory goes that people may cheerfully jump or be ladder-rescued from a first-floor window in a fire, but

not from a second-floor window some 4.5 m or more above the ground.

As theories go, it's not a bad one. A fire-protected escape route has to be formed within the house leading to an external door. The new loft room door should be a fire door but in addition, any existing room doors off this protected route need to be replaced for FD20 fire doors or upgraded to that standard. The good news is that self-closing devices are no longer required (from April 2007) after a review that found most had been disabled or removed anyway because they proved to be such a nuisance.

Decorators

Decorating is for most people a DIY job, but if you are going to employ a professional their work must be outstanding, otherwise you might just as well have done it yourself. They should be people of annoying perfectionism and irritating patience – people who are happy to spend the whole day rubbing down a stair handrail before varnishing it, only to rub it down again the next day to varnish it again and rub it down again the following day, and so on until the handrail appears to have been encased in glass.

A good many builders do not touch decorating work, preferring to leave it to their client for themselves or to employ their own decorator. This may be because builders often prefer as little interference as possible from their customers during the project, and nowhere does the customer feel more able to intervene than in the decorating. And why not – this is the stage that decides whether you can live in the extension or not. It's important to choose the right design and colours.

If wallpaper is to stay on the wall, fresh plaster should be left for six months before papering, while painting can be done after a few weeks when the plaster is touch-dry. Walls that have been dry-lined can be decorated immediately, but they should be sealed with a specialist dry-wall topcoat which will take the absorbency out of the surface and allow you to remove the wallpaper in the future without removing the plasterboard as well.

You would be ill-advised to select the paint colour solely by the label on the tin. Paint manufacturers have recognised this, and provide sample testers which allow you to try out several colours on a test wall before deciding.

Radiators either come plastic-coated white and don't need decorating, or are gloss-painted white and soon go yellowish white in use. A new device for redecorating behind radiators may soon be widely available. It is a hinged fitting that allows the radiator to be pivoted forward so that wallpapering or painting can be done behind it without having to drain down the heating system and disconnect the radiator.

Paint and pollution

Paint has for centuries been an environmentally problematic material, but it is only recently that manufacturers, and indeed suppliers, have tried to do something about it. Lead was removed from paint some time ago, but the problem now is the solvent content. Solvents and other chemicals, or volatile organic compounds (VOCs) to use their scientific term, are

contained in the majority of gloss paints, stains and other timber treatments. Those that offer some degree of fire retarding contain an even more harmful cocktail of chemicals. The only paints which don't contain high percentages of VOCs are water-based ones like emulsion paint.

So what is the problem with solvents? They evaporate during the painting, and continue to do so until thoroughly dry; released into the air, they react with nitrogen oxides and add to atmospheric pollution. You may only be using a one-litre tin and can't be single-handedly responsible for the smog over your city or town, but every little bit contributes. If you're still unconvinced, the possible health risks from regularly painting with solvent-based paints may convince you, particularly if you or your family suffer from asthma or other respiratory problems. Consider also the fact that using these paints in the sealed-up homes of today has us at a disadvantage.

What are the alternatives? There are low-VOC-content paints available now; although paint development in this area is still in its infancy, some retailers are labelling in categories the VOC content on the tin. Minimal content might be anything below 0.3%, while the very-high-content stuff can be extremely high, as much as 80%.

At present the higher the quality of finish required from the paint, particularly with gloss and the like, the higher the VOC content. The first water-based gloss paints tried on the public have not been greeted favourably – the paint goes on a lot less smoothly, resulting in a poorer finish. At present, most painters and decorators tend not to like it, but technology is improving all the time in this area, and the new generation of 'high-solid' gloss paints, that have less than 40% of the traditional gloss solvent content, are marketed as performing equally. Until such times as technology improves to match the two unequivocally, your choice depends upon whether you put your environmental ideologies before your quest for the perfect finish.

It is alleged that as much as a quarter of all paint sold in the UK is never actually used. Think about it: where do you keep the paint left over – in the garage or the shed? And for how long is it going to last before it goes hard? Solvent-based paints have to be disposed of, and that often means landfill sites, which contaminate the ground and may one day leach pollutants into the watercourse, and so on.

Since you should never empty paint or white spirit into the drains, your only safe recourse is to check with your local council, who might have special facilities for disposing of waste or unwanted paint. Alternatively, there may be in your locality a charity that collects waste paint (while it can still be used) and will put it to good use.

Textured paint

This often goes under the name of Artex, which is in fact a trade name but one that is as symbolic to the product as Hoover is to vacuum-cleaning. It was very trendy in the 1980s as a ceiling finish, but has now lost position in favour of the smooth plaster finish. I hope that one day it will return to

fashion, because the professional artexer is a craftsman. A skilled one can cover a ceiling, and himself, in minutes with a perfect regimental pattern using only a comb (or a plastic carrier bag) and a keen eye.

It is, alas, the messiest of trades, and it is rare, if not foolish, for anyone to want to be in the same room as an artexer at work. Indeed, a wise person wouldn't allow one to wash himself or his tools out in the house afterwards. If he or she wishes to stand in the road and be hosed down, make sure that you move your car to a safe distance first.

Wallpapering

As with painting, newly plastered walls need to be prepared before they can be papered. Even allowing for this, it is important to give the plaster a chance to thoroughly dry out, shrink, crack, be filled and be sanded down. All of this can usually be achieved in six months, after which the wall can be given a coat of diluted wallpaper paste (size) before the fun starts.

If you think you've made a short cut here by dry-lining the walls instead of wet-plastering them, make sure that you have coated the plasterboard with the special top-coat solution that will allow you to wallpaper it. If you've tried to save money by missing this out, you will regret it when the time comes to redecorate and removing the paper can't be done without removing some of the wall.

A standard roll of wallpaper is 10.5 m long and 530 mm wide – I have no idea why – and by measuring up your floor to ceiling height, you should be able to calculate how many rolls you will need.

Do not attempt to be frugal here; it is not worth making deductions for doors and windows. A lot of surfeit is needed to allow for imperfect walls, alignment of the pattern and cutting. It is very important to retain the batch number of the paper as, should you need extra, it is the only thing that will guarantee a match.

Coving

This is available in three materials, polystyrene, plaster and timber, plaster being the best: it can be bought plain or moulded to quite elaborate designs. It is common amongst decorators to use a mixture of coving adhesive or plastic (textured) paint and PVA adhesive to glue it into position, held temporarily by nails. The wall should be wetted before the coving is introduced to it. Paper mitre guides usually come with the coving; if you don't have a special mitre block, the guides can be overlaid to draw the cutting line straight on to the coving itself.

The main problem usually comes with the discovery that the walls aren't precisely at 90° to each other. This can be overcome in two ways, first by purchasing premade external and internal corner pieces that cover up dreadful mitre joints, and second, by employing a skilled decorator to do the job in the first place.

Wall and floor tiling

Tiles come in a wide variety of sizes, both metric and imperial (see table opposite), and choosing the right one may be as tricky as choosing the design. The size should reflect the room size and surface area to be covered: large

tiles in small areas look a bit like undersized patios, while small ones over large areas look like – well, like a lot of hard work. In broad terms, the number of tiles required per square metre can be found from the table below; this should help you calculate what you need in advance (in addition, most tile manufacturers print the coverage of a boxful of their tiles on the packaging).

Fixing a straight timber batten one row up from the bottom edge of the proposed tiling and to the sides will enable a straight and square line to be achieved. After tiling the batten is removed, and the bottom and side edge course of tiles can be fixed, safe in the knowledge that they will be level and true. Plastic spacers can be used to achieve the right separation for grouting between the tiles. To avoid any patches of shade variation, it is best to select one tile from each box alternately, thus ensuring a good mix.

Never rely on grout to seal the edges of baths and basins to tiling. Silicone mastic can be applied, or preformed seals can be used. Where GRP baths are

TILE SIZE	COVERAGE (number of tiles per sq m)
$4^1/4 \times 4^1/4$ in	82
6 x 6 in	42
6 x 8 in	32
150 x 150 mm	43
150 x 200 mm	33
200 x 200 mm	25
200 x 250 mm	20

As a general rule, add on 10% to allow for cuts and breakages.

involved, it is a good idea to fill them with water or somebody before sealing them around the edges.

MDF

Joinery details such as picture rails, dados and other mouldings have traditionally been made from timber, but if you intend to paint them you are much better off using MDF (medium-density fibreboard). It has many advantages over wood: it doesn't split and warp or contain knots, and therefore you don't have to spend time searching for good, usable bits at the timber yard.

Once fixed in position it doesn't shrink (provided that it hasn't been left out in the rain beforehand), and you don't have to go around afterwards filling the gaps in with woodfiller before painting it. It has, in fact, only one drawback: being made from compressed particles, if it is cut using an electric saw, the ultra-fine dust flies everywhere and is a possible risk to health. This tends only to be a problem in manufacture, where large quantities of the material is being moulded, but on-site it is worth taking care and wearing a fine gauze mask – if you're carving it up with an electric jigsaw, for example, the dust particles can result in irritation to the skin, eyes and nose.

Heating

In the vast majority of extensions the heating system is simply extended from the house, but care should be taken to ensure that the boiler has sufficient capacity (rated output) to cope with any new radiators. Heating controls are best provided for by thermostatic radiator valves (TRVs), but for optimum control they should be used in conjunction with a roomstat. Water pipes should be accessible, and where they are buried in the floor finishes, ducts with removable covers should be used to house them.

Radiators are measured in terms of rated output (usually in watts, but also in Btu/h) rather than in dimensional size, although the two are related. This output is based upon a hot-water temperature of 80°C in the radiator and a room temperature of 20°C. A calculation is made as to the output needed to heat each room, based on its size and insulation, and from there the radiators can be sized. An experienced heating engineer will be able to advise you in this respect.

If you have a computer, some radiator manufacturers now produce software which will calculate and specify radiator sizes for you. I have recently tried a free DOS version from one leading manufacturer, and found it to be both easy to use and most helpful.

For bathrooms, a radiator which includes a towel rail in one unit is a good choice, as it allows towels and clothes to hang in front of the panel and be warmed without blocking the heat to the rest of the room.

Notching joists for pipes

Water pipes are often run across floor structures beneath the boarding; to do this, the timber joists have to be notched to let in the pipes. Joists should always be notched from the top edge to a depth no greater than one eighth of the joist depth. In package timber-frame construction the floorboarding is

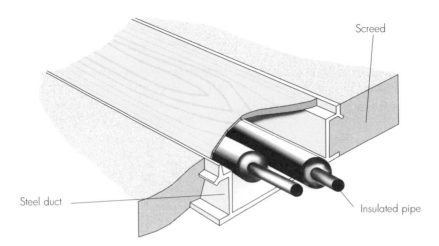

Pipe duct laid within screed.

often fixed down once the joists are built in, making it impossible for the plumber to notch in his pipes from the top. In these situations it must be done from below, but the timber-frame designers should have allowed for this in the joist design. The notches should be cut between 1/14 and 1/4 of the span in from the wall-bearing ends.

Where gas appliances are involved, a CORGI (Council of Registered Gas Installers)-approved gas fitter should be employed. Like the IEE for electricians, this is the governing body for plumbers working with gas, and again like the IEE, membership is voluntary – it is down to the consumer to check that tradesmen are registered.

A wide range of boilers is currently available for mains gas, bottled gas (propane), oil and solid fuel. At time of writing, heating oil is the cheapest fuel, so oil-fired condensing boilers are the

most efficient and hence the cheapest to run. But the price of oil has been suddenly affected before now, and the same could happen again in the future.

If you are installing a new boiler to serve your newly extended home, you can do no better than to select a condensing combination boiler. This kind operates on an efficiency of around 85% compared to that of the standard boiler at 72%, meaning that less heat is wasted and thus smaller fuel bills arrive.

Combination boilers have two drawbacks: one is the initial outlay, and the other is that they are much bigger than the ordinary boiler since they contain a built-in hot-water vessel. Apart from being super-efficient, they also provide you with unlimited hot water on demand, without having to wait for the tank to refill. Because of this, they require no cold-water storage tank either, and are ideal for properties with

137

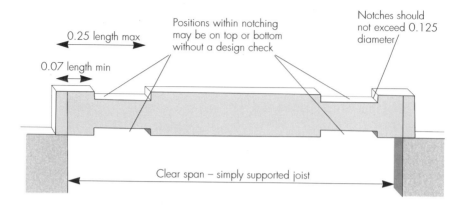

0.25 length max

0.07 length min

Positions within notching may be on top or bottom without a design check

Notches should not exceed 0.125 diameter

Clear span – simply supported joist

Notching limits of joists for pipes.

a restricted roof space.

If you do select a more conventional system, a balanced-flue boiler should still be a priority. These boilers draw their combustion air in from the outer ring of the flue and release exhaust products through the centre. Consequently, they are room-sealed and require no air supply to the room in which they are situated.

Balanced flues obviously need an outside wall, but the flues can be extended in length when they are fan-assisted; recently, vertical ones which can pass through a roof have been developed. Care needs to be taken about where any flue outlet occurs on the outside. It should be away from a window opening, and certainly not beneath one. It should also be sited where a free passage of air will pass over it, and not tucked into a corner or recess.

The Gas Installation Regulations cover all aspects for gas appliances, but in addition the Building Regulations

cover appliances of all fuel types, and manufacturers produce extremely comprehensive installation guides.

Flued boilers and appliances other than balanced ones need combustion air to the room in which they are installed. The greater the rated output of the appliance, the greater the amount of air it will need. This air supply should be permanent and over and above the needs of habitable room ventilation, background ventilation and extractor ventilation. Take care when installing extractor fans in the same room.

Open fires

The fireplace is making a bit of a comeback. When central heating became popular in the early 1960s it almost became extinct, but in the 1980s people came around to thinking that the blank wall in the lounge where the fireplace used to be was lacking a feature. So the fireplace surround reappeared, at first as ornamentation, usually with a flame-effect gas fire in the middle, but now once again as a real fire with a working chimney. Brick chimneys give a bit of character to the appearance of a house, and many new homes today are built with them, to be used as a secondary means of heating.

If your extension includes a lengthy lounge or dining room that is crying out for such a feature, hopefully you will have thought about it before now. Chimneys need a foundation support, and the fireplace itself needs a constructional hearth formed over the floor structure.

Traditionally, brick piers known as jambs are built out either side of the fireplace, and a breastsummer (bresummer) beam or mantelpiece is formed over the top. The hearth projects out about 600 mm in front of these piers and returns about 150 mm or more within them. This enables the open-fire basket to be situated back in the hearth, and any hot coals or logs that fall out will not set fire to the floor covering. Of course, this arrangement only becomes necessary when solid-fuel fires are proposed.

A 19th-century adage goes, 'To talk of architecture is but a joke, 'til you can build a chimney that won't smoke.' It still rings true today, as even the most architecturally designed fireplaces have disappeared under a blanket of smoke once lit. If it is to draw properly, a chimney must be designed with a few basic scientific principles in mind. First, a good supply of air is needed at the bottom, and this is best achieved by ducting pipes through the hearth or floor from external air bricks and bringing them up inside the hearth itself.

One on the inside of each jamb would be good. They can be finished with some brass hit-and-miss vent grills for architecture's sake, and can also be closed for comfort's sake. Second, the same thought must be given to the other end, the pots and the prevailing wind across them. The chimney's position on the roof will make a lot of difference to whether the fire works or not.

Underfloor heating

Underfloor heating is also becoming popular again. In the 1960s it was tried in the shape of unpopular electric heating built into the concrete floors of blocks of flats, with the result of making them highly inefficient from an energy-conservation point of view, and prone to giving the occupants athlete's foot.

Today's underfloor heating is in the form of narrow plastic water pipes laid in loops within the floor covering and, most importantly, above the insulation. They can be embedded in the floor screed (with the water authority's consent) or laid beneath a floating floor of chipboard on insulation. The heat radiates from the whole floor, instead of from the usual isolated wall radiators, making it more efficient. On average an output of around 100W per square metre is achieved, giving a floor temperature of about 29°C and an ambient air temperature of around 20°C. There are no particular restrictions to the type of floor covering you can use, but if you plan on a ceramic or stone-tiled floor throughout the extension, an underfloor heating system could be just the thing, keeping it warm to walk on in winter but cool in summer.

The manufacturers of these systems generally offer a supply-and-fix service. It is quite costly compared to conventional central heating, but should prove to be a much more efficient way to heat your extension if thermostatic room sensors are used to control the temperature.

Soil and waste plumbing

Waste pipes are only effective up to certain lengths dependent on their diameter (see table below), after which they require some additional help from anti-siphon traps, air-admittance valves or vent pipes added to the run.

Soil vent pipe (SVP) is the name given to the main vertical drainpipe which collects the above-ground foul drainage and discharges it to the below-ground system. The SVP provides the whole drainage system with fresh air, and so it should be located at the head of the drain run on the house. Air-admittance valves (AAVs) are no substitute for SVPs, since they do not provide permanent ventilation to the drains. They are instead designed to relieve excess pressure from the system, allowing extra appliances to be fitted around the house.

AAVs are not suitable for outdoor use where they may freeze in winter, but they can be used in cold loft spaces where polystyrene caps may be fitted to them. These consist of a rubber diaphragm which is normally sealed shut, but opens to relieve pressure and admits air into the system before closing again. The SVP is a permanent air vent to the system, and must be terminated outside and well above any window openings to prevent foul smells from

PIPE DIAMETER (and use)	MAX LENGTH of unvented pipe
32 mm (sink or basin wastes)	1.7 m
38 mm (sink, basin, bath or shower wastes)	3 m
50 mm (as above)	4 m

NOTE: the fall of the pipe should be between 18 and 90 mm per metre in all instances above.

100 mm (one WC)	6 m

NOTE: the fall of the pipe for WC wastes should be at least 9 mm per metre.

entering the house.

Plumbers sometimes overlook two elements in waste drainage. The first is the provision of sufficient rodding eyes on bends in the pipework; these are removable screw caps which give access for cleaning out blockages; the second is insufficient support to pipes. Plastic pipes have a tendency to sag over time, and clips should be fixed to walls at least every 500 mm to support them.

As with below-ground drains, plumbing should be tested once all the appliances have been installed, to check for any leaks.

There are on the market a number of quick- or easy-fit WC pan connectors. My experience of these is the same as anything else in plumbing that is fitted quickly – they are quick to leak and often need refixing.

Drains testing

Where an SVP is involved this should be an air test, using rubber-sealed drain plugs at the top of the SVP and the first manhole connection to seal the system airtight. The air pressure can then be checked using a manometer or by carefully filling a connecting WC pan with water – if the system is airtight the water level in the pan will remain constant and not drop away. The latter is something of a pressure balancing act and requires that all traps are water-sealed and that no open pipes (e.g. for washing-machine connections) exist. This method will tell you if there is a hairline crack in the ceramic pan itself, which would otherwise go unnoticed.

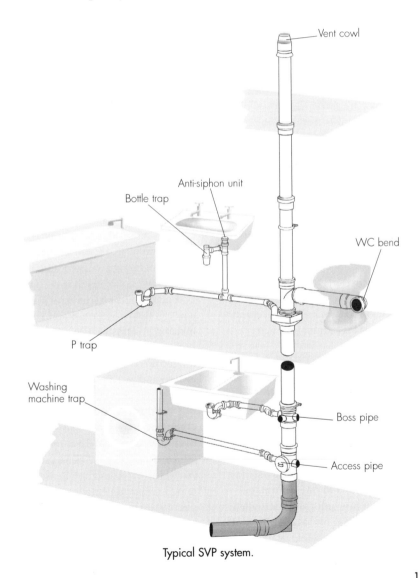

Typical SVP system.

Drain plugs and manometers can bought or hired from some builders' merchants, but tests are better carried out by the person who installed the system and witnessed by the Building Control Officer – this is a statutory inspection with one day's notice, so don't let your plumber forget to invite the BCO. AAVs should be left in position during an air test, since they should be sealed airtight if they are working properly (this is a good way to find out if they are not – before the bad smell arrives). SVPs are fitted with cowls on the top to stop birds from nesting on them, but if your plumber insists on solvent-welding them in position, make sure that the system has been tested first or you won't get the plug in without sawing the cowl off.

Do not attempt to water-test a SVP – once the pipe rises above a metre or so, the pressure can force the joints to leak. A 3 m-high SVP filled with water will exert undue pressure on the joints and risk flooding the house.

Any test on a drainage system should hold up for at least three minutes.

WCs

A standard PVC-U 110 mm-diameter WC branch pipe connecting to a SVP requires a fall of only around 1:100 (10 mm per metre) to work properly. If, however, you are faced with the desire to install a WC suite in a remote area where you can't connect to the existing drainage, there is still one option: an electric macerator unit can be installed. Without getting too biological, the units work on the same principle as a food blender, liquidising solids before

pumping them through a 25 mm pipe full-bore to the SVP. So long as you can get a pipe this size to the existing drainage, you can install a WC anywhere – well almost; they rely on the electric supply, so you can't install one in the extension if you haven't got a conventional gravity-drained WC somewhere in the house.

If you live in an area so remote that you have no suitable water supply or means of foul-water disposal, a chemical closet may be your only option. Environmentalists have tried to push home the benefits of composting closets: here, effluent from the chamber would be pumped into the garden or a reed bed, while the compost from the chamber would be used directly on the soil to improve its condition. Alas, the idea goes so dramatically against the concept of health in the built environment that it doesn't yet stand a chance of being accepted under the Building Regulations in this country.

One of the simplest ways in which you can help conserve water is to install a low-flush WC with a reduced capacity of 6 litres per flush. It is no longer possible to buy a new 9 litre cistern and put a brick (or a water hippo) in it anyway.

Dual-flush WCs, as seen on the continent, have proved unsuccessful over here. The dual-flush mechanism allows you to choose between a full cistern of water and a half cistern, depending upon your needs. However, people just kept flushing them until they got a satisfactory result, which sort of defeated the object. Of course, even if you don't have a water meter fitted, saving water makes a lot of sense, and we may not be able to wait for legislation to save us from water shortages. I'm not convinced by low-flush WCs either; is it a coincidence that the boys and girls at the BSI calculated years ago that 9 litres of water is not only the right amount to clear a WC pan efficiently but also the right amount to put out a 'standard' fire? – those red water-filled fire extinguishers hold exactly 9 litres too. The Water Regulations 1999 have now made low-flush 6-litre cisterns the new standard.

Showers

Still on a water-conservancy theme, showers are meant to be less water-demanding than baths – although it depends on how long you stay under them – but if you are installing a shower, give some thought to the hardness of the water in your area. In my locality, for example, the water is extremely hard and chalky, which has a quick effect on lime-scaling appliances. Electric showers may be cheaper than mixer ones, but in an area like this they are soon useless.

Before you decide on what type of shower to buy, you need to ask yourself a few basic questions. First, do you have a hot-water cylinder in the house (look in the airing cupboard)? If you don't, you may have a combination boiler that heats the water instantaneously – these boilers are ideal for serving mixer showers. If you do have a hot-water cylinder and the water is hard, you can still go for a mixer shower, providing your cylinder holds enough hot water for you. If there isn't enough pressure for your liking, consider power showers that pebble-dash your body up to a pressure of 1.2 bar via a powerful pump. You obviously need a decent-size cylinder to provide the water for one of these if you don't have a combination boiler.

If you prefer a more comfortable shower, take account not only of how much water it delivers per minute and at what pressure, but also of the thermostatic controls available for regulating the temperature. Some will also have an automatic shutdown which will turn it off in the event of either the hot or cold water supply failing, preventing you from getting an unwelcome surprise. These features are important, particularly where young children or the elderly are resident.

Shower trays themselves are commonly available in three materials: acrylic, which tends to be too thin and bows when you stand on it, ceramic, which is a good deal more solid and expensive, and a stonecast material that offers rigidity at a cheaper price.

Finding the right shower door may not be as easy as it seems; a vast array of different styles and opening methods are available. Ensure that the glass is toughened, and if you can avoid the bi-fold ones do so, since they have a reputation for being prone to leaking.

As an option to ceramic tiling, preformed shower panels can be fixed in position complete with soap dishes and the like. These could prove beneficial if the walls around your shower are timber stud rather than masonry. Glazed tiling can be done over plasterboarding, but I'd recommend exterior-grade plywood behind the shower tiles for a timber studwork wall.

Garden taps

Building an extension usually presents the ideal opportunity to install a garden tap. If a kitchen wall with units to hide pipes behind isn't available, the pipework can be run hidden through floor ducts. Wherever the pipes run, there should be a stop valve at the connection, allowing the tap to be isolated and drained in cold weather.

DIY shops have a number of cheap outdoor-tap installation kits on offer, and building an extension gives you the ideal opportunity to avoid them. Often the fittings are so poorly made that you will need to use a lot of PTFE tape and spare olives before you can get everything watertight. Go for quality fittings from the plumbing section or a specialist merchant instead.

10 Expert Points

HERE ARE TEN EXPERT POINTS TO CONSIDER BEFORE FITTING-OUT YOUR BATHROOM:

1 LAYOUT
Consider a layout of appliances that will maximise space and meet your needs. A 'back-to-the-wall' WC, which encases the cistern in a false half-height wall, will also provide a useful shelf above it. Some sanitaryware manufacturers produce cut-outs or templates that will help you to plan the bathroom layout.

2 STORAGE
Setting the hand basin into a vanity unit will provide useful cupboard space beneath the basin.

3 LIGHT
Create additional light and the effect of space with mirrors. Be generous with window sizing if you can, and consider stained or painted glass as well as the obscured variety.

4 FLOORING
Choose a floor covering that is comfortable, splash-resistant and cleanable.

5 EXTRACTOR FAN
If you have a window in your bathroom, make sure that your extractor fan has a humidistat control instead of a switch that comes on with the light, and locate the fan on the opposite side of the room.

6 TAPS
If you have children, consider using the single-lever-type taps with pre-set temperature levers. Modern water cylinders can store extremely hot water!

7 SHOWER
Choose a shower that is compatible with your water quality and your hot-water system.

8 PLAN YOUR PIPES
Agree the layout of appliances with your plumber before setting it in stone – you can only do so much with water and waste pipes.

9 ACCESS TO PIPEWORK
If you want to box in all the pipework, make sure that the boxing is removable, at least in places for maintenance and access to rodding eyes.

10 FLOORS BENEATH BATHS
If you have an original cast-iron bath, it is worth giving some thought to the floor structure beneath it. This may need strengthening or in the worst circumstances, a complete rethink.

Plumbers and heating engineers

In the same way that hygienists have evolved from dental nurses, heating engineers have evolved from plumbers. Indeed, plumbing seems to be becoming more specialised all the time. Now there are gas fitters, CORGI-registered plumbers, plumbers who just do water pipes and waste drainage, plumbers who don't do leadwork, and plumbers who just do central heating – otherwise known as heating engineers.

The reason for this is electrics: central heating has become high-tech over the last decade or so, with sophisticated programmers and boiler-energy management systems, and so the plumber has either had to allow himself to be cross-bred with an electrician or left out of the heating business altogether. It is easy to see why consumers are confused, but choosing the wrong plumber can have disastrous consequences – leaks may not appear instantly, but some time after the plumber has been paid and gone.

I may once again be guilty of over-generalising, but there are plenty of plumbers around who regard digital programmers only as pretty neat places to hang their caps while they set about your rising main with a pipe wrench.

If you are given the opportunity to inspect a plumber's previous work before engaging one, the first thing to do is to make straight for the airing cupboard and look for neatness in the piping. Poor plumbing invariably looks like spaghetti, and a tidy arrangement around the hot-water cylinder, pump and diverted valve is an indication of conscientious, quality work.

Stairs

If your extension is so comprehensively designed that you are planning to install a new staircase between floors, you need to be aware that stairs are covered quite enthusiastically by Building Regulation requirements and other standards – understandably so, as they are dangerous places.

One notable change was made in 1992, when the stair-width requirement for homes in England and Wales was scrapped and left to people to decide for themselves. The standard width is still 800 mm, and although you are free to reduce it, doing so may present problems when it comes to bringing the furniture upstairs. In restricted spaces, such as those forming access to loft conversions, stairs are often only 600 mm wide and frequently of an alternating-tread nature.

Space-saving stairs like these have paddle-shape treads, which means that you have to start off on the correct foot if you are going to make it to the other end in one piece. Treads are referred to as 'goings', and the vertical distance between them as 'risers'. The overall going is thus the total length of the stairs on plan, and the overall rise is the total height. The standard UK staircase bought off the shelf has a 42° pitch, which, by a curious coincidence, has always been the maximum pitch that has been allowed.

Allied with this, each individual riser shouldn't exceed 220 mm and the minimum for each going is 220 mm. The relationship required between the treads and the risers also means that twice the riser plus once the going should be

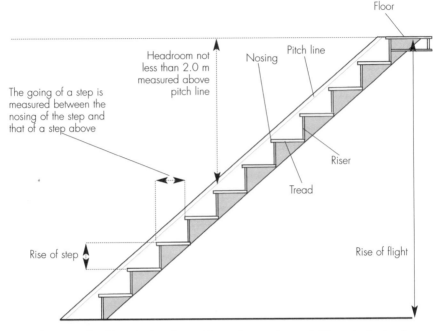

Floor

Headroom not
less than 2.0 m
measured above
pitch line

Nosing

Pitch line

The going of a step is
measured between the
nosing of the step and
that of a step above

Riser

Tread

Rise of step

Rise of flight

The going should not be less than 220 mm for a stairway (225 mm in Scotland).

between 550 mm and 700 mm.

In the case of space-saving stairs, the treads are measured by alternate nosings so that they now comply with the regulations (when they were first invented they didn't, and people wishing to use them were obliged to seek a relaxation of the regulations). Because they are much steeper and more hazardous, they require a handrail on both sides and should only be used as a last resort to gain access to a loft room when nothing else will fit. A fixed ladder would be a safer solution, since it requires you to go down backwards. A space-saving, alternate-tread staircase kids you into thinking you can still go down it forwards, even if you can't. Not only that but, like all open-riser stairs, they can't be carpeted and are left with

polished wood treads to slip on.

Some minor changes in floor level can be designed more freely (without the need for handrails and balustrades) when extending split-level rooms.

Steps which climb less than 600 mm are not considered to present a significant risk, and are thus exempt from most controls.

Landings at the top of stairs are considered to be more important than those at the bottom. A landing at least the width of the staircase in depth should be provided at the top, but at the bottom the depth may be reduced. A fall down a staircase is likely to produce a severe injury at the bottom if you hit a wall or door, and a spacious landing would be an advantage at both ends. In both cases, doors should not open out on to a landing, but should be hung the opposite way into the room.

The headroom on stairs is important. With your eyes watching where your feet are going, it is easy to clonk your head on a low bulkhead or beam. Headroom should be at least 2 m, but if you are taller than this you might want to make life easier for yourself. This height is measured vertically from any tread or nosing on the stair, and also applies to the landings at the top and bottom. If you are building in a new staircase in an old property with low ceilings, beware of extending the floor levels.

Handrails need only to run down one side of a stair, unless it is over 1 m wide, in which case you should have one on each side. They should be positioned at a comfortable height – around 900 mm from the pitch line of the stairs.

Balustrading of stairs has in the past caused some problems, particularly where children are concerned. As a result of the little darlings getting their heads stuck between balusters and railings, a spacing of less than 100 mm shouldn't exist between them; this applies whether they are horizontal, vertical or diagonal. Balustrading to stairs should be at 900 mm height, and outside, where it protects the edge of a roof or a balcony, this is increased to 1.1 m height. Horizontal 'ranch-style' balustrading should be avoided since it is readily climbable by children.

Balustrading is meant to be more than ornamental, and should be strong enough to resist the weight of a person leaning against it. To achieve this, newel posts are normally used. They may also be structurally employed to support the floor-joist trimmings around the stairwell opening, and if this is the case, they will need to be oversized or treated to achieve the fire resistance required.

Speaking of fire, there is one final but important thing you should know about stairs, and this involves knowing where to position them. It may be rather traditionalist, but a staircase is best located in a hall or reception lobby, where it leads directly to the front door, not in a habitable room, and definitely not in a kitchen. Coming down the stairs with the house on fire, you really want to find the door right in front of you. This arrangement is considered sacrilege from a Feng Shui point of view, where some bad vibes may be generated by such a layout – but if your stairs lead down into the open-plan house or room on fire, consider how much ill-feeling you will have with the flames licking around your feet and the door on the other side of them.

Spiral or helical stairs

These types make a stair into an architectural feature, and are often very ornate. They do carry a few problems which need to be overcome before being installed, but they are still an attractive option.

Unless you are replacing a staircase in an original opening (stairwell), a secondhand spiral stair bought from an architectural salvage yard is unlikely to comply with the standards required of it in a new extension. Don't buy one unless you are sure that it does. Spiral and helical stairs take up a lot more room, and require a sizeable stairwell

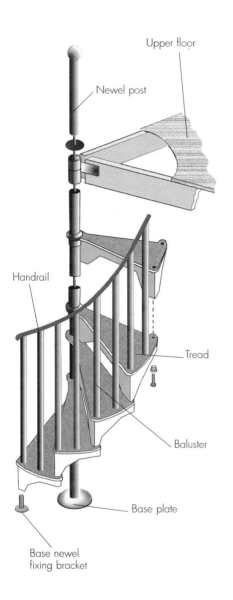

Upper floor

Newel post

Handrail

Tread

Baluster

Base plate

Base newel
fixing bracket

Exploded view of a spiral stair case
supported on an integral central newel post
which means that it does not need to be
positioned against a wall.

opening in the floor. Bear this in mind when designing the floor structure.

Because spiral stairs are supported from an integral centre newel post, they don't need to be located against a wall, and instead are often positioned centrally in rooms. This has the effect of making the room above an 'inner room' for fire-escape purposes. New rooms up there will need escape-size windows if no other stair is available (see Chapter 5). Landings are often odd-shaped at the top and bottom, so beware of doors and other obstacles.

Make sure that the stair complies with BS5395 : Part 2 (Code of Practice for the Design of Helical and Spiral Stairs). This is proof that it will meet the Building Regulations. Some manufacturers offer intricate and ornate balusters, which may not meet the requirement for preventing a 100 mm sphere from passing through the gaps. This is part of BS5395, so double-check with them that it complies before you order. Look for treads which offer some slip resistance.

Kitchens

For many people, planning the fitted kitchen is the high point of building the extension – it may even be the reason for building the extension.

If you are about to start work on planning the kitchen, stop for a moment and ask yourself one question: what sex am I? For most of us this question will be easily answered, but if the answer is male, you might like to consider whether you're the right person for this job. I may have strayed well off the path of political correctness at this stage, but in my experience men have little idea how to lay out a kitchen. Where they have done so without consulting the lady of the house, major alteration works to the extension have followed – doors being moved, drains being extended, and so on. Kitchen design seems to cause a good deal of angst.

The country is awash with fitted-kitchen specialists, hard-selling their range long after the double-glazing people have gone home. Kitchens are easily sold because people want them – they are enticed by the fashion of kitchens hot from the pages of the glossy home magazines, with their glass display units, open-ended niches and half-carousel corner units. And it is these little finishing touches, small though they may be, that boost the price and make the profit for the fitted-kitchen people. If everybody just bought the basic chipboard units without the solid-

10 Expert Points

HERE ARE TEN EXPERT POINTS TO BEAR IN MIND WHEN PLANNING YOUR KITCHEN:

1 HEIGHTS
Make sure that you record the ceiling height and heights of windows, cill positions, etc.

2 PIPES AND PROTRUSIONS
Note the position of pipes, boilers, ducts and other protrusions on the plan, particularly water-supply pipes to the sink and washers.

3 SERVICES
Make sure that your services are correctly positioned and marked for light points and fans (fused isolator switch). Watch out for last-minute extras like waste disposal and under-unit lighting.

4 COOKER POSITION
Never locate a cooker directly beneath a window, beside a sink bowl, or where there isn't a worktop space either side of at least 300 mm.

5 FRIDGE/FREEZER POSITION
Never locate a fridge or freezer directly next to a cooker.

6 WALL-CUPBOARD POSITIONS
Never locate a wall unit directly above a cooker or hob. Consider whether wall-unit positions will obstruct natural light from a window, and if necessary consider slimline depth units. Wall units should not be positioned directly above sink units; even slimline units will interfere with your eyeline.

7 APPLIANCES
Mark the sizes and positions of your appliances in relation to power points and vents.

8 DOOR SWINGS
Consider door swings on all cupboards, and decide whether left- or right-hand hinges are required.

9 MEASUREMENTS
Take your own measurements so you can check the designer's against them. Always measure in metric.

10 ROUGH SKETCH
Use graph or squared paper and work in pencil at first. Alternatively, decide on how much cupboard and drawer space you need, and make scale cut-outs in card that can be moved around between appliances.

Computer aided kitchen design.

wood door fronts or the fancy cornicing, the fitted-kitchen specialist would soon be out of business. But on the whole, we all like a neat, streamlined kitchen where even the appliances are hidden behind the doors and you have to play a game of Pelmanism every time you want to find the fridge-freezer.

If this sounds a little stung, it's because I'm having a kitchen fitted as I write. You, on the other hand, need not trouble yourself with the total refit specialist who will rewire and replumb your existing kitchen, because you have planned your extension and installed the services precisely where you need them. And you can purchase the kitchen you want from a supply-only merchant and fit it yourself or employ your carpenter/joiner to fit it for you. This has

to represent a substantial saving. One thing, though, make sure that the kitchen supplier visits the site and measures up, once the finishings are on, for themselves. Let them design it based on their measurements and not yours. When it doesn't fit, you are going to need somebody to blame.

Allowing for the fact that your supplier is going to measure and design to your needs, you will want to do some planning yourself beforehand to ensure that you get what you want.

Insulating the roof void

Laying glassfibre insulation in roof voids is generally considered to be the worst job in the industry, one which traditionally is given to the trainee, apprentice or gofer. While the manufacturers swear that the product doesn't carry a health risk, most people's skin takes an instant dislike to the stuff, and breathing in the fine airborne particles in large quantities is not going to do you any good at all. Always wear gloves and a fine gauze face mask when handling it with care.

Since reducing heat loss through the roof is so important, you should take the opportunity to upgrade the insulation in the existing part of your loft as well. Old insulation is often contaminated with dust and dirt so it is best gathered carefully up into tie-up refuse sacks before it is taken out and replaced with new material to current standards.

Flat roofs and sloping ceilings are permitted a reduced standard of insulation due to the constructional difficulties. This can currently be achieved by using 100 mm of phenolic or polyurethane foam insulation between the joists and another 75 mm over. Glass fibre is now no longer practical given the excessive thickness it requires.

In a normal loft space, two layers of glassfibre quilt totalling 400 mm laid between and over the ceiling joists will achieve a 'U' value maximum of 0.16W per square metre/degree Kelvin but make accessing the loft very difficult. Two layers of 75 mm phenolic or polyurethane foam board laid between the joists will achieve the same, although at greater expense.

Be careful not to block roof vents with insulation. Special trays are available that allow the air over the top in the eaves where the fit becomes tight.

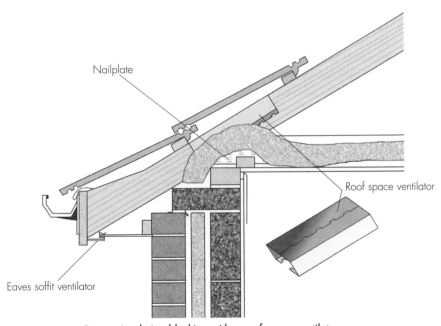

Nailplate

Roof space ventilator

Eaves soffit ventilator

Prevent insulation blocking with a roof space ventilator.

CHAPTER 7

External Work

External (weather) finishings

Remedial cavity trays

With a new single-storey extension butting up against a two-storey house, the existing external cavity wall becomes an internal wall at extension level but remains an external wall above it. With a brick cavity wall this presents a problem, as water can now track down the outer leaf from above to the inside of the house. To prevent this, a remedial cavity tray should be installed just above the abutment. This is quite a laborious job, and builders often shy away from doing it at all. Don't let them – it is an essential and worthwhile part of building an extension, and the job is now a lot easier with preformed cavity trays. These require no shoring or internal making good, as the work is done solely from outside, and they have the added benefit of being relatively inexpensive. Only two courses of brickwork have to be removed (using a conventional, flexible DPC to form this tray would mean cutting out four courses of brickwork), and the tray is fed in in sections with upstands at their ends. If your home is to remain weatherproof, this is a job that must be done before you cut the opening through to the house.

Weatherboarding (lap siding or clapboarding)

Timber weatherboarding can add a lot of character to the appearance of a home extension, and it need not be present on the existing house for it to look right. A two-storey extension with the first floor weatherboarded and the lower brick-faced can look very effective. From a maintenance point of view, if a good preservative is used the timber can last at least 60 years. Low-maintenance decorating, using woodstains or microporous paint, can help to reduce the cost of keeping up its appearance in the future.

Normal square- and feather-edged boards are only suited to horizontal

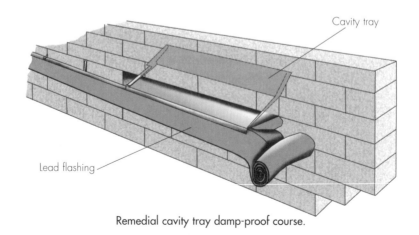

Remedial cavity tray damp-proof course.

boarding, but rebated versions of these can be equally weather-resisting when fixed diagonally. In these instances the overlap can be reduced to 20 mm from the normal 30 mm. Never nail boards through the lap, as this restricts movement and causes the timber to split. Galvanised annular ring-shanked nails are ideal for fixing the boards to timber battens (see Chapter 5).

Plastic (PVCU-E) boarding is becoming popular as a maintenance-free option to timber. It is made from extruded polystyrene and is usually employed as 'ship-lap' rebated boarding, although spin-offs with a cedar-wood-grain effect and a variety of colours have become available. The same material is marketed for replacement fascia boards and soffits, where it can be overfixed to the old timber ones or installed from new. As new fascia it lacks the structural strength of timber, and needs to be reinforced with plywood forms, particularly at the corners.

Cement-fibre products are sometimes also used for external cladding, with the advantage of having a much better resistance to fire spread than wood.

Tile hanging

Vertical tile hanging is done with plain rectangular tiles of either concrete or clay, or using special-shape clay tiles referred to as 'mathematical tiling'. Tile hanging is considered a maintenance-free alternative to timber boarding – since each tile is usually twice nailed to the tiling batten (unlike roof tiling, where a great variety of fixing specifications occur, right down to some situations where only the perimeter tiles

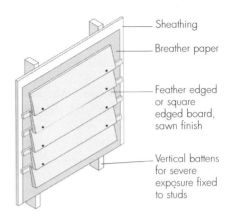

Sheathing

Breather paper

Feather edged or square edged board, sawn finish

Vertical battens for severe exposure fixed to studs

External wall with featheredged boarding shown on single-leaf timber-frame wall.

need nailing and all others can remain unfixed), it doesn't tend to suffer from wind damage. Most plain tiles are sized around 265 x 165 mm, and are suitable for vertical tile hanging as well as pitched roofing over 35°.

Because the gauge between battens is usually slightly greater in vertical

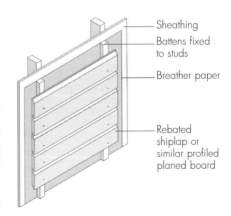

Sheathing

Battens fixed to studs

Breather paper

Rebated shiplap or similar profiled planed board

External wall with rebated shiplap shown on single-leaf timber-frame wall.

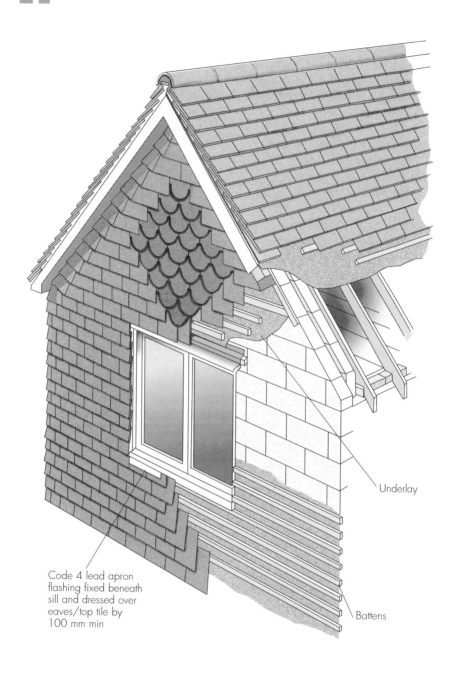

Code 4 lead apron
flashing fixed beneath
sill and dressed over
eaves/top tile by
100 mm min

Underlay

Battens

Tile hanging styles and method.

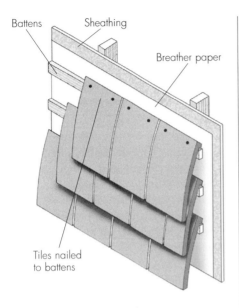

Battens   Sheathing

Breather paper

Tiles nailed to battens

External wall with tiling shown on single-leaf timber-frame wall.

Rendering should be at least 20 mm thick and applied in two coats. It should not be applied during very cold weather, when the frost will cause cracking before it has fully hardened. Forming a bell-drip bottom to the rendered wall at the DPC level is important, as it acts to kick the water out away from the vulnerable sub-DPC wall.

External painting

One drawback to outdoor painting in the UK is the weather: it is often too damp, humid, cold or even sometimes too hot for this job.

The damp and high humidity we suffer from for much of the year delay the drying process, and if the surfaces are also damp they prevent the paint

hanging, less tiles are used per square metre in this situation than on a roof. Vertical tile hanging also has the advantage of being able to utilise ornamental tiles to create a decorative feature that wouldn't be possible on roofs of less than 70° pitch – in other words, most roofs.

Rendering

Rendering the outside of a wall with cement and sand is one of the most effective ways of increasing weather resistance. In areas of extreme exposure, the coarser the grade of sand used, the better. In places such as the west and north of Scotland, a sharp sand render will provide better durability since it requires less water in the mix than a soft (fine) sand.

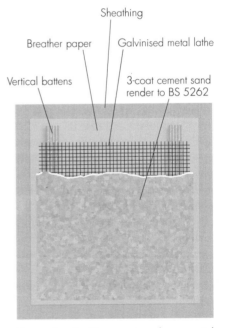

Sheathing

Breather paper   Galvinised metal lathe

Vertical battens   3-coat cement sand render to BS 5262

External wall with cement render on metal lathe shown on single-leaf timber-frame wall.

from adhering properly, leading to peeling. In the worst cases of humidity, such as fog, the paint may lose some of its gloss finish and can even discolour. Cold weather, like damp, slows down the drying process in addition to providing the painter with unpleasant conditions to work in, and hot weather can accelerate drying, causing the paint to blister and making it harder to apply.

What is ideal outdoor painting weather? Dry, preferably overcast, but bright and reasonably warm. In other words, don't plan it unless you have to – just wait for the right day to come along, be prepared, and get on with it. If you've built in timber windows and doors, they should have been primed or stained beforehand.

When applying extra primer, use a brushload, working it into the joints and corners before using a dry brush along the grain to finish it off. Wait for it to dry, and rub down with fine sandpaper. The undercoat should be applied in at least two layers, each one left to dry and sanded down gently before the next coat. With gloss, it is a case of experience to know how much can be applied before it starts to run, and how little can be applied before the brushstrokes disappear. You need a lot of patience to achieve a surface that is both smooth and even, as two or three coats may be necessary.

Masonry painting is often done with a highly durable water-based emulsion that sometimes contains silica or, in the case of some masonry paint, nylon reinforcement. With newly built or rendered walls, it is always necessary to seal the wall first by applying a stabilising solution. If you are painting new brickwork, salts in the clay may have caused it to effloresce, giving it a white, chalky appearance. This may be unsightly and annoying, but it isn't harmful and should wash off. Apply a stabiliser before painting.

Stabilisers seal the wall before you apply the paint; unfortunately, in doing so they can create a glossy surface to which the paint will not adhere. Thinning out the stabiliser with white spirit until the surface gloss is gone when dry is important if masonry paint is going to last.

Time spent in preparing the surface may seem disproportionate to that of painting it, but it is always worthwhile and will span out the length of time before redecorating becomes necessary.

Working from a scaffold tower is a lot safer than from a ladder. These sectional towers can be easily erected and taken down and are available from most builders' plant-hire centres.

Painting awkward surfaces

It is possible to paint plastic drainage pipes, which are only commonly available in unsightly grey or white (in fact, some pipe manufacturers recommend painting to prevent the effects of ultraviolet light from degrading the plastic), but there is one snag: polypropylene pipes are very smooth and shiny when new, and paint simply won't adhere to them. Even the specialised paint sold specifically for this purpose makes a point of having 'weathered plastic pipe paint' on the tin. If you can't wait for nature to do its worst, some fine-grade sandpaper may help to accelerate the process.

Cement-fibre boards are often used for soffit boarding at overhanging eaves. Their natural colour is grey, and cement fibre doesn't like paint. Even the toughest of external emulsions soon begins to peel off. You will only be able to properly coat it by priming it and using an acrylic latex paint.

If you take the opportunity to redecorate your existing fascia boards as well as the new extension's, make sure that you wet-sand the old paint down, rather than burning it off with a hot-air gun. The last two summers in my working district have seen roofs burnt down after hot-air guns had been used on bone-dry fascia boards. In the last incident, the fire spread to the neighbour's roof, destroying that as well.

Even if the roof isn't accidentally set alight, you may still be putting your health at risk by burning off old paint. Prior to 1960, paint contained lead, and burning or dry-sanding it can release a harmful dust. The Paintmakers Association has produced a guide leaflet for painters on how to remove old lead paint safely, which is available from the British Coatings Federation.

By far the most laborious external surface to paint is pebble-dash render. Given the rough stippled surface of pebble-dash or roughcast, there is no quick way to cover it, and the painter will have to resort to stippling on the paint slowly.

Landscaping

By this stage in the proceedings the ground directly around the extension is often compacted and dead – in other words, it is ideal for a path or patio. This presents no problem if it was planned in to start with, by reducing the ground level or raising the DPC position, but as an afterthought it can be a disaster. The finished surface of the patio or path needs to be at least 150 mm below the level of the DPC.

If your builders have taken the existing ground level as the finished surface, you probably won't have the room to raise it by hard-surfacing. Reducing this 150 mm gap will allow rain splashing to cause prolonged dampness that will eventually penetrate the wall. If are in this position, you must reduce the ground level before starting to lay any path or patio. If you are unable to do so, perhaps due to a nearby tree or to shallow drains, your only resort may be to set the hard surface well back away from the extension's walls and form a soft drainage channel of pea-shingle around the perimeter gap.

In any situation patios and paths should be graded away from the house to prevent water from lying against the walls, but an extra fall away in these cases would be beneficial.

In general, Planning Consent is not required for patios, paths or hard standings in domestic use, and so there is no limit to the area of land around your house that you can cover with hard surfacing unless you live in a Conservation Area, Special Interest Area or a Listed Building, in which case Planning Consent will be required.

Planting for security

There are some benefits in planting

HERE ARE SOME EXAMPLES OF GOOD 'SECURITY' SPECIES – AND ONE TO AVOID:

Firethorn (*Pyracantha*) will grow as a bush to around 4 m high and is armed with strong needles. It can also be trained up a wall.

Indigenous **hawthorn** (*Crataegus mongyna*) and **blackthorn** (*Prunus spinosa*) bushes can be used to form natural hedging in a rural location. Hawthorns can also be grown as trees up to 12 m high.

Japonica (*Chaenomeles*) are popular shrubs for their show of spring flowers, but many varieties are also thorned. *C. cathayensis* grows to around a spreading 3 m, and as well as having pink-tinged white flowers has fearsome spines.

Holly (*Ilex aquifolium*) is a typical hedgerow tree but can be grown separately as a shrub; in this, its natural form, the lower leaves are usually spiky, but not the upper ones. In the variegated forms, such as *I. altaclarensis*, however, the leaves are always rounded.

Blackberry (*Rubus fruticosus*) forms, as anyone who has been blackberry-picking will tell you, an impenetrable thicket of vicious spines. This plant can be grown rapidly over hedging, walls, rocks, anything. However, I think you would have to be a little mad to introduce it to your garden; it is aggressive and invasive at the rate of 50 mm a day!

Rambling roses may not be as thorny as their shrub cousins, but will still help to protect a fence or wall.

If you've been thinking height will help, avoid **Leyland cypresses** (*Cupressocyparis leylandii*) at all costs, as they have become the plague of the nation. Once popular for forming a rapid green fence in a few years, they have grown to become the subject of many a neighbourly dispute. Growing at a rate of 1.2 m a year, they will eventually achieve the height of 22.8 m, roughly four times higher than the average house.

Apart from blocking out the light, they are shallow-ball-rooted, and once mature may become unstable in high winds.

small trees and shrubs near your extension, as they provide shade and privacy as well as an attractive vista, but beware of planting anything too close that will grow to become a full-size tree (see Chapter 4). Even if you have a non-cohesive subsoil, a large tree growing a few metres from the house could put it at risk from storm damage or burglary.

From a security point of view, it is possible to deter intruders with the right planting. Plenty of sharp-thorned shrubs make ideal perimeter guards, and some are suitable as wall climbers.

Planting to reduce soil desiccation

With our climate becoming warmer and drier, hosepipe and sprinkler bans have become commonplace during summer. Most of the plants and shrubs we favour, particularly annuals, have a liking for plenty of water in the summer months. While established trees and shrubs can make do without, their roots will be encouraged to grow out further and deeper in search of water, increasing the risk of desiccation to the soil.

If foundations or drains are nearby, this shrinkage of soil can cause damage. Making sure that you avoid species that have a high water demand will help to reduce this risk of damage and increase your plants' chances of survival when water is scarce.

External lighting

If you have children or you just aren't keen on turning your garden into a botanical minefield, open space around the extension coupled with some external lighting could be the answer. A common sight these days is 500W tungsten-halogen floodlights with PIR (passive infrared) detectors mounted high up on house walls, which produce the effect of turning the neighbourhood into Wembley Stadium every time a cat walks by. Although this method is cheap, with care it should be possible to install security lighting with a bit more consideration than this.

PIRs can be positioned so they don't pick up passing traffic, and lights can be placed so that they illuminate only your garden. Mounting the light and sensor at around 2.5 m above ground level with the sensor tilted down will help to reduce the number of false activations. If you're near to a road or footpath, try to arrange the system so that it doesn't pick up on passing cars and people. Reflections from ponds or glass on bright, sunny days, and heat sources such as flue outlets can also start them off. Sensors can be installed remotely from the light itself, and some models can be adjusted so that their sensitivity is reduced.

Other external lights, such as those alongside doors or garden paths, can be both practical, in helping you find your way up to the front door and unlocking it, and architectural, in highlighting plants or garden features. They can be installed with daylight sensors (photoelectric cells) that activate them during darkness, but these tend also to operate when light levels are low, and since that accounts for several months of the year in the UK, they can be switched on unnecessarily. If you do install a photoelectric-cell-switched lamp, make sure that it is also connected to a plate switch inside the house so that it can be kept off when it isn't needed.

If you don't need lamps for security lighting, low-energy bulbs are best. They can easily provide enough light to find a keyhole for a quarter of the energy use, and they will last for up to ten times longer than a standard bulb. They are now available in a bulb shape, as well as the long tubular type, so they should fit any lamp.

Boundary fences and walls

How you treat the boundaries of your property can be a difficult subject. In some situations Planning Consent is

---

A SELECTION OF DROUGHT-RESISTANT TREES AND SHRUBS:

Birch (Betula)
Box (Buxus)
Broom (Cytisus)
Cabbage tree (Livistona australis)
Dwarf pine (Pinus mugo)
Japanese angelica tree (Aralia elata)
Holly (Ilex)
Pea tree (Caragana arborescens)
Privet (Ligustrum)
Strawberry tree (Arbutus unedo)
Yew (Taxus baccata)

These plants all have a low-water demand and, once established, will survive short periods of drought. Mixing in a mixture of gravel and coarse sand to the soil and mulching around the tree will help, particularly in clayey soils.

required, in others restrictive covenants can limit your options, but in most situations you are free to do as you wish. Since a wall or fence is a structure that cannot be easily moved once erected, it is important that you know where the boundary line is before you begin. Let your neighbour know what you intend to do, and make sure that the wall or fence doesn't trespass on their land.

Restrictive covenants and local authority planning controls often demarcate what can and cannot be erected in front gardens, particularly when they abut onto the highway. When your house was built, Planning Consent may have been given conditionally on the basis of maintaining sight lines or visibility splays to the road. These are prescribed zones of clear uninterrupted vision that allow motorists good visibility (many planning applications have an aspect of highway safety to be considered).

In these situations, even planting a new hedge may require a planning application, let alone erecting a fence or garden wall. It is possible to apply to submit an application to the planning authority to remove or relax the condition, but its success will be judged by the proposal's impact on road safety as well as visual amenity. If you live on an open-plan housing estate, the chances are that some restrictions will apply, at least in the front garden.

Other cases where a fence, wall or gate will need planning consent are:

- to a Listed Building.
- where it is over 2 m high (in Scotland, a Building Warrant should also be obtained).
- where it is next to a road (this may mean within 20 m) and is over 1 m high (this is not applicable to footpaths or bridleways).

The heights should be measured from the ground level next to the fence, wall or gate. Where the ground is uneven, you should take the highest point. In any case, always check with your local Planning Authority.

Building Regulations in England and Wales do not apply to garden walls or fences, except where they form protection to the house as a retaining wall. Nevertheless, unsafe garden walls are a danger, especially to children, and they should be constructed with care

---

THE FOLLOWING CAN BE TAKEN AS A ROUGH GUIDE TO BRICK WALL DESIGN FOR ALL BUT THE MOST EXTREME SITUATIONS OF EXPOSURE:

Half-brick-thick (100 mm) walls shouldn't exceed 600 mm height in sheltered locations; in exposed ones 400 mm is a safe limit (barely a wall at all). Use a 400 mm-wide concrete foundation.
One-brick-thick (230 mm) walls shouldn't exceed 1800 mm height in sheltered locations; in exposed ones 1100 mm is a safe limit. Use a 650 mm-wide concrete foundation.
One-and-a-half-brick-thick (330 mm) walls shouldn't exceed 2.5 m height in sheltered locations; in exposed ones 2 m is a safe limit. Use a 800 mm-wide concrete foundation.

Note that in Scotland a building warrant must be obtained from your local Building Control Authority for walls that are over 1.2 m high.

---

and regard to their location and exposure to the wind.

Protecting a garden wall by embedding broken glass or barbed wire in the top is not only crude but dangerous. First, a wall shouldn't be accoutred with anything unless it is over 2 m above ground level. Second, a method of protecting the wall that is less dangerous to cats and wildlife could be adopted; polyester-coated expanded-metal lathing can be secured flat to the top of the wall but turned up vertical on the risk face.

Any security measure should be installed as a deterrent to intruders – setting out to trap or injure them will leave you open to prosecution. An infamous case-law example of building-site security tells of a thief who was able to prosecute a builder for injuring him after he had broken into a site with the intention of stealing materials, only to fall into a hole that had been dug as a trap for him.

Rainwater drainage

Building Regulations require that rainwater drainage be designed to cope with at least 75 mm of rain in an hour. This is quite a deluge – the most intensive rainfall ever recorded in Britain was at Oxford in 1970, when 50 mm fell in 12 minutes. Even so, gutters and downpipes must be sized and positioned to remove this intensity of rainfall from the roof area.

Manufacturers of plastic gutters state that their polypropylene gutters are so frictionless that they will drain water even when laid level. This may be so, but given the structural and thermal

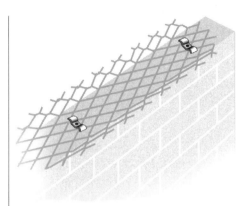

Wall protector made from polyester coated with expanded metal lathing.

movement of buildings, you would be advised to ensure a fall of 1:600 (25 mm in 15 m). Laying them to this fall will also increase the flow rate by around 20%, and will thus also increase the roof area that can be drained. A string line set along the fascia board is the best way to set out the brackets at 1 m centres to achieve this fall.

Some rectangular downpipes are designed to fit flush against the wall, thus making them unclimbable for intruders; if you were planning to use aluminium or cast-iron ones, it might be worth considering these; the standard plastic downpipe is usually flimsy enough to dissuade climbing for all but the slightest of burglars.

To prevent gutters from silting up, downpipes should be placed centrally along a run, rather than located at the ends. This also has a remarkable effect on the amount of roof area that can be drained through one downpipe – if it is placed in the middle with gutters falling to it from either side, the downpipe can

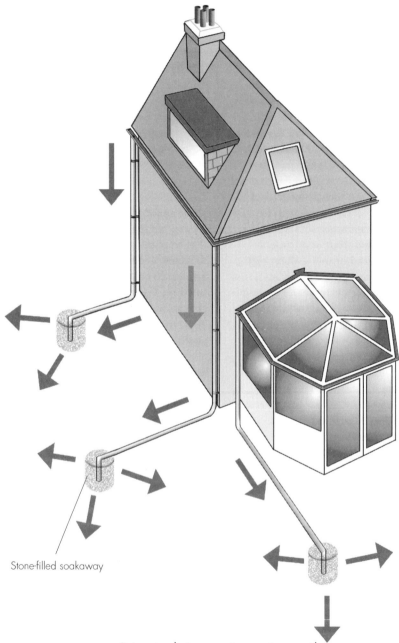

Stone-filled soakaway

Rainwater drainage system must cope with
at least 75mm of rainfall per hour.

carry twice the amount of water (and thus twice the roof area) than if it was stuck at the end of a run on a stop outlet. Downpipes should also be situated at least 2 m away from a corner angle (on a hip roof) for the flow rate to be maximised and for the roof to drain efficiently.

Manufacturers of rainwater drainage provide easy-to-read information on maximum roof areas for their different products. If this information isn't available at your builders' merchants, the suppliers' phone number should at least be, and they will no doubt be pleased to help.

Black plastic rainwater goods should be avoided, as they are subjected to a lot of thermal expansion in hot weather, and the sound of them creaking as they cool down can keep most people awake at night.

Standard half-round gutter widths have increased from 100 mm to 112 mm in the last decade or so, and you may experience difficulties in joining up the new with the old. Universal adapters may make the joint, but my experience of them is akin to that of other 'universal' fittings – they fit all makes roughly, but none of them perfectly. If you can discover the original gutter's manufacturer (most have their name printed on the goods), ask them to supply a purpose-made adapter.

Deep-flow gutters, although more expensive than the standard half-round type, will carry far more water (depending upon the design, up to more than double the flow capacity in litres per second), so if you have a shortage of rainwater pipe positions

available or a large roof area, these are for you.

Gutters need to be cleaned out regularly and should be accessible without having to use your neighbour's property as a ladder base. It is surprising how many extensions are built tight to the boundary, with the gutters overhanging next door.

In areas of heavy snowfall, gutter brackets should be increased in number to a maximum of 750 mm between centres. Additionally, roof snow fencing can be erected along the eaves, not only to prevent those sudden avalanches when somebody knocks on the door, but also to protect the gutters.

I have read about a device for heating gutters to prevent icicles and snow building up, a sort of a linear pond heater, but unless you live in the Highlands such a device is only likely to give you something to talk about at dinner parties.

When working out rainwater goods sizes, the effective roof area should be used. With pitched roofs, this means that the roof is measured on slope, not on plan view. Alternatively, you can measure off of your floor plans and multiply the area by these factors:

- roof pitch at 30°   plan area x 1.15
- roof pitch at 45°   plan area x 1.40
- roof pitch at 60°   plan area x 2.00

Satellite dishes

If you intend to 'plant' a satellite dish on to the side of your house, be aware that in some instances planning permission will be required. Those instances include the following:

- a satellite dish that is over 900 mm in diameter.
- a satellite dish that is installed so that it projects above the highest part of the roof.
- a satellite dish that is located in a Conservation Area and to an elevation that fronts onto a highway.

Note: permitted development laws are prone to change, and you must always check with your local planning authority before proceeding.

Cleaning up

You may not be surprised to see that there is some cleaning up to be done now that the works are complete, particularly outside the house. Brickwork that has been carelessly laid or laid during wet weather may now be splashed with mortar, and be looking quite scruffy, new glass will need the sticky labels removing, and an obsessive amount of hoovering may need to be done.

Obviously you can't make an omelette without breaking a few eggs, but on the other hand, it shouldn't have been necessary to smash dozens of them. It is possible for example to clear up broken bricks and hardened cement as you go – if nothing else, it makes the home a lot safer to work on and live in. It is reasonable to expect the builder to clean off any scruffy brickwork; this can be done with a wire brush and a specialized acid-based cleaner, combined with plenty of elbow grease.

Light fittings and smoke detectors should have been left protected until the work was totally finished (now is the time to test them), and any rubble or waste materials left over should obviously be cleared away from the job before it is practically complete.

Complete or not complete: that is the question

Completion of the work requires a Statutory Notice for Inspection to be sent to the Building Control Officer. Until the final inspection is done and a Completion Certificate has been issued, the work cannot be said to comply with the Building Regulations.

So at what stage can the work be certified as satisfactorily complete by Building Control? It is difficult, if not well-nigh impossible, to generalise, but certainly the insulation must be installed (often the loft space and pipework lagging is the last job to be done), and wall finishings of render, plaster, etc. must be to a finished coat. Any plumbing must be connected up to appliances (with the exception of washing-machine-type connections, where only the traps should be on).

Outside ground levels must be finished off to the right level below the damp-proof course (at least 150 mm); in Scotland the Electrical Installation Test Certificate must be submitted. The walls don't have to be decorated or have any internal painting done unless it is necessary for fire protection; external timber, window frames, doors and fascias, for example, will need to be painted or treated if they are to be weather-resistant.

You should also bear in mind that as a consumer, you are likely to have required a higher standard of workmanship or materials than the Building Regulations require; they are, after all, only the bare minimum considered acceptable for health and safety. If this is the case, then you will also to carry out a snagging inspection and draw up a list of any deficiencies requiring attention before the final bill is paid.

Once everything has been agreed, a satisfaction note should be prepared and signed by both you and your builder. If you have taken out warranty insurance on the work, as recommended, this satisfaction note will most likely have to be sent to the insurers, along with a copy of the final bill.

Since most of these warranties are based on a percentage of the contract sum, if there have been variations during the course of the work and the contract sum has increased from the original quote, it may be necessary to top up the insurance premium at this stage before a warranty certificate can be issued. Once issued, the warranty becomes effective for the duration of the period of cover, commonly ten years.

Both the warranty certificate and Building Control Completion Certificate should be kept in a safe place, along with any other approvals obtained for the extension. If in the future you wish to sell or remortgage the property, it will be necessary to disclose these documents for the conveyance to take place successfully.

As a matter of course, local land searches are made to local authorities during a conveyance, and these will reveal if the extension received planning consent and is in compliance with the Building Regulations. If the search takes place before the extension is certifiably complete, the local authority Building Control Officer should be contacted for an inspection. It may be possible for him or her to provide a list of defects or items that need completing, so that a buyer can be made aware of what is outstanding so that the sale need not be compromised or jeopardised.

For too many people, building a home extension has proved to be a stressful and regretful experience. In 1997, the home-improvement industry generated 93,000 complaints, which is even more than the secondhand car trade. This unfortunate record has prompted the government to look at ways of improving the standard of workmanship and customer care from builders, but undoubtedly whatever measures are introduced will not eradicate the problem entirely. As a home-owner, it is in your interest to look after and protect what is likely to be your life's biggest investment – your home.

Bear in mind also that increasing the property's value can often turn out to be a double-edged sword, since your Council Tax charge is partly dependent upon it – you may be delighted with your extension, but you may have just moved up a band at the same time! If you are unhappy about any such increase, there is a procedure for appealing against the valuation; your local authority will advise you. In addition, check to see whether your buildings insurance, which is based on the rebuilding costs, is still adequate, and increase it if necessary.

Basic House Construction

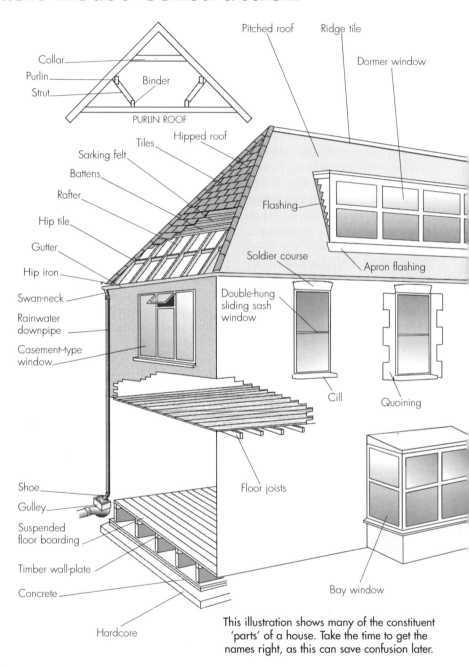

Collar

Purlin

Strut

Binder

PURLIN ROOF

Pitched roof

Ridge tile

Dormer window

Hipped roof

Tiles

Sarking felt

Battens

Rafter

Hip tile

Gutter

Hip iron

Swan-neck

Rainwater downpipe

Casement-type window

Flashing

Soldier course

Apron flashing

Double-hung sliding sash window

Cill

Quoining

Shoe

Gulley

Suspended floor boarding

Timber wall-plate

Concrete

Hardcore

Floor joists

Bay window

This illustration shows many of the constituent 'parts' of a house. Take the time to get the names right, as this can save confusion later.

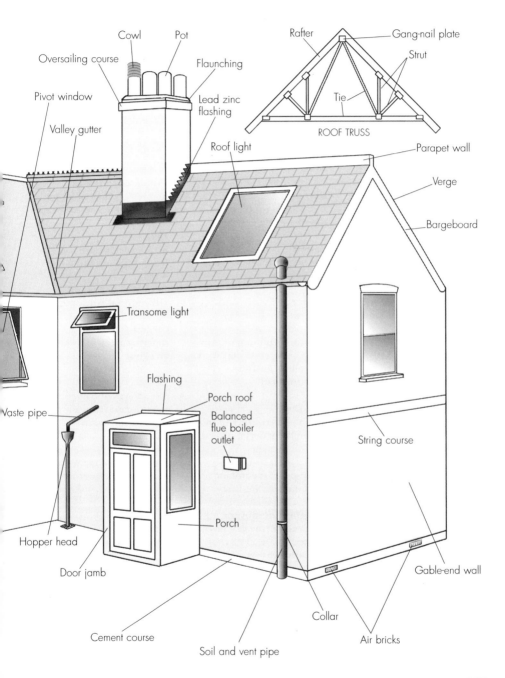

Cowl

Pot

Oversailing course

Flaunching

Pivot window

Lead zinc flashing

Valley gutter

Roof light

Rafter

Gang-nail plate

Strut

Tie

ROOF TRUSS

Parapet wall

Verge

Bargeboard

Transome light

Flashing

Porch roof

Balanced flue boiler outlet

String course

Waste pipe

Porch

Hopper head

Door jamb

Cement course

Soil and vent pipe

Collar

Air bricks

Gable-end wall

167

Glossary

AAV
Air-admittance valve. A valve device to relieve air pressure in above-ground drainage pipes.

Aggregate
Mixed with water and cement to form concrete, coarse aggregate is stone, and fine aggregate is sand. Together they form all-in ballast.

Air test
A test carried out on new drainpipes to see whether they leak.

Architrave
A decorative trim to cover the joint between a frame and a wall.

Ashlaring
A short studwork partition used to support rafters in room-in-the-roof construction.

Attic truss
A trussed rafter that allows the roof space to be used as a room or storage space by leaving it free of internal struts.

Background ventilation
A small amount of permanent but secure ventilation required for a room, often provided by trickle vents or crack positions on windows.

Balanced flue
A double-sleeved type of flue from a boiler or fire that is room-sealed, drawing in combustion air from the outer sleeve.

Ballast
A mixture of aggregates mixed with cement and water to form concrete.

Barge board
A decorative board fitted along the gable-end verge.

Barn hip
A small hip roof formed on top of a gable-end wall.

Batten
A slender timber to which coverings are fixed.

Binder
A longitudinal timber member in a roof structure, running on top of and perpendicular with the ceiling joists to support them.

Blinding
A nominal covering of sand or similar material placed over an oversite preparation before the damp-proof membrane and concrete are laid.

Breather membrane
A vapour-permeable layer applied to a wall or roof beneath weather-resisting coverings.

Breeze block
A name incorrectly given to all building blocks. Coke breeze blocks have not made in Britain since the late 1960s.

Cesspool
A sealed underground tank for storage of foul and waste water.

Combi boiler
A combination boiler which provides instantaneous hot water, omitting the need for a hot-water storage cylinder.

Condensing boiler
An energy-efficient boiler which recycles waste heat.

Dab
A spot of adhesive for fixing plasterboard to walls.

Differential settlement
Where different parts of the building settle at differing rates, causing cracking.

DPC
A damp-proof course incorporated in walls to resist rising damp.

DPM
A damp-proof membrane incorporated in ground-floor slabs to resist damp.

Eaves
The junction of a roof and an external wall.

Elastomeric membrane
An advanced flat-roof material that stretches but regains its shape.

Fascia
A horizontal decorative board fixed along the

rafter ends at the eaves, onto which gutters are usually fixed.

Flashing
A visible strip of material, usually lead, used to weatherproof a joint between a roof and another element.

Flitch beam
A structural beam comprising two timbers with a steel plate sandwiched between and bolted together.

Gable
A triangular-shape end wall between the sloping parts of a pitched roof.

Girder truss
A trussed rafter made up of two or more rafters fixed together to support a hip end or opening trimmer.

Going
The individual tread on a stair.

Hangar
A vertical timber member in a roof which is used to support ceiling joists by connecting between a ceiling binder and the ridge board.

Hardcore
The stone-and-brick rubble used to form an oversite preparation.

Heave
The uplift force caused by swelling of clay subsoil.

Helical stair
A spiral stair without a centre newel post.

Herringbone strutting
A row of criss-crossing struts between floor joists to stop them from twisting.

Hip end
The smaller end of a four-slope roof, as opposed to a two-slope gable-ended roof.

Humidistat
A device for measuring relative humidity as a switch for an extractor fan.

Interstitial condensation
Condensation formed within an element of the external construction, usually on the cold face of the built-in insulation layer.

Intumescent paint
Paint which expands when heated, forming a fire-protective cladding to steel or wood.

Intumescent strip
A strip of foam material which expands when heated, forming a seal around a fire door.

Joist
A horizontal timber member used in forming a floor, ceiling or flat roof.

Lateral-restraint strap
A horizontal metal strap used to tie in walls at roofs and floors.

Lintel
A short beam of steel or concrete over a window or door opening in a wall.

Low-e glass
Low-emissivity glass, coated for improved thermal insulation. Equal to triple glazing.

Marsh gas
Naturally occurring methane.

MDF
Medium-density fibreboard, a timber substitute for joinery.

Methane
A potentially explosive gas generated by decomposing matter from landfill sites.

Noggin
A small piece of timber used between other main structural timbers to stiffen them.

OSB
Oriented-strand board. A woodchip particleboard used as a cheaper alternative to plywood.

Oversite concrete
A ground-bearing concrete floor slab. The name 'oversite' is often given to the hardcore preparation beneath such a slab.

Pad-and-beam foundations
A special foundation system designed with reinforced concrete beams sitting on pads of concrete.

Padstone
A masonry or concrete bearing positioned beneath a beam to spread out the load through the wall.

Percolation test
A test for soakaways and septic tanks carried out on the subsoil to see how well water drains through it.

Pile foundations
A system of columns of reinforced concrete which support reinforced ground-beam foundations.

Polyurethane foam
A high-performance rigid insulation material.

Public liability insurance
Insurance taken out by a builder to protect him against action arising from injury or damage to a third party or their property.

Purlin
A longitudinal member which supports the rafters in a cut-and-pitch roof.

Quoin
A brick or stone face set in an external corner of a wall.

Radon
An inert natural radioactive gas present in certain geological conditions.

Raft foundations
A special reinforced-concrete foundation system, so-called because it floats at the surface, as opposed to excavating deep trenches for foundations.

Rafter
A sloping member which carries the battens and the roof covering in a pitched roof.

Rapid ventilation
Instant ventilation obtained by opening a door or window, or by an extractor fan.

Regularisation Certificate
A retrospective certificate issued as approval under the Building Regulations for work which did not have an application made at the time.

Rendering
A mixture of cement and sand applied to coat a wall. External types include roughcast, pebble-dash and stucco finish.

Ridge
The apex of a pitched roof.

Ring main
An electrical circuit for power points.

Riser
An individual vertical piece on a stair, the height of each step.

Rising main
A cold-water pipe taking water up to the storage tank.

Roof pitch
The angle of a pitched roof measured from the horizontal.

RSC
A rolled-steel channel-shape beam.

RSJ
A rolled-steel joist. The common name given incorrectly to any steel beam, but only relating to one, increasingly rare, type.

Septic tank
An underground tank for foul water where no sewer is available. Unlike a cesspool, a septic tank purifies the water through decomposition, allowing it to drain through irrigation pipes in to the ground. The tank still requires solids to be emptied.

Skew-nailing
A method of driving nails at an angle, often used in cut-and-pitch roof construction.

Skim
A thin coat of plaster over plasterboard.

Soaker
A partly hidden flashing laid on a roof to interlock with the tiles or slates.

Soffit
A decorative horizontal board used to cover the underside of overhanging rafters at the eaves.

Statutory Notice
A notice for inspection to

be given to the Building Control Officer at certain stages of work.

Statutory undertaker
An organisation carrying out a public service such as the supply of water, electricity, gas or sewerage. Technically extinct with privatisation.

Stock brick
A name historically given to the most commonly available type of brick in a locality.

Strut
A diagonal member within a roof structure, usually at right angles to, and supporting the rafters.

Stub stack
A short SVP, sometimes capped with an AAV.

SVP
Soil vent pipe or stack. A vertical pipe, usually 110 mm in diameter, which carries above-ground drainage waste to below-ground drains.

Tanking
The damp-proofing of a wall or room that is below ground level.

Tile hanging
Vertical tiling on a external wall for weather resistance and decoration.

Trench-fill foundations
Foundations that are concreted almost to the surface of the ground,

filling the trench entirely, as opposed to shallow strip foundations.

Truss clip
A metal connector plate used to secure trussed rafters to wall plates.

Trussed rafter
A triangulated, lightweight framework of timbers usually placed at 600 mm centres to form a roof structure.

TRV
A thermostatic radiator valve fitted to radiators to individually control the temperature of each one.

UB
Universal beam. A common I-shape steel beam.

UC
Universal column. A square I-shape steel beam.

Underpin
To prop up an existing foundation/building by forming new foundations beneath the existing ones.

U value
A measure of thermal transmittance – the amount of heat that can escape through an area of a particular element of the building.

Vapour barrier
A thin, impermeable layer, such as polythene, used to prevent interstitial condensation from

penetrating through to the finishings.

Verge
The edge of the roof at a gable-end wall.

VOC
Volatile organic compound. A harmful chemical, such as a solvent present in paints and adhesives.

Wall plate
A timber plate on top of a wall to support the roof or floor in a suspended-timber floor.

Wall profile
A steel connector bolted against an existing wall. allowing new masonry to be bonded to it.

Wall tie
A metal connector for tying together the two skins of a cavity wall.

Weatherboarding
Timber cladding for weather resistance and decoration of an external wall. Sometimes called clapboarding or ship-lap boarding.

Wind post
A vertical metal post incorporated within a wall structure to act as a buttressing support against wind load.

Useful contacts

Arboricultural Advisory and Information Service (AAIS)
Part of the Tree Advice Trust; maintains a directory of registered consultants for advice on problems relating to trees near buildings.
01420 22 022

Association of Building Engineers (ABE)
Maintains a list of member surveyors/engineers.
01604 404 121

British Board of Agrement (BBA)
Set up by the government in 1966; tests and certifies building materials and products.
01923 665 300

British Standards Institute (BSI)
Tests, standardises and specifies materials and practices.
020 8996 9000

Builders' Merchants Federation
Maintains a list of builders' merchants.
020 7439 1753

Building Research Establishment (BRE)
Created by the government in 1971; researches and publishes on building techniques and problems.
01923 664 444

Cavity Insulation Guarantee Agency (CIGA)
Independent body that offers insurance for cavity-fill insulation.
01582 792 283

Centre for Accessible Environments (CAE)
Provides advice on making homes more accessible for the disabled.
020 7357 8182

Chartered Institute of Building (CIOB)
Maintains a list of members.
01344 630 700

Construction Confederation
Maintains a list of builder members and guarantee information.
020 7608 5000

Council for Registration of Gas Installers (CORGI)
Maintains a list of registered members and provides gas safety advice.
01256 372 200

Department of Committees and Local Government (DCLG)
Government department responsible for prescribing and determining Building Regulations, planning orders and circulars; also administers planning appeals in England and Wales
Building Regulations
020 7944 3000
Planning Inspectorate for Appeals 0117 987 8000

Double Glazing Glass and Glazing Federation
Controls glazing industry, with regulations on the supply and fit of glass.
020 7403 7177

Energy Saving Trust
Established by the ODPM; provides advice and administers grant aid on energy-conservation matters.
0345 277 200

English Heritage
Government agency established as custodian of historical properties; advises on listed building/conservation issues.
020 7973 3000

Environment Agency
Established in 1996 as an independent body responsible for controlling air, land and water pollution. Manages the water environment as successor to the National Rivers Authority (NRA).
General Enquiry Line
0645 333 111

Federation of Master Builders (FMB)
Maintains a list of builder members and guarantee information.
020 7242 7583

Health and Safety Executive (HSE)
Advises on safety at work in construction.
01787 881 165

Institute of Electrical Engineers (IEE)
Maintains a list of electrician members and provides electrical safety advice.
020 7240 1871

Institute of Gas Engineers
Maintains a list of members.
020 7636 6603

Institute of Structural Engineers
Maintains a list of members.
020 7235 4535

Lead Sheet Association
Provides advice and technical information relating to leadwork.
01892 822 773

National Association of Scaffolding Contractors (NASC)
Maintains a list of members.
020 7608 5095

National Federation of Roofing Contractors Ltd
Maintains a list of members.
020 7436 0387

Paintmakers' Association
A division of the British Coatings Federation; advises painters on material development.
01372 360 660

Planning Portal
The gateway for submitting and tracking planning applications electronically with advice on planning legislation.
www.planningportal.gov.uk

Royal Institute of British Architects (RIBA)
Maintains a list of members.
020 7251 0791

Royal Institute of Chartered Surveyors (RICS)
Maintains a list of members.
020 7222 7000

Scottish Office
The government department responsible for the prescription and determination on Planning and Building Regulations and Planning Appeals in Scotland. The equivalent of the ODPM.
Enquiry Reporters Unit for Planning Appeals
0131 556 8400

The Stationery Office (HMSO)
Retails government publications.
0870 600 5522

Timber Research and Development Association (TRADA)
Provides advice and technical information relating to timber in construction.
01494 563 091

Index

abutments 87, 15, 16, 115
air bricks 112
all-in ballast 57
appliances 8
  gas 137, 138
applications, see planning
  consent applications, Building
  Regulations applications
archaeological areas 61
Areas of Outstanding Natural
  Beauty 23
Areas of Special Control 23

backfilled ground 10, 11
basements 11
bathrooms 8, 144
bats 41
beams 132
  loadbearing capacity of 64
  steel 132
  supporting 15
bedrooms 27
bitumen 116
blinding 65, 66
boilers 35, 137-138
boundaries 7, 36, 37, 39, 159
  building near 36
  defining 39
breaking through 120
bricklayer 88
brickwork 87, 88-89
  frogs 89
  pointing 89
  profiles 87
  stability 89
  wall ties 91
British Standard 31, 48, 104
builders 42, 51
  choosing 42, 43
  estimate 43, 46
  insurance 43
  quotations 43, 46
  warranty 43
Building Consent, see Planning
  Consent
Building Control Officer 21, 30,
  31, 51, 54, 55

Building Notice 21
Building Regulations 28, 51
  applications 20, 28, 29
    amendments to 20, 28
    rejection notice 29
    time limits 20
    types of 21
  approval 29, 55
  Approved Documents 29
  approved materials 31
  conditional approvals 20, 25,
    28, 29
  conditions 61
  consent 55
  fee 17
  inspection 30, 54, 55, 67
  notice 30, 54, 55
  notification stages 30, 54, 55,
    67, 72
Building Warrant 21, 28

carbon monoxide 130
carpenters 106
car port 30
cavity trays, remedial 152
ceilings 131
cement 57
certificates
  completion 31
  handover 99
  regularisation 55
clay soils 13, 58, 61, 63
compaction 65
completion 164
concrete 56, 57, 66, 70
  for foundations 56, 59, 66
condensation 111, 112, 113
conservation areas 8, 35
  definition of 23
  permitted development in 23
conservatories 29, 30, 96, 97
construction, basic house
  166-167
consultants, planning 25
contracts 48, 51
council houses 23
covenants, restrictive 8, 36
coving 135
cracks 35

damp-proof course 65, 69, 75
  defects 52
  level 57
  notice 75
  recording 52
  in timber frames 78, 79
damp-proof membrane 64, 65,
  66, 75, 75, 77
deathwatch beetle 81
decorators 132
design 27, 34-35
designer 14, 16
  choosing a 14
  agreeing terms 15, 17
development, permitted 21
disabled facilities 54
disputes 51, 52
doors 84-86
  fire 86
  locks 85
drainage 6, 8, 71
  below-ground 71
  rainwater 74, 161
  shared 41, 73
drains 9, 40, 73, 140
  building over 40, 72
  foul 71
  gulleys 73
  invert levels of 18, 75
  private 40
  and trees 73
drainage pipes 6, 8, 40, 73,
  75, 161
  air bubbles in 71
driveway, building over 27
dry-lining 35

electrical installation 124
  and timber structure 126
  and masonry structure 126
energy conservation 111, 123
Environment Agency 6
Environmental Health
  Department 11
European Community mark 31
external work 152

fans, extractor 127
farmhouses 23

fees 17, 43, 46-48, 52, 53
fences 159
fire, open 138
fireplace 138
fire spread 86, 121
   doors 122
   party walls 95
first floor extension 63, 64
flood damage 6
flooding 6
flood plains 6
floor level 6
floors 130-131
floor slab 64, 65, 66
footpath, public 7, 23
foundations 6, 54, 56, 68
   cracks 65
   existing 63, 64
   neighbouring 36,37
   pad-and-beam 58, 59, 61
   pile 58, 61
   raft 58, 59
   special 58, 62
   strip 56, 57, 58
   and trees 6, 8, 9, 61, 62, 73
   trench-fill 56, 57, 58
   underpinning 56, 63, 64
frogs 89

garage, integral 98, 121-124
   insulation of 123
gas appliances 137, 138
gas meter box 6
glazing 30, 83
   for conservatories 97
grants 53-54
ground floor,
   level 90
   suspended 68, 69
gutters 117, 161

hardcore material 65
health and safety 41, 44, 45,
   63, 98
heating 35, 136-140
   underfloor 139
heave
   frost 56
   ground 60, 62

hedgerows 12
highway, public see public
   highway

insects 80, 112
Inspectors, Planning 25, 29
   Approved 45, 46
insulation 65, 70, 95
   in cavity walls 76, 91-94
   foundation 65
   partial-fill 93
   in party walls 95
   in roofs 111, 113, 150
   thermal 123
   timber frame 77
   total-fill 91, 92
insurance, contractor's 44, 110
internal partitions 67
internal work 120
joiners 106
joists 67, 69, 126, 136
   ceiling 104, 105, 107
   flat-roof 107

kitchen 8, 149
kite mark scheme 31, 45

landfill site 12
landscape 157
lateral-restraint straps 93, 103
leadwork 116, 117
light 34
   external 158
   right to 40
lintels 72, 81-82
   loadbearing capacity of 64
   PCC 82
   and point loads 82
listed buildings 23, 28, 35
load capacity 61
loans, home improvement 52
   secured 52
   unsecured 52
location (of extension) 6
loft conversions 63, 132
lounge, sun 98

masonry 76
   construction 76

MDF 136
meter boxes 6
methane 13
mines 8, 56
mini-pump systems 8
mortgage 52, 53

nails 104
National Federation of Roofing
   Contractors 108, 110
National Park, permitted
   development in 23
neighbours 7, 36
noise 95

Ombudsman, Local Authority
   25, 26
ordnance survey maps 7, 18
orientation 34
overlooking 27
overshading 27
oversite material 65, 66
paints 133, 156
   external 155
   textured 134
parking, off street 27
party walls, see walls
passages 34
patio doors 34, 85
payment 49
percolation testing 11
permitted development, see
   development, permitted
Planning Appeal 24
Planning Consent 20
   appeals 24, 25
   applications 20
   conditions 24
   fees 17
   permitted development 21
   refusal notice 24
Planning Inspectorate 24, 25
plans 14, 16, 18
   amendments 17, 20
   approval notice 20, 31
   block 18
   building regulations 16, 17,
   19, 20
   cross-section 18

drawing own 18, 20
elevation 16, 18
location 18
planning consent 17, 19
plants, garden 34, 157-158
plumbers 145
plumbing, soil and waste 140
porches 22, 29, 30
power points 35, 125
public footpath, see footpath, public
public highway 22, 27
development close to 22, 23

quality assurance 49
quotations, building 43, 46, 110

radiators 35, 136
radon gas 13
rafters 103, 107
rendering 155
restrictive covenants, see covenants, restrictive
rights of way 7
river 6
roof area extensions 17
permitted development 23
roofs 99-106, 108
cold 111, 115
coverings 108, 110
cut-and-pitch roof 100, 105
false hip 118
felts 113
flat 34, 110, 114
pitch 109
trussed-rafter 100
trusses 100-102
warm-roof 112, 115
and wind load 100, 101, 103

safety, see health and safety
satellite dishes 163
Scottish legislation 21 see also Building Warrant
security 34, 84-86, 157
services 6, 9, 70
sewers 6, 40, 71
building over 72

showers 143
shrinkage 63, 10
site investigation 6, 9
slabs 64, 66, 68
slates, roofing 108, 110, 112
sloping sites 7, 56
smoke alarms 122, 128-130
soakaways 6, 10, 13, 74
soils 9, 13, 157-157
specifications 16, 17, 18
stairs 145
structural damage 63
struts 70
subsidence 9, 62, 64
subsoil 56, 58, 60, 61, 63, 64, 65, 74
substructure 56
sulphate attack 56, 65
sump holes 13
superstructure 76
survey
site 6, 9
valuation 53
surveyor 31, 37, 51

tank
septic 71, 74
suppports 105
water 104, 137
termites 80-81
tiles
roof 109, 110, 111
fixing 109
wall and floor 135, 153
timber 70, 93, 106
ordering 69
preservatives 69, 80
toilet, see wc
trees 6, 8, 9, 61-62, 73
tying-in 87

underground streams 11
underground works 56
underpinning foundations 56, 63
unprotected areas 86

vat 43
vegetation 6, 65

ventilation 12, 13, 69, 83, 127
background 84
crack 84
rapid 83
roof 111, 112, 113
trickle vents 84
venting 13, 84, 111
roof 112
vibration, ground 61

wallpaper 134
walls 76, 77, 89, 90
boundary 159
buttressing 90
cavity walls 76, 77, 90
insulation in 77, 91-94
external 89
party 36, 37, 39, 94
foundation bearing 67-69
internal 94
load-bearing 68, 69, 105
partition 94
rendering 77, 93
timber-frame 76, 77
wall ties 56, 91
wc 8, 142
weatherboarding 152
wells 10
wildlife 13, 41
wind load 89, 90, 93
windows 34, 35, 82-84, 95
bay 84
dormer 23
French 85
overlooking 27
ventilation 83